INALIENABLE RIGHTS

For Norman,

In appreciation of our years of friendship and for all of the philosophical guidance you have given.

Jerry

October 2000

INALIENABLE RIGHTS

The Limits of Consent in Medicine and the Law

Terrance McConnell

OXFORD
UNIVERSITY PRESS

2000

OXFORD
UNIVERSITY PRESS

Oxford New York
Athens Auckland Bangkok Bogotá Buenos Aires Calcutta
Cape Town Chennai Dar es Salaam Delhi Florence Hong Kong Istanbul
Karachi Kuala Lumpur Madrid Melbourne Mexico City Mumbai
Nairobi Paris São Paulo Singapore Taipei Tokyo Toronto Warsaw

and associated companies in
Berlin Ibadan

Published by Oxford University Press, Inc.
198 Madision Avenue, New York, New York 10016

Library of Congress Cataloging-in-Publication Data
McConnell, Terrance C.
Inalienable rights: the limits of consent in medicine and the law
/ Terrance McConnell.
p. cm.
Includes bibliographical references and index.
ISBN 0-19-513462-1
1. Informed consent (Medical law)—United States. 2. Human
rights. 3. Natural law. I. Title.
KF3827.I5M39 2000
344.73'0412—dc21 99-41540
[ISBN 0-19-462-1 (cloth)]

9 8 7 6 5 4 3 2 1

Printed in the United States of America
on acid-free paper

Preface

I began thinking about the topic of inalienable rights in the early 1980s. While teaching courses in the philosophy of law, I often used books and articles written by Joel Feinberg. As anyone reading this probably knows, Feinberg's works are invariably clear, informative, and provocative. I used his essay on inalienable rights (discussed extensively in chapter 1 of this book) in several of my classes. It stimulated much discussion among students and much thought on my part. Prominent among the issues that Feinberg's essay raised in my mind were questions about the very concept of an inalienable right, questions about the relationship between inalienable rights and paternalism, and wonder about what normative implications follow from a commitment to the inalienability of some rights.

All of this reflection led me to publish a paper in 1984 discussing some of these issues. After that, I began working on other projects, including a scholarly book and the second edition of a textbook. I did not return to full reflection on the issues raised by inalienable rights until the mid-1990s. But in the intervening time, questions about inalienable rights arose occasionally, especially in teaching biomedical ethics. I have finally been able to address these questions in detail in writing this book.

Much of the work done on this book was during the academic year 1995–1996. Generous support for my research and writing was provided by two sources: the National Endowment for the Humanities, which awarded me a Fellowship for College Teachers; and the University of North Carolina at Greensboro, which provided me with a year-long research assignment, thereby freeing me from teaching and administrative responsibilities. Without this support, this book would still be unfinished. I am happy to express my gratitude to both of these institutions.

Some of the positions defended here in chapters 1 and 2 were presented in my paper, "The Nature and Basis of Inalienable Rights," *Law and Philosophy*, Vol. 3 (April 1984), pp. 25–59. Though what is presented in this book is revised and considerably more developed, some ideas from the original essay are used with kind permission from Kluwer Academic Publishers.

An earlier version of chapter 3, entitled "The Inalienable Right of Conscience: A Madisonian Argument," was published in *Social Theory and Practice*, Vol. 22 (1996), pp. 397–416; I thank the editors for permission to use that material. What is presented here is revised and expanded to cover topics not addressed in the original paper. An even earlier version of this paper was read at Davidson College in 1994, and I thank members of the audience there for their questions and suggestions.

Portions of chapters 5 and 6 were presented at a joint meeting of the North Carolina Philosophical Society and South Carolina Philosophical Society at Columbia, South Carolina, February 21, 1998. I thank my two commentators at that meeting, Christopher Wellman and Kyle Hudson, for their stimulating remarks and queries, and I thank members of the audience for their questions.

My colleague, Michael Zimmerman, read and commented on earlier versions of chapters 1, 2, 3, 5, and 6. As always, his suggestions were pointed and on the mark, and I thank him for them. My friends and fellow members of the Ethics Committee at the Moses Cone Health Care System, Kay Hagan, J.D. and Rita Layson, M.D., read and provided feedback on an earlier version of chapter 4, and I am happy to thank them for their assistance.

Throughout much of my philosophical career, Norman Dahl, Thomas E. Hill, Jr., and Laurence Thomas have encouraged and supported my research in many ways; appreciation for the kind of help they have provided is too seldom expressed.

Two anonymous reviewers for Oxford University Press read an earlier version of the entire manuscript and made constructive suggestions that were very helpful. I also want to thank the entire staff at Oxford University Press for their patience and assistance, including Philosophy Editor Peter Ohlin; his assistant Catharine Carlin; the production editor of this book, MaryBeth Branigan; and especially my copyeditor, Marie Milton.

As always, my wife, Marilyn Lee McConnell, was patient and supportive throughout the duration of a project that I allowed to drag out much too long.

Contents

Introduction ix

ONE The Nature of Inalienable Rights 3

TWO The Moral Foundations of Inalienable Rights 23

THREE The Inalienable Right of Conscience: A Madisonian/Jeffersonian Argument 45

FOUR The Right of Informed Consent and Inalienability 65

FIVE The Inalienable Right to Life and Its Implications for Voluntary Euthanasia 79

SIX Assisted Suicide and the Inalienable Right to Life 95

SEVEN Human Organs and Inalienablility 117

EIGHT Concluding Remarks 135

Notes 141

Bibliography 157

Index 167

Introduction

Inalienable rights have seemed to many mysterious and confusing at best, and suspicious or even incoherent at worst. In this book, I hope to remove much of the mystery and suspicion from this venerable notion.

The expression 'inalienable rights' is used multiple ways, which adds to the confusion. In a loose and popular sense, inalienable rights are ones that may never be taken from a person. But in a more focused and somewhat technical sense, inalienable rights are ones that may not be waived or transferred by their possessors. It is inalienable rights in this more focused sense that constitute the subject of this book. And it is inalienable rights in precisely this sense that have aroused skepticism on the part of legal scholars and political philosophers. It is not difficult to understand why.

One way of understanding rights is that they are shields that protect their possessors from various kinds of harms and invasions. But we normally think that it is the possessors themselves who are in control of these shields. They may keep them lowered if they choose, thus remaining protected. Or they may choose to raise the shields and invite selected others to do what is otherwise impermissible. Inalienable rights are different from this, however; for the control that possessors have over their inalienable rights is normatively limited. This seems both puzzling and suspicious.

My goal in this book is *not* to produce an exhaustive list of inalienable rights. When you finish this book, you will not have a list of all and only rights that are inalienable. My goals instead are to explain the concept of an inalienable right, to show why it is morally justifiable to ascribe inalienability to some legal rights, and to examine in more detail some selected rights.

A moral justification for inalienable rights is needed because the normative implications of such rights are more restrictive on possessors than we normally think. To the extent that the metaphor of the shield (or something like that) has dominated our thinking about rights, we believe that the possessors themselves control the degree of protection they wish to obtain from their own rights. If they wish to let selected others infringe their rights, that is their prerogative, we think. But if possessors' own rights normatively limit what they may do, this deviates from the customary metaphor.

Whether these normative restrictions are moral only or are also legal, there should be justification for them. If we are restricting persons' freedoms, especially based on their own rights, we should be able to justify doing so.

The two types of moral justification of inalienable rights that are most common add further to the suspicions. One type of justification restricts the liberty of possessors for their own good. Certain rights are so fundamental that if their possessors were empowered to allow others to invade those rights, they would do irreparable harm to themselves. Paternalism of this sort does not sit well with many. The other justification invokes a divine being. Rights are given to people by God, and squandering those gifts is morally unacceptable. In Chapter IV, section 23, of the *Second Treatise of Government*, John Locke defended such a view. He argued that individuals do not have the power over their own lives to enslave themselves to another nor to give another permission to kill them; such acts would be a misuse of divine gifts. This move seems to many ad hoc.

I shall develop a justification of inalienable rights that is neither paternalistic nor based on theological assumptions. While this book is not a work in early American political philosophy and while I discuss Thomas Jefferson and James Madison only in chapter 3, I do aim in my explication of the notion of an inalienable right to capture at least the spirit of the notion that the founding fathers were talking about. The founding fathers believed that some rights are inalienable; they believed in a wall of separation between church and state; and they were not rampant paternalists. Thus, the justification of inalienable rights that I provide is, I think, one that is at least consistent with the spirit of the political philosophy embraced by Jefferson and Madison.

In chapter 3 I consider the right of conscience. I begin with it because it was widely discussed by political philosophers during the seventeenth and eighteenth centuries and because Madison and Jefferson wrote about it specifically. I try to show that in one sense this right is inalienable because no agent can rid herself of responsibility simply by making a promise to another. I also argue that even if an agent could transfer her right of conscience to another, it would be wrong to do so because of the avoidable moral risks incurred by such an arrangement.

I argue in chapter 4 that the right of a competent patient to be asked for his consent before medical treatment is administered can be neither waived nor transferred to another. This is due, in part, I shall show, to the peculiar content of this right. But that the right cannot be waived also protects patients from certain threats that might otherwise obtain.

Some of the consequences of my account are at least initially surprising. For example, in chapters 5 and 6, I explain what it means to say that the right to life is inalienable and what the normative implications of that are. It has been common to invoke the inalienability of the right to life to justify prohibiting assisted suicide and voluntary euthanasia. I argue that, properly understood, the inalienability of the right to life does not preclude the permissibility of these practices. I also discuss the question of designating another person to serve as one's health care agent in the event that one loses the capacity to make medical decisions. If assisted suicide and voluntary euthanasia are compatible with the inalienability of the right to life, then it is reasonable to think that designating another to serve as one's agent when one can no longer do so oneself would also be compatible. But the law regarding the powers of health care agents varies from state to state, and in a few states agents may make any decision that the patient himself would have been permitted to make. I argue that this version of the law is in fact incompatible with the inalienability of the right to life.

In chapter 7 I discuss the odd but intriguing notion of market inalienability. This notion indicates that something may be given away by its possessor, but it may not be sold. I consider in particular human organs that might be used for transplantation to sick patients. I do not defend outright the policy that permits gifts but not sales; but I do try to show what I think is the most promising line of argument in favor of this view. This position will suggest approaches that might be taken to related issues, such as whether women may be paid to be surrogate mothers and whether subjects may be paid to participate in research protocols that offer no therapeutic benefits for them and put them at some risk.

If I am successful, I will have provided a framework and context for future discussions about inalienable rights. Other particular rights not mentioned in this book may indeed have this status.

INALIENABLE RIGHTS

ONE

The Nature of Inalienable Rights

The task of this chapter is principally conceptual; the goal is to explain the notion of an inalienable right. In carrying out this task, it will help to explain other notions, including the idea of an absolute right and the idea of a forfeitable right. Various distinctions will be drawn along the way and alternative accounts will be critically examined. But in the end the hope is to arrive at a reasonably clear account of the nature of inalienable rights.

I shall begin, however, with some brief remarks about the nature of rights[1] in general.

Rights

Whatever else one might say, rights are normatively advantageous to their possessors, and any analysis must reflect this.[2] In explaining part of what is advantageous about possessing rights, it is common to contrast rights with privileges.[3] Privileges are favors granted to one by another. Privileges cannot be claimed as one's due and may be withdrawn by the grantor at any time. If I allow you to drive my car, I have extended to you a privilege. By contrast, rights are entitlements one has. Rights can be claimed as one's due and form the basis of legitimate demands against others. Rights may not be withdrawn capriciously by others. This notion is what has been called "claim-rights" (in contrast with rights as mere liberties).

Following jurist Wesley Hohfeld, many have analyzed rights in terms of other normative positions, especially in terms of claims, liberties, immunities, and powers.[4] The idea is that rights cannot be analyzed simply in terms of claims, or simply in terms of liberties, or simply in terms of immunities or powers. Rather, typically rights involve several of these notions in various combinations. Some refer to these as "rights packages." So, for example, the right of free speech may involve immunity from legislative regulation of speech plus certain liberties. The right to make a will may involve a power to dispose of one's property as one wishes. And the right to vote may include claims against one's fellow citizens that they not prevent one from voting and claims against the state official working during the election that they provide one with a ballot.

The nuances here are many and the literature is rich. But these complexities need not concern us here. For what is central to my purposes is the fact that claim-rights (hereafter, rights) impose obligations or duties on others.[5] We may take as canonical this scheme: P_1 has a right against P_2 regarding R. In this scheme, P_1 is the *possessor* of the right, P_2 is the bearer of the duty correlative with that right, and R is that to which P_1 has a right. The bearer of the correlative duty, P_2, may be a specifiable individual(s). If Anna has signed a valid contract to buy Timothy's house, then Anna owes Timothy the agreed upon sum of money on the date indicated. When there are determinate, specifiable individuals on whom the correlative duties fall, such as Anna in this example, the right is said to be *in personam*. By contrast, some rights are said to hold against the world, to hold against all moral agents. Examples include a person's right not to be assaulted[6] and a landowner's right to exclusive enjoyment of his property. Such rights are said to be *in rem*. The variable R designates the *content* of the possessor's right. The content of a right—what is owed to the possessor—may be divided broadly into two categories. A *negative* right is a right to other persons' omissions or forebearances; negative rights impose duties on others to refrain from doing something. A *positive* right is a right to other persons' positive actions; positive rights impose duties on others to do something for the possessor of the right.[7] Timothy has a positive right against Anna that she pay him for his house, as she contracted to do. Maria has a negative right against everyone that they not assault her.

One other distinction is important for our purposes. This is the distinction between *moral rights* and *legal rights*. Providing precise difinitions of these terms is quite difficult, in part, because there is not agreement among philosophers on this matter. Legal rights, it is usually said, derive from the customs, various legal systems, and institutional arrangements for promulgation. Moral rights are not products of conventional design and exist as standards independently of legal implementation.[8] L.W. Sumner puts it this way:

> [L]egal rights are the creatures of legal institutions, and especially of legislatures and courts. Since legal institutions and legal systems are themselves subject to assessment for the extent to which they respect basic rights, their pronouncements cannot provide an authoritative standard of authenticity for such rights. In normative debates on public issues appeals to rights are not, or are not only, appeals to legal rights. Instead, or additionally, they are appeals to moral rights which cannot, by their nature, be authoritatively declared by any legal institution.[9]

Later Sumner provides an example of this point: "We say that black South Africans have the moral right to full representation even though this right has not been accorded legal recognition, and in saying this we mean to point to the right as a moral reason for changing the legal system so as to accord it recognition."[10] Legal rights, then, are conventional products of deliberate human decisions. Of course, legal rights are not the only rights that are conventional; clubs, universities, and all sorts of organizations may accord their members rights in virtue of membership. Moral rights, if there are any, provide standards against which such conventions may be assessed.

The legal rights that a society grants to its citizens are among the conventions that can be assessed by utilizing moral rights and other resources provided by moral theory. Let us say that rights granted to citizens by a particular society are *morally defensible legal rights* if they are genuine moral rights or if plausible moral principles require this society to extend such rights to its citizens. This leaves open the possibility that morally defensible legal rights may differ from society to society. This is as it should be, I think, for circumstances in various societies may be radically different; what is easily granted in one society may not be at all feasible in another.

The so-called *correlativity thesis* (of rights and duties), in its strongest form, holds that all rights imply duties and all duties imply rights. Each half of the thesis is controversial. Some hold that there are duties to oneself, even though one cannot hold a right against oneself; and some hold that there are duties of charity, though no one else can make a claim against a person that that person owes him charity. If either of these examples is plausible, this casts doubt on the contention that duties imply rights. And some maintain that so-called manifesto rights—ideals portrayed in political documents as rights—are genuine rights, even if they cannot currently be satisfied and therefore imply no duties on others. For our purposes, however, the controversy about the correlativity thesis can be avoided. While we need not make assumptions about all rights, we simply note that the subset of rights to be considered here are rights that imply duties or obligations on others. For, as will soon become clear, a principal focus of this work will be on conditions under which it is permissible not to act on a duty generated by a right.

Rights and Correlative Duties

Restricting ourselves to rights that imply duties on others, we now introduce certain terminology to describe various possibilities. The terminology is standard.[11]

Let us say that a right is *fulfilled* when the duty correlative with that right is discharged. What constitutes discharging the duty will depend on the content of the right. In the case of a positive right, discharging the duty will involve the performance of some required action. In the case of a negative right, fulfillment depends on others refraining from the prohibited action in the appropriate context.

Let us say that a right is *infringed* when the correlative duty is not discharged.[12] This means either that the required action is not performed, or the prohibited action is performed. If Anna does not pay Timothy the amount of money specified in the contract at the appropriate time, she has infringed his right. If Hans attacks Maria, he has infringed her right (not to be assaulted).

Infringements may be either justified or unjustified. If an infringement of a right is morally unjustified (and so wrong, or impermissible) and the victim of the wrong is the possessor of the right, then let us say that the right has been *violated*. If an infringement of a right is morally justified, then the right has not been violated. So understood, all violations are infringements, but not all infringements are violations. And all violations are wrong, but not all infringements are wrong. If I infringe someone's right, I go beyond the *usual* limits; my act is *normally* wrong because it is not in accord with the obligation correlative with the right. But it need not be wrong.

When, then, are infringements justified? Some might say that with respect to selected rights infringements are never justified. To hold such a view is to say that the right in question is *absolute*. An absolute right is exceptionless; there are no circumstances in which one is justified in infringing that right. Judith Jarvis Thomson characterizes an absolute right as follows. "That is, it is the inclination to take it that if a man has a right that such and such shall not be the case, then if we bring about that it is the case, we act wrongly in so doing. As the point might be put, every infringing of a right is a violation of a right."[13] Explaining the same concept, Joel Feinberg writes:

> An absolute right (if there is such a thing) is a right that would remain in one's possession, fully effective as a ground for other people's duties to one, in all possible circumstances. If my right to X is absolute, then there are no circumstances in which it is "subject to legitimate limitation" or in which the correlated duties of others to me in repect to X are suspended.[14]

Some might hold that all rights, when rights are properly understood, are absolute.[15] A more common position is to hold that a narrowly selected subset of rights are absolute.[16] If some (or many) rights are not absolute, then we may ask when it is that infringements of those rights are justified.

One way in which others may be justified in infringing an individual's right is if that person has *forfeited* that right. Some say that a person who has forfeited a right has lost that right because of some offense or wrongdoing on his part. For reasons that will emerge soon, I prefer to say, not that the person has lost the right, but that the duty correlative with the right is suspended because the possessor has engaged in wrongdoing. This means that others are permitted to infringe the person's right because of his wrongdoing.[17] A right that can be forfeited is, in one sense, conditional: to retain the normative advantage that the right gives the possessor, the possessor must not engage in certain improper behavior. When a person has forfeited a right, others are permitted to treat him in a way that would otherwise be impermissible *simply because* of his wrong action.

This account of forfeiture leaves several issues unaddressed. One important issue concerns how we determine *what* right a person forfeits when he engages in the conduct that brings about the normative change. Presumably if a person is assaulting you, you are permitted to do what is necessary to repel the attack; but you are not permitted to torture the attacker. And someone who engages in criminal activity has at least forfeited his right to freedom; but we do not think that the person has forfeited his right to an attorney. A second issue is whether there are some rights that cannot be forfeited. Some might think, for example, that a person cannot forfeit his right not to be tortured no matter what he does. A third issue not dealt with here is *who* may engage in otherwise impermissible behavior because the possessor of the right engages in wrongdoing. Perhaps the answer to this question depends on the context. If Hans attacks Maria, it may be that anyone is permitted to do what is necessary to stop the attack, thereby infringing certain of Hans's rights. But if Susan takes Walter's baseball, perhaps only Walter is permitted to take it back. And that gives rise to a fourth issue not addressed here: it may well be the case that not all wrongdoing results in the forfeiture of a right. If William breaks a promise to meet Mary for lunch, he has done something wrong (assuming that he had no justification for failing to keep the promise) and is subject to moral criticism. But it is not clear that William has forfeited any of his rights. A complete account of forfeiture would address these issues; they will not be pursued here, however.

A second way in which an infringement of a person's right may be justified is if the obligation correlative with that right is overridden or defeated by competing moral considerations. Perhaps this occurs only in rare circumstances or emergencies, but if it is possible then the right in question is *defeasible*—it can be overridden. If an obligation correlative with a given right cannot be overridden by competing moral considerations, then that right is *indefeasible*. While it is possible that some rights are indefeasible, many hold that at least some rights are defeasible. To establish this, typically examples are given. An excellent illustration of this strategy is manifest in an often-cited passage from Feinberg.

> Suppose that you are on a backpacking trip in the high mountain country when an unanticipated blizzard strikes the area with such ferocity that your life is imperiled. Fortunately, you stumble onto an unoccupied cabin, locked and boarded up for the winter, clearly somebody else's private property. You smash in a window, enter, and huddle in a corner for three days until the storm abates. During this period you help yourself to your unknown benefactor's food supply and burn his wooden furniture in the fireplace to keep warm. Surely you are justified in doing all these things, and yet you have infringed the clear rights of another person.[18]

The right that has been infringed is the cabin owner's right to property. If the infringement is justified, as most will agree, then at least property rights are defeasible. What rights are defeasible and what moral considerations defeat the correlative duties are no doubt complicated questions, questions answered differently, one suspects, by different moral theories. But these issues need not be pursued here.

What I have said here implies that the possession of rights is not the only—and maybe not the most important—morally relevant feature about people and their circumstances. For one thing, I am willing to grant (though I have not discussed it here) that it may be wrong in some circumstances for a person to exercise some of her rights. Some say, for example, that in certain situations it may be wrong for a person to exercise her right to procreate.[19] Second, and more significant for my project, acknowledging that people have rights does not settle the issue of what conduct toward them is proper. Instead, if our treatment of someone is contrary to his rights, we can only say that such conduct is unjustified *unless* there is some special reason to justify it.[20]

Given these concepts, if a right is absolute, then it is not forfeitable and is indefeasible. If a right is not absolute, then there are some circumstances in which it is permissible to infringe that right and act contrary to the duty correlative with that right. One type of a nonabsolute right is a right that is forfeitable. Another type of nonabsolute right is a right that is defeasible. Of course, the same right may be both forfeitable and defeasible, but for all that has been said here that need not be so. And there may be circumstances other than or in addition to forfeiture and defeasibility in which it is permissible to infringe a right. Indeed, we now turn to such a possibility.

Alienable Rights and Inalienable Rights

As we have just seen, whether the failure to discharge a duty correlative with a right is impermissible depends on several factors. One possibly relevant factor not yet discussed, however, is important. Suppose that the rights-possessor herself gives another agent permission to infringe one of her rights. Does the assent of the possessor render infringement permissible?

The answer to this question might vary, depending on the nature of the right in question. But at least in some cases we are inclined to answer the question affirmatively. This is made clear in the following:

> Ordinarily, others may not enter your house or have sex with you or slice open your body in surgery unless you consent to their doing so. If they proceed without your consent, they violate your rights. Consent thus allows us selectively to admit different people to different sorts of intimacy and to repel those we're not interested in. That others need your permission in such contexts identifies you as an independent agent deserving of respect, with plans and projects of your own.[21]

The examples identified—entering another's house, having sexual intercourse with another, and performing surgery on another—seem to be such that with the possessor's consent infringement is (prima facie) justified, and without the possessor's consent the infringement is (prima facie) unjustified. Other examples can be cited. Loren Lomasky gives this one: "Consent renders licit what otherwise would be in violation of rights. To assault someone with your fists is impermissible—unless that person has agreed to step into a boxing ring with you."[22] Indeed, *the very thing* that distinguishes boxing from illegal assault is the voluntary consent of the participants. And one might make the same point about medical research that puts human subjects at risk.[23] George Fletcher puts the point succinctly: "Consent affects our relations with others by vesting in them the power to act toward us in ways that would otherwise be wrong and prohibited."[24]

In all of these cases, then, the possessor's consent seems to be a permission-generating activity. We might put it this way: "In giving consent to another's actions, however, our primary purpose is to authorize those actions and in so doing create for or accord to another a special right to act . . ."[25] This, then, suggests a third possibility for justifying infringements of rights: because the possessor's consent was obtained.

We might reasonably wonder, however, whether all rights are such that the possessor's consent authorizes infringement. For as we have just seen it is not unreasonable to think that some rights might not be forfeitable and some might not be defeasible. And, indeed, in our own legal system, it seems that some rights are such that the consent of the possessor does not authorize others in infringing that right. The right not to be killed provides an example.

Consider the case of Susan Potempa.[26] Potempa was (in 1993) a 50-year-old woman racked by pain after a mastectomy for breast cancer. Her breast cancer was diagnosed in 1992, and the mastectomy was performed then. Unfortunately, this surgery left Potempa in excruciating pain. Neighbors reported that they had often driven her to the hospital because she was too sick to drive herself. When Potempa's husband and son returned from a Thanksgiving (1993) football game, they found her dead in their garage. She had been beaten to death. The police initially called her death a random act of violence. Further investigation, however, revealed that this was a much more bizarre case. Reginald Williams, an 18-year-old who lived fewer than three blocks from the Potempa family, was identified as the killer. What was bizarre is that Susan Potempa had paid Williams $2100 in cash to kill her. Indeed, she had approached at least four other neighborhood men about arranging this murder before Williams agreed. Susan Potempa gave her consent to Reginald Williams; she paid him to kill her. Yet in this case consent was not a (legal) justification for killing.

While the case of Susan Potempa seems a bit strange, a more recent case of murder with consent seems downright weird. In the autumn of 1996, Sharon Lopatka left her home in Hampstead, Maryland.[27] In a note to her husband, Lopatka said that she would not be returning; she also asked her husband not to pursue the person who would kill her. On October 25, 1996, Lopatka's body was found in a shallow grave behind the mobile home of Robert Glass in the town of Collettsville, North Carolina. She had been strangled to death. More than 100 e-mail messages between Lopatka and Glass were retrieved. Many of these messages indicated that Glass had promised Lopatka that he would torture her sexually and then kill her. Others were privy to some of the exchanges that occurred in so-called Internet chat rooms. Tanith Tyrr of Berkeley, California, a self-described bondage enthusiast, said that she and others had communicated with Lopatka and had tried to convince her not to act on her death wish.

Robert Glass has acknowledged that he killed Sharon Lopatka. Prosecutors have charged him with first-degree murder, a charge to which he is pleading not guilty. Glass claims that Lopatka was killed accidentally during rough, consensual sex. Assuming that Lopatka was not mentally ill, the existence of numerous e-mail messages and the fact that she traveled to North Carolina to rendezvous with Glass both suggest that Lopatka did indeed consent to be killed. In addition, in the note to her husband, Lopatka said, "If my body is never retrieved, don't worry, know that I'm at peace." Yet her consent, even if genuine, will not get Glass off the legal hook. Indeed, prosecutors intend to use the e-mail communications as evidence of premeditation!

The cases of Susan Potempa and Sharon Lopatka both suggest that infringing the right not to be killed is not justified (at least in the legal system of the United States) simply because the possessor consents. Consent at most authorizes infringement of a right only sometimes. Let us explore this further.

To waive a right is to give up that right knowingly and voluntarily. Waiver involves the intentional or voluntary relinquishment of a right, or conduct that warrants the inference of relinquishment of that right.[28] In order for waiver to be valid, the possessor must understand what he is doing and his choice must be voluntary. When valid waiver occurs, the duties correlative with the right are suspended because of the possessor's consent (or conduct on the part of the possessor that warrants the inference of consent). If the police properly inform Sabrina, her voluntary agreement to answer questions without the presence of legal counsel constitutes a waiver of that right. In this sort of case, waiver is formal, effected by Sabrina's freely uttering certain words with understanding in an appropriate context. To cite another example, individuals have a right that the police not search their person or home without first obtaining a proper warrant. But this right may be waived. If Frances knows that she has this right but voluntarily allows the police to search her home without a warrant, she has waived the right.

Waiver may also be informal and inferential, however. If having read a newspaper at the airport, George lays it on an unoccupied seat and walks away, others may appropriately infer that he has relinquished his right to that paper. Perhaps a better example of waiver that is informal and inferential is this. Suppose that last winter Mr. Kowalski specifically told the neighborhood children that they could go sledding on his nicely sloped driveway. He even shoveled a path along the side of the driveway so that they could easily retreat to the top after a successful run. This year, after the first snow, Mr. Kowalski again shovels a path on the side of the driveway. He does not explicitly give the children permission to use his driveway for sledding, but they take his behavior as evidence that he will allow them to do so. The inference is reasonable.

Waiver has normative force in that it authorizes others to act in specified ways. When valid waiver occurs, a correlative duty is suspended and others are permitted to infringe the right in question. When Sabrina waives her right to legal counsel, *that* is what authorizes the police to question her about her activities, even in the absence of her attorney. Of course, Sabrina may regain her right to have counsel present any time she chooses; in virtue of the waiver, Sabrina is under no *obligation* to answer questions. And though the children in Mr. Kowalski's neighborhood reasonably inferred that he had waived his right regarding the use of his driveway, Mr. Kowalski could at any time deny the children permission to continue playing in the driveway. Like Sabrina, Mr. Kowalski is under no obligation not to regain his right in full.

When waiver has occurred, I maintain that the possessor still has the right in question; what has changed is that the correlative duty (vis-à-vis at least some others) has been suspended. Some prefer to say instead that the possessor no longer has the right. Thus, Thomson says that it does not follow from the fact that P_1 owns the land that he has a right against P_2 that P_2 stay off the land. This does not follow *because* P_1 might have given P_2 permission to enter his land.[29] By contrast, I claim that P_1 still has the right to the land, but the correlative duty for P_2 has been (temporarily) suspended. There are two reasons why I say this. First, P_1 has a right against all other agents (to whom no such permission has been granted) that they stay off his land; so P_1 must still have the right. And second, ordinarily P_1 can take back the permission that he has given to P_2. But surely P_1 has the authority to take back the permission only if he still has the right in question.

It should also be noted that waiver may be either specific or general. When waiver is *specific*, a selected individual (or individuals) is authorized by the possessor to infringe his right. Sabrina gave only the police questioning her at that moment the right to do so without presence of her legal counsel. When waiver is more *general*, multiple but not a definite number of individuals are authorized to infringe the possessor's right. This seems to be what is going on in the case of Mr. Kowalski.

Waiving a right is one way of alienating it. *Transferring* a right to another is a second form of alienation. To say that something is alienable is to say that it is transferable to the ownership of another.[30] A person's right to the property he possesses is paradigmatically alienable because it is transferable. If Helen is the owner of a book, she may transfer it to another by sale, trade, or gift. As with waiver, in order for transfer to be valid the possessor must have acted freely, with understanding, and with no fraud on the part of others. If Helen does transfer her book to Otto, then all claims and correlative obligations (based on property rights) regarding the book that were owed to Helen are now owed to Otto; Otto is now the possessor, and even Helen has obligations regarding the book that are owed to Otto.

Waiver is *unilateral* and brings about one significant normative change, namely, that (selected) others are now authorized to do certain things because of the waiver. Transfer involves at least two parties; it is *bilateral* and brings about two normative changes. First, it authorizes another specific individual(s) to do things that were previously not warranted. And second, it imposes new obligations on the original possessor (though these obligations are selfimposed, in a sense). A good example from the classical philosophical literature is provided by John Locke.[31] As an advocate of the social contract theory, Locke holds that no one can be legitimately subjected to political power without his consent. But if an individual does consent to join a state, that voluntary act effects two significant moral changes: it transfers the right to punish offenders of the laws of nature from that individual to the state; and it places the consenting individual under an obligation not to attempt to punish reputed offenders of the law.

The explanations just given may leave one with the false impression that transfer is always permanent; but that need not be so. If a person has signed a lease on a apartment with a term of one year and makes the monthly payments, that authorizes the lessee to live in the apartment for that year (assuming that he abides by all terms of the agreement) and places an obligation on the landlord (at the very least) to allow the occupancy. At the end of the year things may change; transfer need not be forever.

What is common to waiver and transfer is that the possessor's consent (or behavior that warrants the inference of consent) authorizes others to infringe the possessor's right; the infringement is justified *because of* consent. When transfer occurs, not only are others authorized to infringe the possessor's right, but in addition the possessor has incurred an obligation (typically an obligation not to interfere) to the individual to whom the right has been transferred. An individual has alienated a right if she has waived it or transferred it to another. A right is *alienable* if that right may be waived or transferred to another. In some cases it may make sense to talk about waiver but not transferrence: For example, while we may sensibly talk about a person waiving her right to have an attorney present while being questioned by the police, it makes little sense to talk about transferring such a right to another.

There can be instances where one neither asserts nor claims one's rights, yet alienation is not involved. In some cases, a person may simply choose *not to exercise* a right that she possesses. Citizens have the right to vote, but they may (legally) choose not to vote if they wish. And an individual who is married may have a right to sue his or her spouse for divorce, yet choose not to exercise that right. Simply not exercising a right does not authorize others' infringing that right in the way that waiver or transfer does. Citizens who do not exercise their right to vote nevertheless retain it, and others are not permitted to prevent them from voting should they change their mind. They continue to have the choice to vote in any particular election until the polls close, and in subsequent elections if they choose. And though an individual does not exercise his right to file for divorce, he retains the right to do so and others may not interfere with this.

Some may hold that there are rights that it is not permissible for the possessor not to exercise. Such rights are called *mandatory*; they are rights that must be exercised by their possessors. Examples of allegedly mandatory rights cited by Feinberg include the right to education and a student's right to be vaccinated against certain contagious diseases.[32] He says that these rights involve "half-liberties" with respect to their objects, since the possessors have a duty (not merely a liberty) regarding the object. If there are any mandatory rights, then the possessor may neither waive, transfer, nor refrain from exercising those rights.

Let us now turn to the notion of an *inalienable right*. If certain rights are correctly said to be inalienable, this tells us "something about how the rights may be treated, either by the rightholders or by others . . ."[33] Simply put, an inalienable right is one that is not subject to alienation. An inalienable right is one that may not be waived nor transferred by the possessor to another.[34] If a right is inalienable, the possessor's consent does not normatively authorize others to infringe that right *and* the possessor's consent does not obligate the possessor with respect to the activity in question. Consider as an example a citizen's right to vote. A citizen may not transfer this right to another either by sale or gift. Even if I sign an agreement with you not to vote in the upcoming election in exchange for a sum of money, this puts me under no (legal) obligation not to vote; this is not an enforceable contract. Nor is a person's right to vote waivable. Of course, a person may choose not to exercise her right to vote. And in the legal system of the United States, prisoners forfeit the right to vote. But giving permission to others to stop one from voting does not authorize others to do so. With regard to inalienable rights, the possessor's consent lacks normative efficacy. So understood, we can now see that an inalienable right is one that may neither be transferred nor waived by its possessor. Here I take transfer and waiver to be different ways of alienating a right. For transfer and waiver both authorize others to infringe a right; but transfer, in addition, places obligations on the original possessor. So if a right is inalienable, then the possessor's consent lacks normative efficacy with respect to the obligation correlative with that right.

Thomson says that "if there are inalienable rights, then we each of us have some immunities against ourselves."[35] An immunity is the absence of vulnerability to some change in one's legal (or moral) position.[36] A property owner possesses an immunity against others when they are not empowered to dispose of his property. Given my account of inalienable rights, Thomson's claim is correct in this sense: If there are inalienable rights, each of us has immunities against ourselves in that we lack the power to authorize others to infringe our (inalienable) rights merely because we consent *and* we lack the power to obligate ourselves by mere consent to allow such infringement.

Explicating the notions of waivability and transferability as I just have does leave open the possibility that a right is waivable, but one of the conjuncts defining transferability is not satisfied. This would occur if the possessor's consent did authorize others to infringe the right in question, but it was impossible for the consentor to obligate himself (through consent) to allow the infringement to occur (or to continue). Again, an example is waiving the right to have legal counsel present when being questioned by the police. At any point the person being questioned may stop the process until an attorney representing her is on the scene.

It should be acknowledged that the phrase "inalienable right" is sometimes used in a looser and more popular sense. According to this popular usage, an inalienable right is one that may never be taken from the possessor. Revolutionaries and persons protesting abuses of rights sometimes assert, usually against governments of whose activities they disapprove, that citizens have certain inalienable rights. This is to use the term in a looser sense. Scholars too sometimes understand inalienable rights in this looser way. Germain Grisez, for example, writes, "If I have an unalienable right to life, then it is always wrong for others to kill me. If it is sometimes justified for them to kill me, then my right to life is not unalienable."[37] So understood, this designates what I earlier called "absolute rights." And, of course, Grisez is not alone in employing the notion of an inalienable right in this broad sense.[38]

It should also be acknowledged that others have given accounts of inalienable rights that are broader than mine, but less broad than the popular sense. Diana T. Meyers, for example, explains inalienable rights as follows: "It is impossible for anyone who has these rights to lose them."[39] Meyers later identifies various ways that persons might lose rights, including renunciation, conditional waiver, forfeiture, and revocation,[40] and says that inalienable rights cannot be lost in *any* of these ways. This, in effect, counts forfeiture as a case of alienation; and Meyers is not alone in explicating the notion in this way.[41] Obviously, philosophers are free to stipulate how they will use various terms. My reason for distinguishing forfeiture from alienation, and therefore defining 'inalienable' more narrowly than Meyers, is that I want to focus on one kind of justification that might be cited for infringing a person's right—namely, that the possessor gave consent. And that the possessor gave consent (or engaged in conduct that warranted the inference of consent) is what I take to be common to waiver and transfer. When an individual forfeits a right, he is not giving others consent to infringe his rights; rather, it is his wrongdoing that authorizes their behavior. It is true that his behavior is voluntary, but that does not mean that he has given consent. For presumably in most cases the individual who forfeits a right wants to "get away with" his offense.

Still, those who understand inalienability to preclude forfeiture may argue for the superiority of their account over mine by pointing to the fact that an individual may forfeit a right intentionally. Thus Meyers argues, "Provided that right-holders can opt to forfeit their rights and can elicit revocation of them, their rights are renounceable since intentional forfeiture or deliberately provoked revocation is nothing other than indirect renunciation."[42] The idea here is that if a right is forfeitable and if the possessor wishes to divest himself of that right, then he can do so by engaging in whatever prohibited behavior will effect the result of losing that right. So it seems that this is just a special way of alienating a right. Others have noted this too.[43] But the fact remains that what *justifies others* in infringing the right in question is different in the two cases: in the case of forfeiture, it is the possessor's wrongdoing; in the case of alienation, it is the possessor's consent. And it is possible that there may be good reasons to support a public policy that allows infringement when the possessor has engaged in certain offenses, but does not allow infringement simply because of the possessor's consent. It is not inconsistent with the supposition that all persons have an inalienable right to life to say that governments are justified in executing criminals who have forfeited that right.[44]

Moreover, there is another problem with regarding forfeiture as one instance of alienation. There is an important difference between transfer and waiver, on the one hand, and forfeiture, on the other. Declaration of one's intentions (in a way that constitutes consent), if done knowingly and voluntarily, is sufficient for alienation (assuming, of course, that the right in question is alienable). But this is not the case with forfeiture. Suppose that Otto believes that engaging in act *A* will result in his forfeiting right *R*, and Otto engages in act *A* for the very purpose of forfeiting *R*. Suppose too that though right *R* is forfeitable, it is not forfeited by engaging in acts of type *A*. Given these suppositions, others are *not authorized* in infringing Otto's right to *R* simply because Otto intentionally performed act *A*. This suggests that we will do well to keep the notions of forfeiture and alienation separate.

Even among those who restrict the account of inalienable rights along the same lines that I have suggested, there are differences of explication. And I now turn to one of the most influential accounts that varies from my own.

Feinberg's Account of Inalienable Rights

Joel Feinberg, in a seminal essay, "Voluntary Euthanasia and the Inalienable Right to Life,"[45] has sketched an account of inalienable rights that is somewhat different from the one offered above. A detailed examination of Feinberg's account will be useful both because of its influence and because such an examination will enable me to clarify my own views.

Feinberg's principal motivation is to show that voluntary euthanasia is permissible, even if the right to life is inalienable.[46] Feinberg distinguishes two ways of giving up a right.[47] One might waive a right that one continues to possess, or one might relinquish the very possession of the right itself. Waiving a right, according to Feinberg, involves giving it up temporarily; in so doing, one retains "the right to change one's mind *at any point* and thereby nullify the transaction."[48] By contrast, relinquishing the very possession of a right is permanent and irrevocable. To clarify the notion of an inalienable right, Feinberg says, one must ask whether it is X itself or the right to X which may not be given up. If a right may be waived but not relinquished, it is the right to X and not X itself which may not be given up. If people are only prohibited from relinquishing but not waiving their inalienable rights, there will be more liberty associated with the doctrine of inalienable rights than many have previously supposed.

To illustrate this difference, Feinberg discusses the rights to property, liberty, and life. In each case, the purpose is to demonstrate the difference between giving up X and giving up the right to X. Begin with property. Imagine a person giving away his land and money and living the life of a beggar. Such a person has given up his right to specific possessions, but he has not given up the very right to acquire property. For a person to be able to give up the very right to acquire property, we have to imagine a system in which the right to acquire property can be relinquished irrevocably in a legally binding way, perhaps in exchange for a large sum of money to be paid to a third party. In such a system, once the exchange occurs the individual may never again own possessions, unless the individual with whom he contracted frees him to do so.

Turning to the right to liberty, we can envision many situations in which a person seems to waive his right to liberty temporarily. Feinberg describes a case reputedly of this sort in which an individual has locked himself in a room and has thrown away the key. The person has arranged to have food put through a small window, and his garbage is taken away daily. The person may terminate this arrangement and regain his freedom simply by informing the delivery persons of his desire to do so. Such an individual continues to possess the right to liberty, even though he has voluntarily given up his freedom temporarily. By contrast, to relinquish the very right to liberty is to become the permanent slave of another. Were such an arrangement possible, one might contract to become a slave in exchange for a large sum of money to be paid to one's beneficiaries.

The right to life is much trickier because life itself cannot be given up temporarily and then regained. What Feinberg does is to describe a situation in which the (correlative) *duty* of others not to kill a person is suspended temporarily. He asks readers to imagine a community whose members celebrate an annual spring rite. Included in the tradition is a contest in which all males of a certain age are encouraged to participate. Each of the participants is armed with lethal weapons. For a fixed period of time—say, an hour—each participant roams the forest in search of others. The object of the game is to stay alive for the duration of the contest and to kill as many of the others as possible. Feinberg contends that voluntary participants have waived their right to life (vis-à-vis the other participants) while the game is in progress; they have released other participants from the duty not to kill them during that time. But what would it be like to relinquish permanently the right to life? Such a situation could obtain, Feinberg claims, in a legal system that allowed a person to give to another the *irrevocable* right to kill him, again in exchange for some benefit, presumably a benefit bestowed on some third party designated by the individual who is relinquishing his right to life.

If Feinberg's case illustrating waiver of the right to life seems strange and concocted, a different example might be produced. Suppose that two persons have a bitter dispute. Each wants to settle the matter and settle it quickly. They agree that the best method of resolution is to have a duel. If each is participating voluntarily, then it seems plausible to say that each has waived his right to life vis-à-vis the other participant; each has suspended for the other participant only the duty not to kill or maim.[49] If one (or both) survives, then presumably he (or they) regains his right to life in full when the duel ends.

To relinquish a right, then, is to abandon one's discretion; one no longer has control over the thing in question. To waive a right, though, is merely to exercise one's discretion in a certain way; one decides to give up temporarily that to which one has a right or the protection that is bestowed by the right.[50] Feinberg spells out this distinction so carefully because he believes that failure to do so will render the doctrine of inalienable rights ambiguous. On one account an inalienable right is one that may not be relinquished by its possessor, though it may be waived. On another account an inalienable right may be neither waived nor relinquished by its possessor. Once one is clear about this distinction, Feinberg thinks that the three major points that he wants to establish can be made.[51] First, he wants to show that if the right to life is inalienable only in the sense that it may not be relinquished by its possessor, then voluntary euthanasia need not be impermissible. This is so because the doctrine of inalienable rights, so understood, will prohibit a person from allowing another to choose whether he lives or dies; but it does not forbid the person from choosing death for himself and enlisting the help of others to carry out the choice. It is not life itself but the right to life that may not be relinquished. Second, he suggests that the doctrine of inalienable rights understood this way is plausible and certainly more defensible than if it were contrued as proscribing even the waiver of certain rights. This is so because the doctrine, construed in the former way, is less paternalistic and exhibits greater respect for personal autonomy (than if the doctrine is interpreted in the latter, stronger way). Third, Feinberg contends that this account of the doctrine of inalienable rights closely resembles that which Jefferson and the other founding fathers had in mind.

In the previous section, I suggested that inalienable rights are best understood as follows: if X is an inalienable right, then others are not justified in infringing X simply because the possessor consented, and the possessor is not obligated to allow others to infringe X simply because he has given consent. On my account, both waiver and transfer are prohibited if a right is inalienable. This is incompatible with Feinberg's contention that the inalienability of a right only precludes the possessor from giving up the right itself, and not the thing to which he has a right. There is significant agreement between the two accounts, but the chief point of disagreement between them is this: Feinberg is committed to saying that even if the right to X is inalienable, others may in certain circumstances still be justified in infringing X simply because the possessor has consented. This is so because, according to Feinberg, even inalienable rights may be waived. While Feinberg's account of waiving is different from what I have offered, the distinction that he draws between waiving and relinquishing rights is genuine. It is doubtful, however, that this distinction does the work that Feinberg wants it to do. In the remainder of this section, I shall argue that there are three difficulties with Feinberg's account of inalienable rights.

To explain the first problem, it is instructive to ask what actions or contractual arrangements are prohibited if a right is inalienable. This is to inquire about the normative effects of inalienable rights. According to Feinberg, the most plausible version of the doctrine of inalienable rights permits the possessor to waive but not to relinquish an inalienable right. Applied to the right to liberty, this version of the doctrine prohibits a person from voluntarily becoming the permanent slave of another. That is a desirable result given that in our legal system such a relation is prohibited and seems to be so because the right to liberty is inalienable. When applied to the right to life, however, Feinberg's version of the doctrine proscribes only bizarre possibilities. What is forbidden is the contractual relationship between two parties in which one is given *irrevocable* permission to kill the other any time he chooses. It is difficult to imagine circumstances in which two parties would voluntarily agree to such a contract. It is even more difficult to believe that this is all that the founding fathers intended to prohibit when they proclaimed the right to life to be inalienable. Yet Feinberg claims to have described the doctrine of inalienability enbraced by those admired ancestors.

There is a second problem regarding the right to life. If we regard the right to life as inalienable only in the sense that Feinberg thinks is plausible, then it cannot be employed in circumstances where it is most natural to appeal to it. The paradigmatic situation in which the inalienability of the right to life is cited is that in which one person asks another to kill him for no apparent reason. In our legal system that second party is not permitted to kill the person because consent alone does not justify taking human life. The cases of Susan Potempa and Sharon Lopatka, described earlier, show this, though of course Potempa apparently had an understandable reason for consenting. Feinberg's account of the doctrine of inalienable rights will not yield such a result, however. To ask another to kill one for no good reason is not the same as relinquishing the right to life; until the act is performed, the possessor can change her mind. Of course, Feinberg can argue that there is *some other reason* for prohibiting the killing of another when he asks you to do so for no good reason; utilitarian considerations might be cited, for example.[52] But since this is a situation in which the inalienability of the right to life is most naturally invoked, it is a weakness of Feinberg's account that it cannot be so employed.

Finally, when discussing the difference between giving up X and giving up the right to X, there is an obvious asymmetry between the rights to property and liberty on the one hand and the right to life on the other. Feinberg acknowledges the asymmetry, but thinks it causes no problems. I contend, however, that it does have an adverse impact on his argument. Consider the person who gives up his property or freedom but retains the relevant right in question. That person can acquire new property or regain his lost freedom. But even if a person only temporarily waives the right to life, if another takes his life the loss is irrevocable. The importance of this disanalogy becomes clear when one compares the examples of waiving the rights to liberty and to life that are provided by Feinberg. Concerning the case involving the right to liberty, the person has given up his freedom but may regain it whenever he wishes. What is given up in the case in which the right to life is waived, however, is not life itself; rather it is the *protection* of life that that right bestows on its possessor. A voluntary participant (in the spring rite or in a duel) has released other participants from the duty not to kill him for the duration of the contest. Moreover, while the game is in progress the participants cannot change their minds and reclaim the protection provided by the right to life. These differences are significant and may provide grounds for making different judgments about the situations.

The latter difference—that one cannot change one's mind—is apparently removed in the second example of waiving the right to life furnished by Feinberg. This is a case in which a person signs a "living will," a document directing others either not to take steps to sustain one's life or to take positive steps to kill oneself provided that specified medical conditions obtain.[53] Here, until the person's life is ended, it seems that he can change his mind and reclaim the right to life in full. The former difference, however, remains: where the right to liberty is waived, *freedom itself* is lost *temporarily*; when the right to life is waived, only the *protection* that bearers of that right possess is lost, but if life is taken the loss is *permanent*. Since these are arguably normatively relevant differences, the example involving the right to liberty should be changed. In fact, in the case presented by Feinberg one might well say that the person has not really lost his freedom at all but is merely exercising it in an unusual way; to escape the locked room he need only convey his wishes to the delivery persons. To make the cases analogous, the situation must be altered so that the one who has waived (but not relinquished) the right to liberty has given others permission to make him a slave for the duration of the time agreed on. And if while the permission is in effect others succeed in enslaving the person, his freedom is lost forever (unless his captors choose to release him).

To understand why it is important to make these cases analogous, recall what Feinberg's strategy is. After articulating the distinction between waiving and relinquishing, Feinberg wants to show that the doctrine of inalienable rights is plausible only if it forbids possessors to relinquish certain rights; waiving those same rights should be permitted. To support this, he provides examples of waiving the rights to property and liberty. In these two cases, most will agree that the arrangements should be permitted. So, the argument goes, consistency requires that we approve of waiving the right to life too. The case involving property rights need not concern us. It is not surprising that we approve of waiving property rights since they are uncontroversially alienable. But the examples of waiving the right to liberty and the right to life must be relevantly similar since each is thought by some to be inalienable. When the case concerning the right to liberty is reconstructed, however, so that the loss of liberty can be permanent, then it is not obvious that most will approve of waiving that right. And if one is not convinced by this (reconstructed) case, then one is not compelled to grant that waiving the right should be allowed.

It is important to note that even if one agrees that others should comply with the wishes of a person who has executed a living will, it does not follow that the right to life is alienable. For typically living wills instruct others that certain medical procedures should not be started, or if they have already been initiated then stopped, when certain specified conditions obtain.[54] And not initiating or withdrawing treatment is usually not regarded as killing a person. So one may be comfortable with the moral appropriateness of complying with the instructions in a person's living will, even if one is not sure whether the right to life is inalienable.

It is also important to notice that arrangements made in living wills are not actually instances of waiver, as Feinberg understands that notion. With genuine waiver (according to Feinberg), the rights-possessor can change his mind at any time and regain the right in full. But living wills and other advance directives go into effect *only when* the person who executed the document lacks decision-making capacity—only when he is not competent to make his own medical decisions.[55] While not competent, the individual cannot regain the right in full because he lacks the capacity to exercise that right. In some instances, of course, he may regain that capacity and *then* he will be able to regain the right in full. In a very important kind of case, however, he will *never* regain the relevant capacity. This is when the person who executed the document is irreversibly incompetent. The most widely discussed example is the patient who is in a persistent vegetative state. Other examples include individuals who are irreversibly comatose and those with irreversible dementia. In none of these cases can the person change his mind and regain the relevant right. This is ironic. For it is only *waiver* of an inalienable right that Feinberg approves of. Yet a case that nearly everyone who executes a living will wants covered—namely, the case of a persistent vegetative state—is a case that cannot count as waiver once the condition obtains. If waiver is relevant to living wills, as Feinberg and many others assume, this is an unwelcome result.[56]

Feinberg, then, understands inalienable rights in terms of irrevocable agreements. If a right is inalienable, then the possessor may not transfer it irrevocably to another, nor may he suspend irrevocably the duty correlative with that right. I do not deny that irrevocability may sometimes be important; but I deny that it is part of the *concept* of an inalienable right. Instead, I suggest that if a right is inalienable, then the possessor's consent lacks normative force that is present if the right is alienable. If the right to R is inalienable, then P_1's consent does not justify P_2 in infringing P_1's right to R, nor is P_1's consent sufficient to put P_1 under an obligation to P_2 to allow such an infringement. It is worth noting that each of these aspects of inalienability that I have highlighted are discussed by legal scholars. In providing accounts of inalienability, some legal scholars emphasize prohibited transfers between consenting parties,[57] while others focus on the idea that the possessor's consent does not create an enforceable obligation and so limits his ability to make enforceable contracts.[58]

Clarifications

According to my account, then, an inalienable right is such that the possessor's consent does not justify another in infringing that right and that consent does not bring about any new obligations on the possessor. The possessers of inalienable rights lack the normative authority to effect such changes.

Earlier I said that mandatory rights are ones that must be exercised by their possessors. A child's right to education, according to Feinberg, is mandatory. If there are any mandatory rights, then possessors of those rights may not waive, alienate, nor refrain from exercising them. But if a right is inalienable, does it follow that it is mandatory? Some have answered this question affirmatively. James Nickel writes: "A claim that human rights can neither be given up permanently nor waived temporarily would have very paternalistic overtones since it amounts to an assertion that one must keep and use on every possible opportunity all of one's human rights."[59] But this seems incorrect. An inalienable right may neither be waived nor transferred to another by its possessor; but there is nothing about inalienable rights that requires the possessor to exercise them.[60] A citizen's right to vote is a clear example. A citizen may not transfer her right to vote to another, nor may she incur a contractual obligation to another not to exercise that right. But still a citizen is not (legally) required to exercise her right not to vote (at least in the United States). So inalienable rights need not be mandatory.

A second clarification concerns limits. Even if two consenting individuals are forbidden (either legally or morally) from engaging in certain behavior, it does not follow that inalienable rights are involved. Sexual intercourse between two consenting persons, each of whom is married to someone else, may be forbidden (morally and legally), but this has nothing to do with inalienable rights because infringement of the right of one of the consenting parties has no relevance to why the behavior is forbidden. Similarly, the mere fact that a contract between P_1 and P_2 creates no enforceable obligations does not necessarily indicate that inalienable rights are involved; the reason, again, is that infringement of a right of P_1 or of P_2 may have nothing to do with why no obligation is created. For example, if P_1 contracts with P_2 to kill P_3, this creates no new obligations on either P_1 or P_2; but the doctrine of inalienable rights has no bearing on why no new obligation is incurred because no right of either consenting party—P_1 or P_2—is infringed, permissibly or otherwise. And again, the mere fact that a person's permission does not authorize an act need not signal the existence of an inalienable right; for the contemplated action may be wrong for other reasons. Arthur Caplan discusses a case in which a man charged with sexual assault requests surgical castration instead of incarceration.[61] Caplan cites multiple reasons against complying with this request, including doubts that such a choice is voluntary and qualms about physicians being used by the state to mete out punishment. It is possible to find these reasons convincing without necessarily supposing that any inalienable rights are involved.

Nothing I have said so far precludes the possibility that some rights are neither alienable nor inalienable. This is the third point of clarification. My account implies that in order to qualify for possession of an inalienable right, one must be capable of giving genuine consent; the same is true of alienable rights. But I do not assume that beings incapable of giving consent cannot possess rights. Perhaps irreversibly comatose individuals possess some rights. Or maybe anencephalic neonates have selected rights. Or maybe sentient nonhuman animals have rights. If in any of these cases we have a possessor of rights, then presumably the rights possessed are neither alienable nor inalienable.

By way of a final clarification, I should also say something about my general approach here. As I said, I am limiting myself to rights that imply duties on others, and I am interested in when such correlative requirements are suspended and when they are not. In particular, if a right is waivable or alienable, then the possessor's informed and voluntary consent alone is sufficient to suspend the correlative duty and to justify the person to whom the consent was given to infringe the right. If a right is inalienable, then the possessor's consent alone does not have the normative force to suspend the correlative duty. My approach assumes that rights are the basis of certain duties, understood as prohibitions or prescriptions, but that acting in ways other than what these prohibitions and prescriptions dictate is sometimes permissible. When such behavior is permissible, I call the act a *justified infringement*. And depending on the right in question and the nature of the circumstances, an infringement might be justified because the possessor forfeited his right, because the right was over-ridden by more important moral considerations, or because the possessor consented to the infringement.

One might take a different approach to account for the same "data." Consider again the case (described by Feinberg) in which you are stranded in the mountains due to a ferocious blizzard. You break into an unoccupied cabin and use the owner's food. I have said that you have infringed the owner's property rights, but it is a case of justified infringement because the duties associated with the property rights have been defeated by more important moral considerations. An alternative approach would be to specify further the content of the right. In this *specification*, one might deny that property rights give their possessors rights against others when the lives of those others depend on the use of one's property. So once the right is fully specified, the behavior is *not an infringement* at all; the right does not even pretend to preclude the behavior in question. The "further specification" account makes all rights absolute.

I prefer the "justified infringement" approach rather than the "further specification" approach for two reasons. First, I am not at all convinced that all of the necessary specifications could ever be executed; the possibilities seem too numerous. And even if it were possible, the resulting right would be incredibly complex. Second, I am not sure that the "further specification" approach can account for some of the things that we would like an adequate view to account for. For example, if you do use the cabin owner's food, once you return to safety, it seems that at the very least you should compensate the owner for his losses. But on the specification view it will be difficult to say why; for on this view you have neither violated nor infringed his right at all. Advocates of the "further specification" view may say that there is some other basis for this duty. But I would argue that the duty is best explained as existing *because* of the infringement of the right, and only the "justified infringement" approach squares with this.[62] A third, and related, criticism is that conduct that many hold is justifiable is nevertheless an infringement of a right. One might argue, for example, that it is justifiable to warn the spouse of an HIV-positive man about his medical condition if he refuses to do so himself and says that he will not alter his sexual practices and use condoms.[63] Most will agree that this is an infringement of his right to privacy, though many maintain that it is a *justifiable* infringement.

I do not here pretend to have shown that the "justified infringement" approach is superior to the "further specification" view. I have merely explained which approach I am taking and why. But on either approach, one would have to wrestle with some of the same questions—though they would be put differently. I am interested in what rights are alienable and what rights are inalienable. So my focus is on when the possessor's consent justifies infringing his right. But the same issue would arise, in a different way, within the "further specification" view. For example, if the right to life is inalienable, then presumably the possessor's consent does not justify killing him. So when the right to life is specified, it will say something about an obligation not to kill the possessor, but will say *nothing* to the effect "unless he consents." On the other hand, a person's right to privacy gives him (among other things) a right against his physician that she not reveal information about his medical condition to others. But presumably this is a waivable right; with the patient's consent, the physician is permitted to convey information about the patient to his spouse. So a full specification of *this* right will include the proviso "unless he consents." So, since one must face the issue one way or the other, one suspects that it does not really matter (to the issue I am interested in) whether one adopts the "justified infringement" approach or the "further specification" view. But for reasons already indicated, I prefer the former.

On my account, at least some rights—and perhaps many—are nonabsolute. Some object to this because they think that it implies that rights are merely prima facie; but, they insist, the *right* remains the same, even when others permissibly deny a person that to which he has a right. I agree that the right remains the same, and so the rights themselves are not merely prima facie. What varies in strength is the correlative duty associated with rights. And indeed I should think that this must be the case if we are to make sense of the world in which talk about rights is invoked. For notice that the duties correlative with rights are duties *on others* vis-à-vis the possessor. But these other agents are subject to all sorts of different duties in different contexts, and obviously these various duties may sometimes conflict. Unless one is willing to say that in all of these cases of conflict there are genuine moral dilemmas—and I am not willing to say this[64]—then these different duties *must* sometimes vary in strength. To deny this seems solipsistic. For assuming that duties correlative with a person's rights at least sometimes bind others, then if their relative strength is invariant they must always bind others. But once a conflict between rights of multiple individuals occurs, then the hypothesis that the relative strength of associated duties is invariant can be maintained only if we allow for genuine moral dilemmas or we give an account of rights in the "further specification" tradition. Since I reject both moral dilemmas and the "further specification" view, I hold that the strength of the duties associated with rights varies in strength from context to context.

TWO

The Moral Foundations of Inalienable Rights

An inalienable right may neither be waived nor transferred by its possessor. Waiver is a unilateral activity in which the possessor of the right suspends for others the obligation not to infringe the right in question. Transfer is a bilateral activity in which the possessor transfers the right (or the object protected by the right) and the accompanying normative advantages to another. If a right is alienable, valid waiver or transfer changes the normative landscape; infringing a person's right is rendered permissible because of his consent. If a right is inalienable, the consent of the possessor alone does not justify infringing that right.

The focus of this chapter is on the normative foundations of inalienable rights. If a right is inalienable, the behavior of consenting individuals is restricted. What justifies such a restriction is the topic of this chapter.

The Challenge

Others have recognized that a moral justification is needed for inalienable rights. Henry Sidgwick, in *The Method of Ethics*, notes that such rights are frequently invoked in moral debates, but says that there is a serious "difficulty of deducing these inalienable rights from any clear and generally accepted principles."[1] Sidgwick is suggesting that such rights require a normative foundation and to date none has been forthcoming. It should be noted, however, that Sidgwick seems to be using the notion of 'inalienable right' in a rather broad sense, designating the idea that *others* may not take the right from the possessor.

Judith Jarvis Thomson poses the challenge for those who want to defend inalienable rights in the more technical sense (that is being employed in this work). In *The Realm of Rights*, Thomson distinguishes three different senses of 'inalienable right', the second of which is a right that a person cannot make himself cease to have by sale or other form of trade; so understood, inalienable rights *limit* the powers of their possessors to make themselves cease to have the rights. Thomson declares "that no right is inalienable" in this sense. She admits that she has no argument for this view, but says "I see no good argument against it."[2] Construed charitably, Thomson is suggesting that the burden of proof is on defenders of inalienable rights. Since they are imposing additional restrictions on individuals, they owe us a justification for doing so.

One way to respond to Thomson's challenge is to deny its legitimacy. Perhaps those who hold that rights are basic would do just that. To say that rights are *basic* in a theory is to say that rights "are not supported by yet more fundamental principles that make no mention of rights."[3] Even if rights are basic, however, it need not be inappropriate to demand a moral justification for inalienable rights. For their status of inalienability deprives possessors of options they would otherwise have (with other rights); and it seems appropriate to seek a justification for such deprivation.

Assigning the burden of proof in philosophical debates is tricky. It is often hard to ascertain any principled basis for assigning the burden to one side or the other in such debates. And, not surprisingly, in the debate about inalienable rights, Daniel Callahan asserts a claim about where the burden lies that is in conflict with Thomson's position. "Is our right to life just like a piece of property, to be given away or alienated if the price (happiness, relief of suffering) is right? . . . The idea that we can waive our right to life, and then give another the power to take that life, requires a justification yet to be provided by anyone."[4] Thomson and Callahan might both be right, of course. There may not be any good arguments for inalienable rights (at least none that Thomson *has seen*), and perhaps no plausible justification for the alienability of the right to life has been produced either. Since I intend to defend the claim that some rights are inalienable, I will assume the burden of proof and try to respond to Thomson's challenge.

When valid waiver occurs, an agent is permitted to infringe a right because of the possessor's consent. If a right is not waivable, the behavior of consenting individuals is restricted. (In the case of legal rights, the restriction is imposed by the state; in the case of moral rights, by morality.) When transfer occurs, the possessor conveys her right to another. The second party is now the possessor because of the transfer and the original possessor is under new obligations as a result of giving her word. If a right is inalienable, no such obligations are created and none will be enforced. In asking why this should ever be so, we are asking for a moral justification of inalienable rights. Arthur Kuflik puts it this way: "*Why* should the state adopt a policy of not enforcing contracts in which certain rights are putatively given up? And what is it about those rights, but not others, that warrants the view that a person should not have the right to trade them away?"[5] These are questions that defenders of inalienable rights must answer. And these questions are appropriate whether we are talking about moral rights or morally justifiable legal rights. Many think that there is no plausible answer to these queries. It is with these opponents of inalienable rights that we begin.

Arguments Against Inalienable Rights

Some reject inalienable rights explicitly; others do so by implication. But either way, there is significant and powerful opposition to inalienable rights. Understood one way, these opponents of inalienable rights maintain that the state should enforce contracts between consenting parties when one freely and knowingly transfers some of his rights to another. Here three different arguments against inalienable rights will be discussed. One of these arguments is conceptual; the others are normative. The next section will indicate how defenders of inalienable rights might respond to these challenges.

The first and most serious argument against inalienable rights is *conceptual.* According to this argument, it is a part of the very concept of a right that its possessor may waive or transfer it to another. Just as it is a conceptual truth that rights imply obligations, so too it is a conceptual truth that the consent of the possessor suspends that obligation; genuine consent is a permission-generating act.

Among others, Allen Buchanan has given voice to this argument. He claims that "part of what is distinctively valuable about rights is that they may be invoked or not invoked or waived."[6] Buchanan immediately adds that it is because right-holders have these options that "allows rights to function as nonpaternalistic protections of the invidual's interests, and, indeed, allows rights to function as nonpaternalistic protection against paternalism." Dan Brock conveys these same points when he writes: "A more important aspect of rights is that their possessor may waive them, or give consent for acts that would otherwise violate them, for reasons that need not accord with the best available estimate of his long-term interests."[7] Both Buchanan and Brock hold, then, that part of the concept of a right is that its possessor may waive it if he chooses.

Perhaps the most forceful advocate of the conceptual argument against inalienable rights is Baruch Brody. Brody agrees that rights imply obligations. To make this point, he offers the following matrix: P_1 has a right to R against P_2 if and only if P_2 has an obligation to P_1 not to deprive P_1 of R or to withhold R from P_1.[8] But this correlative obligation is such that P_1 can relieve P_2 of it. Brody asserts that "rights are *always* waivable."[9] To illustrate what he takes to be a conceptual truth, Brody asks you to imagine that you have lent someone else some money which she has agreed to return to you on a given day. If this is the case, then you have a right to the money on that day and she has an obligation to repay it. But you may waive that right; if you do, she no longer has an obligation to repay you on that day. And depending on the nature of the waiver, she may have no obligation to repay you at all. This is but one example and involves a right that all will acknowledge is alienable. Brody recognizes this and is aware that some will still hold that certain rights are inalienable. But he retorts, "I cannot accept such a claim; it turns a right into something you are stuck with, and that is not the proper way of understanding rights."[10] Rights are normatively advantageous to their possessors. But if some rights were inalienable, they could be burdensome to their possessors. Therefore, no rights are inalienable.

Brody asserts that the rights not to be killed, not to have bodily injury inflicted on oneself, and to make one's own medical decisions are waivable,[11] but in each case he reminds readers that this is a feature they share with *all* rights. The aspect of rights that Brody focuses on is control; right-holders call the shots with respect to their own rights. Thus, Brody concludes: "When your action is wrong because it infringes on the rights of others, then it is wrong because you have wrongly interfered in an area that is theirs to control, and that person's consent can eliminate the wrongness of your action. That is why there are no inalienable rights."[12] Brock too claims that the idea of control is crucial to understanding rights. He says, "Rights protect our freedom to act in the areas the right covers even in ways that may not be in our overall best interests." And this feature of rights "reflects a value placed on our autonomy or self-determination in making such choices and directing our lives. . ."[13]

So, Buchanan, Brody, and Brock endorse the conceptual argument against inalienable rights. If some rights were inalienable, individuals would lack the control necessary for understanding why rights are advantageous to their possessors.

Two other arguments against inalienable rights will be discussed; these arguments are normative. The first is the *antipaternalistic* argument. This argument attempts to link the endorsement of inalienable rights with a commitment to paternalism, and then rejects paternalism. One who articulates this argument is Robert Nozick.

> A person may choose to do to himself, I shall suppose, the things that would impinge across his boundaries when done without his consent by another. (Some of these things may be impossible for him to do to himself.) Also, he may give another permission to do these things to him (including things impossible for him to do to himself). Voluntary consent opens the border for crossings. Locke, of course, would hold that there are things that others may not do to you by your permission; namely, those things you have no right to do to yourself. Locke would hold that your giving permission cannot make it morally permissible for another to kill you, because you have no right to commit suicide. My nonpaternalistic position holds that someone may choose (or permit another) to do to himself *anything*, unless he has acquired an obligation to some third party not to do or allow it.[14]

Like Brody, Nozick holds that all rights are alienable; genuine consent always gives permission to others to infringe an individual's right. But Nozick's defense of the alienability of all rights is not based on the conceptual argument. Instead, he maintains that those who hold that some rights are inalienable are committed to paternalism. The idea, I gather, is this. If some rights are inalienable, then the consent of the possessor does not justify another in infringing that right. But if the possessor's consent does not justify such infringement, then the purpose must be to protect the possessor against his own foolishness. To protect persons from their own foolishness is paternalism. Nozick rejects paternalism; therefore, all rights are alienable.

Nozick is not alone in linking inalienable rights and paternalism. James Nickel, for example, says, "A claim that human rights can neither be given up permanently nor waived temporarily would have very paternalistic overtones since it amounts to an assertion that one must keep and use on every possible opportunity all of one's human rights."[15] And, as was noted above, Allen Buchanan says that it is the fact that individuals always have the option of not invoking or waiving their rights that "allows rights to function as non-paternalistic protection against paternalism."[16]

The paternalistic argument against inalienable rights might be summarized as follows:

(i) If right R is inalienable, the rights-possessor's consent is not sufficient to authorize another in infringing R.
(ii) If a rights-possessor's consent is not sufficient to justify another in infringing his rights, then a competent individual's options are being restricted for that person's own good.

(iii) If a competent individual's options are restricted for his own good, then those who are engaged in restricting his options are engaged in paternalism.
(iv) But treating competent individuals paternalistically is unacceptable.
(v) So, no right is inalienable.
(vi) If no right is inalienable, then all rights are alienable.
(vii) So, all rights are alienable.

It is now commonplace to distinguish between two kinds of paternalism—soft paternalism and hard paternalism.[17] Roughly, soft paternalism is restricting a person's freedom for his own good only when that person's behavior is substantially nonvoluntary (due, for example, to mental defect, lack of maturity, compulsion, or ignorance). Paternalism toward an incompetent is typically soft paternalism. Hard paternalism is restricting a person's freedom for his own good, even when his behavior is substantially voluntary. Paternalism toward a competent individual is typically hard paternalism. This argument against inalienable rights is based on rejecting *hard* paternalism. Premise (iv) should be understood as opposing hard paternalism, but not necessarily soft paternalism.

The third argument against inalienable rights, like the second, is troubled by what it takes to be one of the implications of endorsing inalienable rights. This argument claims that those who endorse inalienable rights must affirm that there are duties to oneself; but, the critics claim, the notion of duties to oneself is implausible. The reason that inalienable rights imply duties to oneself, the critic claims, is this. If a right is inalienable, then certain relations between even consenting individuals are prohibited; and if these relations are prohibited, then individuals have a duty not to engage in them. This argument against inalienable rights might be summarized as follows:

(i) If right R is inalienable, then the rights-possessor's consent is not sufficient to authorize another in infringing R.
(ii) If the rights-possessor's consent is not sufficient to authorize another in infringing R, then consenting individuals are prohibited from engaging in a relationship in which one infringes R simply because the other consents.
(iii) If consenting individuals are prohibited from engaging in a relationship in which one infringes R simply because the other consents, then the prohibition imposed on the would-be consentor is a duty that he has to himself.
(iv) But individuals cannot have duties to themselves.
(v) So, no right is inalienable.
(vi) If no right is inalienable, then all rights are alienable.
(vii) So, all rights are alienable.

This, then, completes our explanation of the three main arguments against inalienable rights. We turn now to the issue of whether these arguments are plausible.

Assessing the Arguments Against Inalienable Rights

If any of these arguments is sound, then we may quickly conclude this inquiry; for each of the arguments concludes that all rights are alienable.

Assessing the first argument—the conceptual argument—is the most complex task; evaluating the other two arguments is much simpler.

The conceptual argument is based on a general understanding of the nature of rights. In order to explain that, we need to raise a basic question: What is the normative function that rights perform? Two fundamentally different answers to this question have emerged, answers that can be understood as advancing different conceptions of rights. We will call these the "interest conception of rights" and the "choice conception of rights."[18] These two accounts concur that rights serve as one kind of constraint on the pursuit of social goods. They agree that rights protect their possessors by imposing constraints on others. They differ, however, by offering alternative accounts regarding the point or function of rights. The interest conception holds that rights are devices for promoting individual welfare.[19] Rights imply duties on others, and according to the interest conception the rights-possessor is the beneficiary of a set of duties. The interest conception implies that an individual can have rights only if it has interests, interests that can either be advanced or thwarted. A right-holder must have a good of its own and the duties correlative with rights protect that good.

By contrast, the choice conception maintains that rights are devices for protecting individual autonomy.[20] Rights delineate an area over which an individual has control, and the duties that rights imply prohibit others from usurping this control. On this view, the rights-possessor is pictured "as the active manager of a network of normative relations."[21] Within the designated domain, the rights-possessor is authorized to make choices and rights function to protect individual choices. The choice conception implies that an individual can have rights only if he is capable of making choices with which others might interfere. This presumably means that only autonomous individuals are rights-possessors. It seems clear that the interest account distributes rights more widely than does the choice account.

The dispute between the interest conception of rights and the choice conception of rights is related to the debate about inalienable rights. Indeed, some proponents of the choice conception have asserted that it alone can make sense of rights as the sort of thing which can be exercised or not exercised; and some proponents of the interest conception have argued that it alone can make sense of inalienable rights.[22] This may lead some to conclude that the issue of whether all rights are alienable will depend on whether the interest conception or the choice conception of rights is correct. And that suspicion is further fueled when one recognizes that those who advance the conceptual argument against inalienable rights presuppose the choice conception.

Defenders of the conceptual argument against inalienable rights hold that what is normatively advantageous about rights is the control that is accorded to the possessor of the right in his relations with others. And this control includes alienability. At this point, one obvious option for defenders of inalienable rights to adopt is to argue for the interest conception of rights. While it may not follow immediately from adopting this option that some rights are inalienable, doing so at least blocks the conceptual argument *against* inalienable rights. And one suspects that a positive argument *for* the inalienability of some rights would be easy to construct, given the interest account. I shall not take this option, however. Instead, I propose to grant (for the sake of argument) that the choice conception of rights is correct.

This position will enable us to tangle with advocates of the conceptual argument on their own turf. But a more important reason for adopting the choice conception of rights is one of philosophical economy; for if inalienable rights can be defended on the choice conception of rights, they can be defended on the interest conception too.[23] This follows if we grant the modest assumption that autonomy is a part of individual welfare for those individuals who are capable of choice. Granting this, we may say: "Because autonomy can be treated as a particular component of individual welfare, anything which counts as a right under the choice conception will also count as such under the interest conception."[24] And given this, any right that can be defended as inalienable under the choice conception can also be defended as inalienable under the interest account.

Granting the choice conception of rights, then, what can be said in response to the conceptual argument against inalienable rights? Recall that in part the argument is fueled by the idea that rights cannot be burdensome baggage for their possessors. As acknowledged at the outset of this book, rights are normatively advantageous for those who have them. But what does it mean to say that rights cannot be burdensome to their possessors? Most will grant that rights cannot *always* be burdensome to their possessors; for then it is hard to see how they would be advantageous. But does the defender of the conceptual argument hold that rights can *never* be burdensome to their possessors? Such a claim is implausible. Parents have rights to make certain decisions regarding their children, rights that have associated with them responsibilities. Most of the time these rights are not burdensome; indeed, they bring joys and rewards to parents. Surely, however, these rights are sometimes burdensome. I speculate that the same is true of many other rights.

Addressing the conceptual argument more directly, we may begin with a simple point that even defenders of the choice conception of rights do not think that individuals have unbridled freedom with respect to rights. Since others too have rights, those rights may restrain what the rights-possessor may do or how she may exercise her rights. If exercising a right in a certain way infringes the rights of others, there is at least a reason to believe that exercising the right in that way is wrong. And even defenders of the choice conception will concede that certain agreements between consenting parties are inappropriate and should not be enforced. Again, the uncontroversial case here is when two parties contract to violate the rights of a third individual. If I pay you a sum of money because you agreed to kill Frederick, such an agreement is inappropriate and unenforceable; and this is so, of course, because carrying out the agreement will violate the rights of Frederick. This points the way to an *in principle* argument for the inalienability of some rights that even defenders of the choice conception can accept. If P_2's infringing the right of P_1 simply because P_1 consents causes harm or infringes the rights of some innocent third party or seriously puts those rights at risk, then there are at least prima facie grounds for prohibiting such a relationship. It is important to emphasize that this "in principle" argument for inalienable rights requires the defender to show that the rights or well-being of a third party are jeopardized *simply because* one individual, P_2, is permitted to infringe the right of P_1 whenever P_1 genuinely consents. The burden of showing this may not be easy. One would guess that advocates of the choice conception of rights would work from the presumption that rights are alienable; the burden of proof is on those who hold that some rights are inalienable. And the in principle argument envisioned here is one for a certain social policy. Put in the abstract, the argument for inalienability that even proponents of the choice conception can accept is this: If allowing P_2 to infringe right R of P_1 simply because P_1 consented will endanger the rights of nonconsenting persons, then it is justifiable not to allow such a relationship. In any given case, it may be difficult to make this argument; and the burden is on the proponent of inalienable rights. But this at least shows that the notion of an inalienable right is not ruled out conceptually if we adopt the choice account of rights.

It is worth noting here that advocates of the choice conception of rights are no doubt opposed to mandatory rights, rights that the possessor must exercise. But as was explained in chapter 1, inalienable rights need not be mandatory. The right to vote may not be alienated, nor may the right to sue for divorce (if grounds exist). No agreement not to vote and no antenuptial agreement not to sue for divorce is binding. No such agreement creates a legal obligation; nor, one suspects, a moral obligation.[25] Yet possessors are not legally required to exercise either of these rights, and they are surely not always (if ever) morally required to exercise them. To the extent that the conceptual argument strikes a responsive chord, it may be due to one's inclination to reject mandatory rights, not inalienable rights.

Let us now turn to the other two arguments against inalienable rights. Here our discussion can be brief. Consider first the antipaternalistic argument against inalienable rights. One obvious way to respond to this argument is to embrace hard paternalism. To do so would be to reject premise (iv) of the argument. But I do eschew such a strategy here. This is not necessarily because I am opposed to all instances of hard paternalism; when, if ever, paternalism is warranted is a complicated issue on which entire volumes have been written.[26] Rather, I adopt a different approach so that the issue of paternalism can be put aside. The weak link in the antipaternalistic argument against inalienable rights is premise (ii). According to this premise, if a rights-possessor's consent is not sufficient to justify another in infringing his rights, then a competent individual's options are being restricted for his own good. This, in effect, says that the *only* ground for not permitting infringement on the basis of consent alone is hard paternalism. But this is doubtful. Indeed, the response to the conceptual argument just sketched shows this. If the basis for denying that consent alone justifies infringement is to protect the rights of nonconsenting third parties, then the normative foundation for inalienable rights is not paternalistic. Again, the burden of proof is on the defender of inalienable rights. But if he can show that nonconsenting third parties are threatened, his position need not rest on paternalism.

It is worth noting that the connection between inalienable rights and paternalism might be much stronger if one were to adopt the interest conception of rights. Or, to put the point somewhat differently, if one holds the interest conception of rights, defending inalienable rights seems easier. For if the purpose of rights is to protect the welfare of rights-possessors, then it is not hard to imagine that this goal might better be achieved by denying alienability to at least some rights. But here the interest conception of rights is not employed.

I shall take it as a condition of adequacy, then, that a proper defense of inalienable rights must not be based on (hard) paternalism.

The other argument against inalienable rights is based on the rejection of duties to oneself. Again, the most obvious response to this argument is simply to *deny* that persons cannot have duties to themselves. To adopt this strategy would be to reject premise (iv) of the argument. And though philosophical opposition to the notion of duties to oneself is considerable, it is at least worth noting that some have recently defended this idea.[27] It is also worth noting that at least some of the arguments against the notion of duties to oneself are based on the *assumption* that all rights are alienable. For example, Marcus Singer's well-known argument against duties to oneself is based explicitly on the following assumption: "If *B* has a right against *A*, *B* can give it up and release *A* from the obligation."[28] So unless there are arguments against duties to oneself that do not make this assumption, it is question-begging to appeal to premise (iv) in order to reject inalienable rights.

But here I shall not reject premise (iv), at least with respect to inalienable rights that are morally defensible in a *legal* context. For it at least seems strange to utilize the coercive apparatus of the *law* to *enforce* duties to oneself.

The initial response to this argument that I shall pursue here is to question premise (iii). According to this premise, if consenting individuals are prohibited from engaging in a relationship in which one infringes a right simply because the other consents, then the prohibition imposed on the would-be consentor (the rights-possessor) is a duty (in the form of a prohibition) that he has to himself. But this can be questioned on either of two grounds. First, though inalienable rights do give rise to certain prohibitions, these prohibitions *need not* be on the rights-possessor. If right R is inalienable, the possessor's consent alone does not justify another in infringing R. It may be that the only prohibition generated by the inalienability of a right is on others: *they* are prohibited from infringing a person's right if they have no other reason than that he consented. But even if prohibitions associated with inalienable rights are also imposed on rights-possessors, there is a second basis for questioning premise (iii); for the prohibition on the would-be consentor need not be understood as a duty that he has to himself. Again, the response to the conceptual argument above can point the way here. If in selected cases permitting infringement on the basis of consent alone will put nonconsenting parties at risk, then the duty may be owed to the state, or to nonconsenting third parties. As before, the burden is on the defender of inalienable rights; but it need not be an impossible burden. Premise (iii) is certainly not true merely on conceptual grounds.

I shall take it as a condition of adequacy, then, that a proper defense of inalienable rights, at least in a *legal* context, must not be based on prohibitions that are duties to oneself.

The "Volenti" Doctrine

Before turning to a positive defense of inalienable rights, let us discuss one other possible objection. This will enable us to provide a broader framework for presenting the issues.

There is a maxim found in ancient Roman law and most modern legal systems: *Volenti non fit injuria.* This is typically understood to mean: To one who has consented, no wrong is done.[29] Endorsing this doctrine seems to provide a basis for holding that all rights are alienable. To see how, consider this. Suppose that right R is inalienable. If so, then P_1's consent alone does not justify P_2 in infringing R. But now suppose that P_2 does infringe P_1's right to R with P_1's consent. If the right to R is inalienable, then it seems that we must conclude that P_2 has violated P_1's right to R. But such a charge seems unwarranted. As John Salmond has put it in explaining the "volenti" maxim, "No man who consents to a thing will be suffered thereafter to complain of it as an injury. He cannot waive his right and then complain of its infringement."[30] And indeed John Simmons has suggested that the "volenti" doctrine shows that consent theorists (in political philosophy) cannot easily embrace inalienable rights. The "volenti" doctrine, Simmons says, implies that consent is sufficient to transfer any right, but if some rights are inalienable consent is not sufficient to transfer them.[31]

Against this appearance, I want to argue that one can affirm the "volenti" doctrine—that is, one can agree that to one who has consented, no wrong is done—without being committed to the claim that all rights are alienable. The claim that some rights are inalienable is not incompatible with the "volenti" doctrine.

In order to explain this, recall the difference between infringements and violations. If P_2 infringes P_1's right to R, that infringement may be justified or unjustified. An infringement of a right may be *justified* for any one of at least three reasons: P_1 may have forfeited her right to R; P_1's right to R may have been overridden by a more important consideration; or R may be alienable and P_1 may have validly alienated or waived her right to R. Suppose, however, that P_2's infringement of P_1's right to R is *unjustified*. In that case, it is natural to think that P_2 has *violated* P_1's right to R. But this need *not* be the case. All violations of a right are unjustified infringements; but it is not the case that all unjustified infringements are violations. As was explained in chapter 1, in order for P_2 to violate P_1's right to R, it must be the case that P_2's infringement of R is unjustified *and* that P_1 is the victim. But this leaves open the possibility that P_2's infringement of P_1's right to R is unjustified but not a violation of R because P_1 is not properly regarded as the victim.

If P_2's infringement of P_1's right to R is unjustified, then the act is wrong. But if P_1 is not the victim, who is? There are two possibilities here. One possibility is that there is no victim at all; P_2's action is wrong, but there is no one to whom a wrong is done. If P_2's act were criminal, then it would be a victimless crime. The other possibility is that someone other than P_1 is the victim. The most obvious candidate here would be some nonconsenting third party. In suggesting how defenders of inalienable rights might respond to arguments against such rights, I pointed out that if nonconsenting parties were adversely affected because P_2 is permitted to infringe P_1's right to R merely because of P_1's consent, then this provides a legitimate nonpaternalistic basis for disallowing such a permission. If P_2 proceeds anyway, then presumably society at large is the victim.

All of this shows that we can agree with Salmond when he says that a person cannot "waive his right and then complain of its infringement" without thereby being committed to holding that all rights are alienable. For if P_2 infringes P_1's right to R with P_1's consent, P_1 need not have any grounds for complaint, *even if* the right to R is inalienable; in that case, it may be others who are warranted in complaining.

We turn now to some positive defenses of inalienable rights.

How Utilitarians Might Defend Inalienable Rights

In this section I want to show that a utilitarian moral theory can allow that some rights are inalienable. Detailed arguments for the inalienability of specific rights will not be given here; those will be explored in subsequent chapters. Instead, here I simply want to show the kinds of considerations that can be cited to support the inalienability of some rights. And I will observe the restrictions discussed above: an adequate defense of inalienable rights must not be based on hard paternalism and must not impose duties to the self on citizens. In addition, I will be looking at the issue from the social perspective, seeking arguments that will justify inalienability from the *legal* perspective. So conceived, the focus is on what counts as a morally defensible *social policy*.

Utilitarianism is a consequentialist moral theory. Consequentialist theories judge the rightness or wrongness of actions in accord with the value of the consequences the actions produce. Simply put, consequentialists instruct agents to perform the act among the options available to them that produces the best consequences. But best for whom? Utilitarianism counsels agents to do what is best for all affected parties; each counts for one, and no one counts for more than one.

Matters are more complicated than this, however, because there are many forms and variants of the utilitarian moral theory.[32] Two versions of this theory are most important for purposes here: act-utilitarianism and rule-utilitarianism. *Act-utilitarianism* holds that act X is right if and only if doing X will have consequences at least as good for all affected parties as the consequences of any alternative act open to the agent. *Rule-utilitarianism* holds that act X is right if and only if doing X is in accord with a set of moral rules the general acceptance of which will have consequences at least as good for all affected parties as the general acceptance of any alternative set of rules. Since our concern here is with social policy, and in particular with the legal status of certain rights, it is natural for us to focus on rule-utilitarianism.

It should be noted that many are skeptical that consequentialists in general, and utilitarians in particular, can properly account for rights within their theories.[33] Others have argued that consequentialists/utilitarians can adequately accommodate rights.[34] I assume here that at least rule-utilitarianism can provide a place for rights within its general theory.

To establish a right within a rule-utilitarian system, one would have to show (at least) that all agents have duties to each other with respect to the thing in question. If it is a negative right, these will be duties to refrain or leave alone; if it is a positive right, these will be duties to provide assistance or services. The utilitarian justification for such a rule will be that the consequences for all affected parties of everyone's accepting this rule will be better than the consequences of everyone's accepting some alternative rule. Whether the right should be *legally enforced* is a separate issue. Again one would have to ask about the consequences for all affected parties. To enforce a right legally is to use the coercive apparatus of the law to ensure (to the degree possible) that citizens comply with the duties correlative with the right in question. In some cases, it may not be worth it to society to enforce a right. The matter may be so small, for example, that more is lost than gained if society's resources are utilized to ensure that correlative duties are complied with. Promises, we may suppose, give rise to rights (for the promisee), but in many cases it would be foolish for society to police such matters. On the other hand, it seems clear that the consequences for all affected parties are better if society enforces duties generated by the right not to be killed and by property rights. Of course, detailed arguments need to be given here. But I take it that my suggestions accord with common sense.

Among those rights whose correlative duties should be legally enforced (should, that is, according to rule-utilitarianism), other questions may be asked. One such question concerns the conditions under which these correlative duties might be suspended. With respect to alienation, the issue is whether rights-possessors are permitted to dispose of their rights through gift, trade, sale, or waiver. If waiver is allowed, then the possessor's valid consent is sufficient to suspend the duty that others have regarding this right; or, to be more accurate, valid waiver suspends the duty for those to whom the consent was given. If transfer is allowed, not only is the correlative duty suspended (again, for those to whom the consent is given), but in addition the original rights-possessor incurs new obligations as a result of the consent.

We can readily see why, within a rule-utilitarian system, alienation of some rights will be permitted. For in some cases it appears that the consequences for everyone are better if rights-possessors are permitted to dispose of certain rights by gift, trade, or sale (better, that is, than if such activities were prohibited). Property rights provide a good example. Of course, 'property' must be defined within the law (of any given society); doing that will determine the rules of ownership. This assumes the prior existence of a rule-utilitarian argument for private ownership, an argument that one suspects will appeal to considerations such as maximizing the supply of things valued by persons. Given the likelihood that various individuals will have more of certain things than they need or can use and less of other things than they need, allowing them to trade, sell, or give away their possessions seems to be the policy that will most likely produce the best consequences for all affected parties. This is oversimplified, obviously, but I take that the general line of argument is familiar enough.

But within this same rule-utilitarian system, what kind of argument could be given for the inalienability of certain rights? Any successful rule-utilitarian argument for inalienability will have to show that consequences for all affected parties will be better if the relations between a rights-possessor and others are limited (with respect to the right in question). An adequate rule-utilitarian defense of the inalienability of right R will have to show that the consequences for all will be best if the law does not recognize the possessor's consent as a legitimate reason for others' infringement of R and does not allow consent alone to impose an obligation on the consentor not to exercise right R. And, in accord with our avoidance of hard paternalism, the considerations cited cannot appeal merely to protecting the well-being of the would-be consentor.

Legal scholars who have written about inalienability have pointed to a number of considerations which might be employed by the rule-utilitarian to assign the status of inalienability to at least some rights. The general idea here is that there may be certain goals that benefit all of society, and those goals are only achievable, or at least most efficiently achievable, if certain rights are inalienable. We may begin by noting that even the alienability of property rights may be limited. And though limiting alienability is not the same as pure inalienability, the rationale for the former is apt to provide a clue for an adequate argument for the latter. Susan Rose-Ackerman provides some examples, where alienability of property rights is limited because of legitimate social goals. She suggests that prohibiting the sale of selected game is an appropriate way to facilitate the conservation of the species.[35] Of course, a society might attempt to achieve this same goal by proscribing possession and ownership of the species; in some cases, this prohibition may more efficiently achieve the end of conservation. But one can imagine circumstances in which conservation of the species is more likely to be achieved if possession is permitted but sale is forbidden. If this possibility were to obtain, then society would have a utilitarian reason to limit alienation.

Calabresi and Melamed, working with this same idea, suggest that one individual, Taney, may be prohibited from selling his land to another, Chase, a known polluter, because this would harm Taney's neighbor, Marshall, by lowering the value of his property.[36] This may seem a bit far-fetched since the same goal could be achieved by making polluting illegal or very costly to polluters. But if for some reason this would not work, then restricting alienation would serve a good social end.

Other examples can be cited where a similar rationale for limiting the alienability of property is present. Societies may, for example, limit the size of gifts that can be made to another (without the recipient having to pay taxes on the gift) in order to prevent individuals from avoiding inheritance taxes.[37] Assuming that inheritance taxes serve a legitimate social end, or at least an end that can be defended within a rule-utilitarian system, then such a restriction on the size of gifts permitted makes good sense. Yet another example of restricting alienation is found in the prohibition of certain gifts or the sale of items substantially below market value before filing bankruptcy.[38] If such gifts or sales were permitted, persons in serious debt could adopt an obvious strategy (provided that they could find a cooperative partner) of eliminating the debt while retaining (by regaining) the valuables that they possessed prior to the filing of the bankruptcy. By prohibiting such gifts and sales, the legitimate interests of creditors are protected. But arguably this prohibition is needed not just to protect creditors' interests; it may be necessary to protect the very institution of borrowing or lending. For if borrowers could so easily avoid repaying a debt, surely few would be willing to make loans. And if the institution of lending benefits society, then the limitation on alienation is necessary in order for society to be able to have this beneficial institution.

A utilitarian argument for proscribing waiver in certain cases has been articulated at length by Russell Hardin.[39] Hardin describes the strategy of rendering certain rights inalienable as a response to a collective action problem. The idea in general is this. If right R were waivable, though at some cost to the possessor, and some individuals would benefit from or be willing to waive R, then circumstances would likely develop so that nearly all people (or all people in certain socioeconomic classes) would have little choice but to waive R. Consider this example.[40] Current occupational safety laws do not allow an employee to waive his right to work in a safe environment. Even if an employee signs such a waiver, it has no effect; it does not relieve the employer of his legal obligation to provide a safe working environment, nor does it make the employer immune from civil suit. Suppose, however, that employees could waive their right to a safe working environment; suppose that such a valid waiver were legally efficacious and did relieve the employer of his obligations in this area.

The impact on at least unskilled workers is not hard to imagine. For any workers whose bargaining power was limited, prospective employees could demand that a waiver be signed as a condition of employment. Economic needs and lack of other options might quickly give (at least) unskilled workers little choice but to sign the waiver. So merely making waiver an option in this kind of case places an entire class of individuals in a bad position. Only if waiver is not an option for any of them will they be able to retain the protections guaranteed by the right to work in a safe environment.

The argument just given will work in cases where one group of people are at a serious disadvantage in bargaining with a second group and when what is at issue is something persons in the first group cannot plausibly choose to forgo. The same argument might be used to establish the inalienability of the right to minimum habitability of one's rented domicile.[41] If affordable rental units are scarce, then landlords could demand, as a condition of renting to another, that renters sign a waiver of their right to the habitability of the unit (with respect to safety matters, etc.). If such a waiver were legally efficacious, then landlords renting (at least) to the poor could demand that lessees sign such a waiver. Given a shortage of affordable units, few could refuse to agree to the landlord's terms. Thus, if waivability is an option here, the whole class is worse off, one might argue. This situation can be avoided only by denying any legal efficacy to a waiver.

Yet another application of this argument can be found in the emerging field of genetic testing. Already through various techniques many genetically based maladies can be detected prior to the advent of any symptoms. And with the relentless progress of the human genome project, it is not far-fetched to suppose that nearly all genetically based maladies will be discoverable well in advance of their onset—presumably as soon as genetic material can be extracted. Such information could be extremely useful to companies that sell life insurance or medical insurance. For by refusing to sell life insurance policies to persons whose deaths are apt to come while they are young and by refusing to sell medical insurance to persons who will be afflicted with an illness that is very expensive to treat, such companies can increase their profits considerably. As a result, some citizens would be unable to purchase health insurance or life insurance. An obvious way to handle this problem is to make it illegal for insurance companies to require genetic testing of prospective buyers. But if that is all that is done, these companies are apt to develop an obvious counterstrategy. If it is merely *permissible* for individuals to be tested and to give the results to others, insurance companies will provide an incentive for many to do just that. They will offer "reduced rates" for those who have a "clean" genetic test. A two-tiered cost structure will develop rapidly, and eventually those who are unwilling to undergo genetic tests or unwilling to give the results to the company will either be priced out of the market or forced to pay exorbitant rates. This practice is unfair and can be prevented only by restricting the options of consenting parties. Charles Culver explains the point this way:

> In order to prevent discrimination by life insurance companies, one would have to prohibit them from even using the results of tests that the person tested *wants* them to use, for if such tests could be submitted in order to get lower premiums, then discrimination is possible even without anyone requiring genetic testing. Thus allowing individuals to use their own tests as they want can have serious effects on others.[42]

Here one can probably also make a Rawlsian argument[43] for prohibiting the consensual relationship in question. For none of us knows what his genetic makeup is (will be). And the worst-off position in society that allows this consensual relationship is apt to be very bad off indeed!

While more details are needed to make any of these examples convincing, again the point is merely to show a kind of argument for the inalienability of some legal rights that is available to the utilitarian and does not appeal to paternalism.

We have sketched so far two kinds of reasoning that (if adequately filled out) show that the inalienability of certain legal rights can be defended within a utilitarian framework and without resorting to paternalism. The first argument is based on adopting the most efficient means to a desirable social goal. The second argument is a response to a collective action problem that will put unequal parties in certain situations in more nearly equal bargaining positions.

A third argument—available not only to utilitarians, but to others too—appeals directly to the interests of innocent third parties. In the abstract, the argument says that if P_1's consent alone permits P_2 to infringe P_1's right to R, then other individuals' right to R will be threatened because of this. This sort of argument will be most plausible when it is difficult to determine after the fact whether the original rights-possessor did in fact consent to the infringement, and if so, whether the consent was genuine—that is, freely given and adequately informed.

The right to life, understood minimally as the right not to be killed, provides an example. If this right is inalienable, then the possessor's consent is not sufficient to justify killing. As is sometimes said, the consent of the victim is no defense for the act of killing. Again, while details are needed that will not be provided in this chapter, one can see how the argument might go. If consent alone did justify killing, abuse would seem all too easy. Murderers would try to make it appear that their victims consented, and if successful they would be off the legal hook. And among the many obstacles to determining whether the person who was killed did genuinely consent is the fact that this person's testimony is not available to us. It may not follow from this that voluntary euthanasia ought to be forbidden; that is a matter that will be discussed later (in chapter 5). But we can see why some may want to hold that consent alone should not be allowed as a defense for killing.

One other example will be cited to illustrate this third type of argument. It is now widely accepted in law and medical ethics that competent patients have the right to informed consent regarding medical treatment. This means, among other things, that their refusal of treatment must be honored, and when treatment is recommended, patients must be informed of the likely risks and benefits, the alternatives available, and the likely consequences of refusing treatment. It is also held by many, however, that this right may be waived by patients. Valid waiver—which must be freely given and informed—relieves health care practitioners of the obligation to secure the patient's consent before treatment is administered, or of the obligation to provide the patient with information, or both. And one might justify allowing waiver of this right by appealing to the patient's right to self-determination.[44] But in spite of such an argument, allowing waiver to relieve obligations as a matter of *legal* policy may cause problems. The general concern is that allowing valid waivings of the right will lead to illegitimate denials of that same right. The existence of such a policy may prompt some physicians to fail to inform patients who want to exercise that right and decide for themselves. Unless safeguards can prevent such abuses, perhaps waiver should not be allowed to relieve health care professionals of the obligation to solicit competent patients' informed consent before administering treatment.

What this third argument says is this: If allowing waiver or transfer to permit persons to whom consent has been given to infringe an individual's right puts other rights-possessors at risk (because, for example, it will make it difficult to prevent abuses), then society has legitimate (nonpaternalistic) grounds for not recognizing the legitimacy of such alienation. But for this argument to be convincing, it must show more than the mere possibility that abuse will occur. Defenders of inalienability who employ this argument must show that *more harm* will result from allowing alienation (that is, allowing consent to justify infringement) than if alienation were not allowed. For it may be that harm to nonconsenting persons will result no matter which of the two policies is adopted. And in that case, the utilitarian will presumably urge the adoption of the policy with which less harm, on balance, is associated. One can see this by looking at a different case. Self-defense is allowed as a justification for killing. Yet clearly the self-defense justification can be abused; persons can commit cold-blooded murder and make it appear to be a case of self-defense.[45] To disallow self-defense as a justification for killing, however, would be unwarranted; for it is quite likely that even more innocent persons would be harmed if this were our social policy. So advocates of this third type of argument have a burden that is greater merely than showing that abuse is possible if alienation is legally allowed.

There are, then, at least three types of arguments that might be employed from a utilitarian perspective to justify the inalienability of some rights. One argument applies when restricting alienability—partially or wholly—is necessary to promote a legitimate social goal. The second argument applies when ascribing inalienability to certain rights is the best collective action strategy that a group of persons can adopt to protect their own welfare. The third argument applies when allowing alienation to justify others in infringing a person's right will put innocent third parties at risk.

It is not unlikely that if the inalienability of right R can be justified by any one of these rationales, then situations might occur in which the utilitarian appears to be caught in a dilemma. Putting aside, for now, the distinction between act-utilitarianism and rule-utilitarianism, and working within what one might call the "spirit" of utilitarianism, a situation may occur in which P_1 gives P_2 consent to infringe R and P_2 judges correctly that the consequences for all affected parties will be better if she infringes P_1's right to R because P_1 consented, but the best social policy is not to allow consent alone to count as a justification for infringing anyone's right to R. In other words, a utilitarian justification for a certain legal policy can be given, but in a particular situation acting contrary to that legal policy is what is best. Eighteenth-century British moralist Francis Hutcheson saw this possibility. Hutcheson wrote that

> many laws prohibit actions in general, even when some particular instances of those actions would be very useful; because an universal allowance of them, considering the mistakes men would probably fall into, would be more pernicious than an universal prohibition; nor could there be any more special boundaries fixed between the right and wrong cases. In such cases, it is the duty of persons to comply with the generally useful constitution; or if in some very important instances, the violation of the law

would be of less evil consequence, than obedience to it, they must patiently resolve to undergo those penalties, which the State has, for valuable ends to the whole, appointed.[46]

Hutcheson's position here is that normally one should follow the law; but if the consequences of obeying the law in a particular case are very bad, one should disobey the law and accept punishment if the disobedience is detected. This is a clear answer that averts dilemmas, though it puts the agent unfortunate enough to face such circumstances in a difficult position (because if caught he will be punished, even though he has done the morally right thing).

As was acknowledged at the outset of this section, I have not presented a detailed utilitarian defense of inalienable rights. But I have shown how this moral theory can, in principle, make sense of rights that their possessors may not alienate; and the arguments need not appeal to paternalistic considerations, nor be based on duties to oneself. If the argument can be filled in, this is a promising defense of a social policy that renders selected rights inalienable. All of this will be examined in subsequent chapters.

A Kantian Defense

Utilitarianism is not the only moral theory that one might appeal to in defending inalienable rights; indeed, it is not even the most obvious candidate. Looking at key historical figures who have advocated the inalienability of certain rights,[47] one might conclude that a Kantian defense is more promising.

As was explained in chapter 1, rights are often portrayed as being in opposition to utilitarianism. Rights, it is said, make the government's job of securing the general benefit more difficult and more expensive. The institution of rights recognizes several important ideas, at least one of which is Kantian in nature. As Ronald Dworkin puts it, "The first is the vague but powerful idea of human dignity. The idea, associated with Kant, but defended by philosophers of different schools, supposes that there are ways of treating a man that are inconsistent with recognizing him as a full member of the human community, and holds that such treatment is profoundly unjust."[48] These individual rights put obligations on others. So a government may have to forgo actions or policies that would benefit the majority of its citizens if that good can be achieved only by invading the rights of a few. And the things to which we have rights—life and liberty—are things associated with or constitutive of human dignity. Thus, we might say that the institution of rights "represents the majority's promise to the minorities that their dignity and equality will be respected."[49] Though the notion of human dignity is vague, it seems to strike a responsive chord in many to say that rights somehow are based on or protect this same dignity.

But how does this relate specifically to inalienable rights? Again, the idea is murky, but still appealing. Kuflik seems to see the connection when he says "respect for personhood must include respect for the person in oneself; certain rights are so fundamental to, or indeed, constitutive of, the moral dignity of the person, that even the individual himself is without title to give them up or trade them away, *no matter how good* the expected consequences of striking such a bargain."[50] There is a certain fundamentality about inalienable rights, and agents themselves do not have the authority to dispose of them in certain ways. Alan Gewirth emphasizes this same fundamentality when he speculates about why Thomas Jefferson included life, liberty, and the pursuit of happiness among the inalienable rights of persons. Gewirth writes, "If 'happiness' is understood as well-being, these rights are inalienable because, being necessary to all action, no agent could waive them or be deprived of them and still remain an agent."[51]

In spite of the eloquence of Kuflik and Gewirth, the connection between dignity and inalienable rights is still difficult to grasp. Perhaps looking at a more specific right will help. Thomas E. Hill, Jr., who is sympathetic with the Kantian tradition, makes a helpful contribution here. Hill acknowledges that many rights may be waived; in these cases, a person's consent releases others from correlative obligations, but only if the consent was autonomously given.[52] But perhaps some basic rights may not be waived. If so, then there are some rights that others are bound to respect regardless of what the possessors say. And given this, persons should avoid even the appearance of consenting to give up these rights; for to act as if we could release others from their obligations regarding these rights would be "to fail to respect morality."[53] Along these lines, Hill explains, a Kantian might argue that a possessor of the right to life cannot release others from the obligation to refrain from killing him: Consent is no defense for murder. This seems to put rights in a certain framework. Quoting Hill, "To accept principles of this sort is to hold that rights to life and liberty are, as Kant believed, rather like a trustee's rights to preserve something valuable entrusted to him: he has not only a right but a duty to preserve it."[54]

So conceived, inalienable rights, if there are any, put special obligations on both their possessors and on others. Others may not infringe the right simply because the possessor consents; and possessors may not give even the appearance of consenting to infringement. Such an account need not be paternalistic. But it seems to imply that individuals have duties to themselves, since they have duties to preserve whatever it is that the inalienable right protects. But appearances here *may* be deceptive; for the duty to preserve in this case may be a duty *regarding* oneself, but not owed *to* oneself.[55]

Hill does not necessarily think that the rights to life and liberty will qualify as inalienable. He does suggest, however, that one formal right may qualify. This is the right that individuals have to some minimum degree of respect from others. And if such a right is inalienable, it puts obligations on both the possessors and on others. Concerning others' obligations, Hill says, "No matter how willing a person is to submit to humiliation by others, they ought to show him some respect as a person."[56] And if the possessor himself seems to consent to such humiliation, he is guilty of acting in a servile manner, behavior that Hill argues is contrary to the demands of morality. If such a right is plausibly regarded as inalienable and if Hill's account is correct, it does seem that this particular inalienable right is one that possessors must exercise. This may be cause for suspicion, since I argued earlier that the inalienability of a right does not entail that the possessor is also required to exercise that right. Of course, inalienability does not preclude that possibility. Still, if defense of the inalienability of a particular right includes the claim that the possessor is required to exercise that right, one would like to have an account of why this is so.

Kant himself held that autonomy, or one's status as an equal among all citizens, could not be alienated. Kant argued that self-enslavement contracts were without legal or moral force. While a person might lose his status as a free and equal being because of wrongdoing, he cannot lose such a status through contract. No contract in which a person agrees to be the mere instrument of another can be binding.[57] It is far from clear, however, how one can defend these claims made by Kant.

Norman Dahl attempts to construct such a defense of Kant's prohibition of self-enslavement contracts, though acknowledging that it rests on crucial Kantian premises that themselves need additional support.[58] As Dahl sketches the position, an adequate ethics must provide grounds that curtail people's pursuit of their own ends. According to the Kantian view, a person is justified in acting on a desire or end, provided that doing so does not conflict with a rational constraint arising from people's ability to take a more detached view of themselves. Rational prudence provides an example. If a person's present desire conflicts with a long-term end, the person must step back from the present desire and weigh each from this detached perspective. But people also have the ability to reflect on their long-term ends. Kant, as Dahl understands him, assumes that rational ends are those that people would want for themselves after such reflection. These are ends that people ought to have, ends that they would pursue if they were fully rational. This process provides content to imperatives, which direct a person to do what he would were he fully rational. One such rational end, Kant holds, is the desire to determine what happens to oneself by means of one's own decisions, decisions determined by one's own conception of the good. This is a desire for autonomy.

People also have the capacity to regard themselves as one person among others, and this provides other rational constraints. From an impartial perspective, people want others to have a fair opportunity to pursue their own rational ends. From this, one can conclude that it is reasonable to pursue an action or end provided that it is not incompatible with principles that everyone would choose that everyone adopt and act on. This is roughly Kant's categorical imperative, that one should act only on maxims that one can will to be a universal law. Given this and given that autonomy is a rational end, one can speculate reasonably that only maxims that forbid agents from interfering with the autonomy of others will pass the Kantian test; and it may even follow that agents ought, to some extent, to promote the autonomy of others. And, finally, because autonomy is a rational end, it seems that one cannot consistently will to be a universal law any maxim that allows people to enslave themselves; for were this permitted, people would be free to undermine what is taken to be a rational end.

I do not know if this Kantian defense of the inalienable right of autonomy is plausible. As Dahl himself acknowledges, the account rests on Kantian assumptions that themselves are controversial and for which independent argument is needed. When relevant to particular cases (in subsequent chapters), we will explore this Kantian position further. For now, we merely note it as a possibility; if defensible, it can provide a nonpaternalistic defense of inalienable rights.

Clarifications

I conclude this chapter with several points of clarification.

I have provided an account of inalienable rights which has two broad implications: first, that reasons normally relevant for justifying others' infringement of a right are not relevant for inalienable rights; and second, that acts which normally obligate a person do not do so when what is at stake is the object of an inalienable right. More specifically, if a right is inalienable, then the possessor's consent alone does not justify others in infringing that right, and the possessor cannot obligate himself by consent to allow others to infringe that right.

A related but different account has been offered by Diana T. Meyers. According to Meyers, "an inalienable right has an object that it is never obligatory, though it may be supererogatory, to sacrifice altruistically."[59] Meyers holds this in part because she believes that inalienable rights protect fundamental goods, goods that individuals need to function as agents. This, of course, is in accord with the ideas of Kuflik, Gewirth, and Dahl discussed above.

In contrast with Meyers, my account does not imply that an individual can never be obligated to sacrifice the object of an inalienable right. Instead, my account holds that a person can never incur such an obligation merely by giving consent. In this sense, the good protected by an inalienable right cannot be contracted away. But nothing I say precludes the possibility that one might be obligated to sacrifice such a good for a *different reason*. Suppose that the right to life is inalienable. If so, then on my account a possessor's consent alone cannot put her under an obligation to sacrifice her life. This, however, does not preclude the possibility that she is required to sacrifice her life for some other reason. We can imagine circumstances, for example, in which the lives of other innocent persons will be lost unless a person sacrifices her own life; for example, suppose that it is the lives of her own children that are at stake. Surely, in some such scenarios, we would say that the person's sacrificing her own life was required, not supererogatory. Perhaps the often told story of Captain Oates is such a case.[60]

The first point of clarification, then, is this. If a right is inalienable, then the possessor's consent alone cannot put her under an obligation to sacrifice the object of that right or to allow others to infringe the right. But this does not rule out the possibility that the possessor may be required to sacrifice the good for some other reason.

The second point of clarification concerns the role of the possessor's consent in justifying infringing that individual's rights. According to the account of rights that I have given in these first two chapters, without additional normative inquiry one cannot say with confidence that the possessor's consent is either necessary or sufficient to justify infringing her right. One cannot say it is sufficient because if the right is inalienable, then consent alone does not justify infringement. One cannot say it is necessary because there are at least two kinds of cases where infringement is justified without consent. The first case involves forfeitable rights. If a right can be forfeited and if the possessor engages in the relevant wrong behavior, then others are justified in infringing the right simply because the person has engaged in the behavior. And though the behavior is voluntary, engaging in it is not the same as consenting to infringement. The second case concerns the situation where the obligation correlative with a right is overridden by a stronger moral consideration. If this occurs, then others will be justified in infringing the right apart from whether the rights-possessor consents or agrees.

Suppose we hold for the moment that all rights that are plausibly regarded as inalienable are such that they may be forfeited or overridden (one or the other, but not necessarily both). On that supposition, one might be tempted to say that if a right is inalienable, then the consent of the possessor is *not relevant* to determining whether infringing that right is permissible. Consent is not relevant because it is neither necessary nor sufficient to justify infringement. It is not necessary because the right can be forfeited or overridden; it is not sufficient because the right is inalienable; therefore, consent is irrelevant. Granting the supposition, I of course agree that consent is neither necessary nor sufficient to justify infringement of these selected inalienable rights; but I deny that it follows from this that the possessor's consent is irrelevant to the issue of permissible infringement. Let me explain.

Suppose (for the sake of argument) that the right to life is inalienable, but may be forfeited or overridden. Now consider the following statement on the issue of euthanasia endorsed by the American Medical Association (AMA) in 1973. "The cessation of the employment of extraordinary means to prolong the life of the body when there is irrefutable evidence that biological death is imminent is the decision of the patient and/or his immediate family. The advice and judgment of the physician should be freely available to the patient and/or his immediate family."[61] This part of the statement seems to be referring to what was once called *passive* euthanasia, which involves withholding or withdrawing life-sustaining medical treatment. The statement seems to say that passive euthanasia is permissible only if two conditions obtain: (i) the patient (or his immediate family) has consented and (ii) biological death is imminent. But if the right to life is inalienable (and relevant to the issue of passive euthanasia) and if inalienability means that the possessor's consent is irrelevant to the issue of the permissibility of infringing that right, then those who issued the AMA statement are confused in believing that condition (i) is relevant. That the person consented is neither necessary nor sufficient to justify doing something that will hasten her death. And if that is so, then presumably to assess the AMA statement we need only to determine whether hastening a person's death is permissible when biological death is imminent; condition (i) adds nothing that would make the act acceptable.[62]

But if it does not follow from the fact that consent is neither necessary nor sufficient to justify infringement that consent is also irrelevant to whether infringement is permissible, then a more charitable construal of the AMA statement is possible (continuing to maintain the assumption that the right to life is inalienable). For the following position is not only coherent, but it also may even be plausible. Because of the inalienability of the right to life, the *mere fact* that the patient consented does not justify removing medical interventions when that will hasten his death. But it may also be impermissible to stop these treatments without the patient's consent. It may be that consent must be *combined with* something else—the imminence of biological death, according to the AMA statement—for doing that which will hasten the patient's death to be permissible.

But if consent in combination with something else shows that infringement is justified, doesn't that show that consent is indeed necessary? The answer is no. Consent is not necessary to justify infringement because we are assuming that the right in question may be forfeited by its possessor or overridden by other moral considerations. We can put the point this way. For the sort of right being considered here, a *disjunctive* list of conditions will justify infringement. (And we need not assume that we can complete the list.) One of the disjuncts is that the right has been forfeited by its possessor. Another disjunct is that the right has been overridden by competing moral considerations. And another disjunct is itself a conjunction: that the possessor consented *and* death is imminent (here, accepting the AMA statement uncritically for the sake of illustration). Any one of these disjuncts is sufficient to justify infringement. If the right in question were alienable, then consent alone would be sufficient. But if a right is inalienable, that is not the case.

The second point of clarification, then, is this. If a right is inalienable, then the possessor's consent is neither necessary nor sufficient to justify infringement.[63] But it does not follow that the possessor's consent is irrelevant to the issue of whether the infringement is permissible.

The third point of clarification concerns the relationship between inalienable rights and so-called natural rights. Not all natural rights are inalienable. I have no special account of natural rights to offer. I think of natural rights as a subset of moral rights. Presumably natural rights, at the very least, are rights that one possesses simply because of some central aspect of one's nature. One account puts it this way: In calling a right "natural," we mean (i) that it is possessed by all X and (ii) that it is not the product of human convention or some voluntary act.[64] The "X" here will vary in content, depending on one's account of what is essential about rights. "X" might be filled in with "human beings," or "rational agents," or "agents capable of choice." Presumably, something like the last of these three is congenial with the choice conception of rights discussed earlier.

The reason for saying that not all natural rights are inalienable is not deep. It simply seems, at the intuitive level, that there are examples of rights that are natural (and moral) but not plausibly said to be inalienable. John Simmons cites as an example "the right of self-government."[65] This is understood as a right, or a cluster of rights, to formulate and to pursue one's own plan of life within the bounds of the moral law. Yet, by consent, one can limit this right by binding oneself to a government. Supporting the same theoretical point, James Nickel cites the following: "A[n] . . . example is accepting certain permanent limits on what one can say and publish in order to receive a security clearance for government intelligence work. Although one does well to be suspicious of government secrecy regulations, it does not seem to me that agreements of this sort can be precluded wholesale."[66] Either of these examples, I think, is sufficiently plausible to lend considerable credence to the view that not all natural rights are inalienable. As we have already seen, some philosophers who readily accept that people have moral rights deny that there are any inalienable rights. It should hardly be surprising, then, that defenders of inalienable rights do not think that all (moral) rights have this status.

Having given an account of the nature and normative foundations of inalienable rights, we turn now to examining some particular rights and their status. We shall begin with the right of conscience—something that, while perhaps initially strange to us today, was of central importance to such founding fathers as James Madison and Thomas Jefferson.

THREE

The Inalienable Right of Conscience

A Madisonian/Jeffersonian Argument

In *Civil Disobedience,* Henry David Thoreau writes about the importance of conscience and its relationship to obligations.

> Can there not be a government in which majorities do not virtually decide right and wrong, but conscience?—in which majorities decide only those questions to which the rule of expediency is applicable? Must the citizen ever for a moment, or in the least degree, resign his conscience to the legislator? Why has every man a conscience, then? I think that we should be men first, and subjects afterward. It is not desirable to cultivate a respect for the law, so much as for the right. The only obligation which I have a right to assume is to do at any time what I think right.[1]

Some might construe this as endorsing the subjective claim that a person's only real obligation is to do what he believes is right. Such a position is paradoxical because it implies that wrongdoing occurs only when agents act against their considered moral judgments. Perhaps this is Thoreau's view; but another thesis may be at work here—that the right of conscience is inalienable. Indeed, some of Thoreau's predecessors, in particular, writers of the late eighteenth century, held that the right of conscience is inalienable. Here I shall explore this thesis, ignoring whether or not Thoreau endorsed it.

The Right of Conscience

Characterizing conscience is difficult. The way that this term is often used makes it sound like it is a special power possessed by people. Bishop Butler seems to have held that conscience is a special faculty that is a source of moral knowledge; but I follow more recent authors in not assuming this.[2] Instead, when we speak of conscience we speak of the act of applying one's moral beliefs to one's own conduct.[3] Conscience is not itself a standard; rather, appeals to conscience involve an agent reflecting on his own past or (projected) future behavior and assessing that behavior in light of his own standards.[4] A person who, in conversation with another, invokes conscience as an apparent justification of a proposed course of action has already made a judgment about that action. Such an appeal borrows its effectiveness from the conviction that one ought (in some sense) to think for oneself about moral matters and then act on one's considered judgments.

So conceived, conscience does not support any particular moral theory. The purpose of praising those who act on conscience is presumably to encourage agents to act on their own moral judgments. One who is said to have a well-developed conscience has a disposition to act in accordance with his moral beliefs. Such a person is sometimes said to have integrity, and this means that the person has properly integrated his actions and beliefs. There is a proper harmony between his moral beliefs and actions. If conscience were some mysterious power or faculty, perhaps we could be confident that its pronouncements were unerring. But, according to a more contemporary understanding, praising conscience can do no more than encourage agents to do what they believe they ought to do. Even when there is proper harmony between agents' actions and their moral beliefs, those actions may still be objectively wrong. And when actions and beliefs are not in proper harmony, agents may not know whether to change their beliefs or their actions.[5]

Appeals to conscience occur typically in cases of conflict. Agents who are tempted to act contrary to their own moral beliefs may invoke conscience in hope of bolstering their strength of will. Here the conflict is within oneself.[6] But there may be conflicts with others too. In such a conflict, an agent might, for example, refuse to do something that another wants him to do on grounds of conscience. Such appeals are typically a last resort, made only when the other will not accept other reasons given by the agent for refusing.[7]

But what, then, does it mean to speak of a right of conscience? It is presumably a negative right, a right not to be interfered with in certain ways. In part, it is the right of agents to act on their own moral beliefs. One document which explicitly affirms this right is the *International Covenant on Civil and Political Rights* (1966).[8] Such a right, if there is one, places duties on others not to prevent persons from acting in certain ways. The *International Covenant* in Article 18 lumps together "the right to freedom of thought, conscience, and religion," and says that such a right gives to the individual the freedom "to manifest his religion or belief in worship, observance, practice, and teaching."[9] It would be surprising, however, if these duties of noninterference were absolute; one suspects that on occasion they may be overridden by more pressing duties. And the *International Covenant* recognizes explicit limitations on the right when necessary "to protect the public safety" and "the fundamental rights" of others.[10] So if there is a right of conscience, there is a moral presumption, albeit overriddable, that agents should be free to act on their own moral beliefs.[11]

In order to explain the notion of an inalienable right of conscience, let us review some of the ways that agents may divest themselves of rights explained earlier in chapter 1. To *waive* a right is to give up that right knowingly and voluntarily. When valid waiver occurs, the duties correlative with the right are suspended because of the possessor's consent. If the police properly inform a person, he may give up the right to have legal counsel present while he is being questioned by authorities. Waiver is unilateral; it authorizes others to act in specified ways. To *alienate* something is to transfer it to another. An alienable right is one that may be transferred by its possessor. Property rights are typically thought to be alienable. If I own a copy of Plato's

Republic, I may give it to you. My merely giving (not lending) you the book transfers rights I had to you. The correlative obligations that all others have regarding this book are now owed to you. My consent alone transfers to you rights that I previously possessed. Prior to the transaction, you (and all others) had, for example, a moral requirement not to tear the pages from this book; I had no such requirement. After the transaction, you no longer have this obligation; but now I am under such a requirement. Transfer is bilateral; it permits another to do what was previously a violation of a right and it puts the consentor under a new obligation. What is common to waiver and transfer is that the possessor's consent is permission-generating. As John Simmons puts it, "In giving consent to another's actions, however, our primary purpose is to authorize those actions and in so doing create for or accord to another a special right to act. . . ."[12]

As explained in chapter 1, an *inalienable* right is one that may not be waived or transferred by its possessor. The possessor does not have the moral authority to give up the right deliberately. Such a *transaction* between the possessor of the right and another is impermissible. With inalienable rights, my consent lacks normative efficacy; it is not sufficient to transfer to you what I possess or have a right to. If the right to life is inalienable, my consent alone does not give you justification to kill me, nor do I incur an obligation to resist your attempts. It should be noted that there are different ways to understand the notion of an inalienable right, ways that were not discussed earlier. One way says that transference of such rights is *morally wrong*. Another way says that inalienable rights are ones that literally *cannot* be alienated. Here I am following the former account, though later I shall have something to say about the connection between the two.

So, if the right of conscience is inalienable, then it is morally wrong for an agent to alienate it.[13] But we need to say more about this; for there are different ways to understand what particular moral commitments this places on agents. Understood one way, the inalienability of the right of conscience implies that each agent always ought to follow his own conscience. This account is unattractive, however, because it implies *either* that agents' beliefs about what they ought to do are infallible *or* that there are genuine moral dilemmas. The argument to demonstrate this is as follows. Assume that agents' beliefs about what they ought to do are fallible and that they sometimes have erroneous consciences. If it is still true that an agent ought always to follow his own conscience, then we get the following result. Suppose that an agent's sincere belief that he ought to do X is erroneous; in the situation in question, he ought to do Y, which is incompatible with doing X. But since he always ought to follow his own conscience, he also ought to do X. Such an agent has incompatible obligations; he is in a moral dilemma. If, however, there are good arguments against moral dilemmas, as some maintain,[14] then something has gone wrong.[15] Either agents' consciences *are* infallible after all or it is *not true* that one always ought to follow one's own conscience. Since I deny infallibility, I conclude that it is not true that agents always ought to follow their consciences.

If the right of conscience is plausibly regarded as inalienable, then there must be a different understanding of the moral requirements associated with it. The alternative that I suggest is this: to say that the right of conscience is inalienable is to say that an agent should not bind himself *irrevocably* to follow the commands of another. This is a negative moral requirement, one not to undertake a certain commitment. An agent's agreement always to obey another neither permits the other to determine how the agent should act, nor is it sufficient to create an obligation on the consentor. This also places on others a duty not to act as if an agent were so obligated. Alienating the right of conscience is giving up *completely* the right to act on one's own moral decisions. If this right is alienable, such a transaction is permissible. As a result of the transaction, the agent who alienates the right is strictly obligated to act in the way that the person to whom he transfers the right instructs him (either for a fixed period or time or permanently). The agent's consent shifts the power of decision making from that agent to another. The task here is to show that alienating the right of conscience is not a morally acceptable option. This is a transaction that is prohibited on moral grounds.

The Madisonian/Jeffersonian Argument in Context

Eighteenth-century writers were principally concerned about a particular instance of the right of conscience, namely, the right of religious freedom. And they were concerned about this right being surrendered not to another individual, but to civil society. It will be helpful to place their concern in its historical context.

After the Revolutionary War, during the period of the Articles of Confederation, the proper relationship between governments of the thirteen States and religion was fiercely debated. Nowhere was that debate more spirited than in Virginia during the 1780s. While all seemed to agree that government should be neutral (in some sense) with respect to religion, exactly what that implied was a serious point of contention. In Virginia, three different positions regarding the appropriate relationship between government and religion were advanced. One position was that government should support all religions. On this view, no single religion would be established and so neutrality would be maintained. A second position, favored by Patrick Henry, held that all Christian religions should be supported by the state. This view is not neutral since all non-Christian religions would be at a distinct disadvantage. But presumably the assumption was that the overwhelming majority of Virginians were Christian, and so with respect to them government would remain impartial. The third position, defended by James Madison and Thomas Jefferson, was that government should support no religions; this is the "disestablishment" position, the view that there should be a wall of separation between church and state. For this position, Madison and Jefferson received important support from the Reverend John Leland, a minister from Massachusetts who preached in Virginia from 1776–1791.

As intellectual descendants of Hobbes, Locke, and Rousseau, Madison, Jefferson, and Leland subscribed to the social contract theory. Legitimate civil government emerges from a compact among the people; the consent of the governed is necessary to render political authority legitimate. But what does that have to do with religion and the right of conscience? The Reverend Leland, in a 1791 sermon, addressed this question explicitly. He argued that though civil government is based on a contract, nevertheless, people entering into that contract do not surrender their rights of conscience to society.[16] Nearly a decade earlier, Jefferson, in his *Notes on the State of Virginia*, had made a similar point: "But our rulers can have authority over such natural rights only as we have submitted to them. The rights of conscience we never submitted, we could not submit. We are answerable for them to our God."[17]

What emerges from this is the following argument.

(1) The government has authority over a matter only if the people, through consent, have given it that authority.
(2) But the people have not given the government authority over religious matters.
(3) Therefore, it is not the case that government has authority over religious matters.

Premise (1) of this argument involves an appeal to social contract theory, and Leland, Jefferson, and Madison might reasonably have expected those to whom the argument was addressed to share their commitment to it. So to make this argument convincing, they must defend premise (2). But how?

It would be unconvincing to defend premise (2) by making a historical claim about what people in fact did; nor is that the way that social contract theorists typically proceed. Instead, a conceptual argument is needed for premise (2). And it is clear that Leland, Jefferson, and Madison agree about why premise (2) is true. No question even arises about whether the people did in fact give government power over religious matters because the people lack the authority to do so. As Jefferson put it in the passage quoted above, "The rights of conscience we never submitted, we *could not* submit" (emphasis added).

But the full argument for the inalienability of the right of conscience is left to be provided by Madison in his "Memorial and Remonstrance against Religious Assessments."[18] Madison asserted that "the duty which we owe to our Creator and the manner of discharging it, can be directed only by reason and conviction, not by force or violence." Madison goes on to say that the "Religion then of every man must be left to the conviction and conscience of every man; and it is the right of every man to exercise it as these may dictate." According to Madison, this right is inalienable (he says "unalienable") for two reasons: (1) "because the opinions of men, depending only on the evidence contemplated by their own minds cannot follow the dictates of other men"; and (2) "because what is here a right towards men, is a duty towards the Creator." Madison elaborates on (2): "It is the duty of every man to render to the Creator such homage and such only as he believes to be acceptable to him."

According to Madison, then, the duty that people owe to God is the basis for the inalienability of the right of conscience. The duty cannot be discharged if the right of conscience is alienated; and to give government authority over religious matters would constitute alienating that right. This duty has an objective component, paying homage to God, and a subjective component, rendering the homage that one *believes* is acceptable to God. Even with the built in belief-component, this need not be radically subjective; for acting on one's own belief about what is proper may be necessary but not sufficient for fulfilling this duty. Madison's view seems to be that one is not genuinely paying homage to God, unless one believes that the act one is performing is the *proper way* to pay homage. Sincerity is necessary for genuine homage, though no doubt not sufficient. This is not all that unusual, as examples show. One does not forgive another merely through words and deeds; the one doing the forgiving must also have certain beliefs and attitudes. And we can say similar things about displays of gratitude and humility. One might chide Madison for asserting (1) on grounds that he is unaware of things like brainwashing, psychosurgery, and the like.[19] But that would be off the mark, I think. Madison may well have been naive about the factors that influence people's opinions. But in the end his point is that the duty to pay homage requires that one act on one's own beliefs, however those beliefs were acquired.[20]

Madison's argument for the inalienability of the right of conscience, then, is based on a duty that he claims people owe to God. If an agent were to transfer his right of conscience to another, he would be unable to discharge his duty to pay homage to God. And doing that which makes the fulfillment of a duty impossible is itself prohibited. Indeed, as John Locke suggests in *A Letter Concerning Toleration*, such alienation may compound one's wrongs.

> Whatever Profession we make, to whatever outward worship we conform, if we are not fully satisfied in our own mind that the one is true, and the other well pleasing unto God, such Profession and such Practice, far from being any furtherance, are indeed great Obstacles to our Salvation. For in this manner . . . we add unto the number of our sins, those of Hypocrisie, and Contempt of his Divine Majesty.[21]

Jefferson put the point more succinctly than Locke: "Constraint may make him worse by making him a hypocrite, but it will never make him a truer man."[22] Madison, Jefferson, and Locke seem confident that those to whom their argument is addressed will agree that words and deeds offered as homage but not endorsed by the agent are contemptuous of God. Madison, Jefferson, and Leland were concerned to argue that citizens did not transfer to the *state* rights to worship as they please. It was their contention that religious opinions are not the proper objects of civil government. More to the point, government cannot answer for individuals on the day of judgment.[23] Based on this, one can understand why revolutionaries might use the phrase 'inalienable rights' in the loose sense that I described in chapter 1. What is common to Madison, Jefferson, and twentieth century revolutionaries is a concern about government's usurpation of or failure to comply with people's rights. Since Madison and Jefferson believed in government by consent and since they held that the people themselves lack the authority to transfer their right of conscience to the government (or anyone else), it follows that the government is not authorized to make pronouncements in the area of religion. But it does *not* follow that every time a government exceeds its authority, it is thereby infringing on an inalienable right. For, to take an obvious case, governments may impermissibly infringe property rights, even though they are paradigmatically alienable.

In a sense, then, Madison, Jefferson, and Locke are saying that alienating the right of conscience is not only wrong, but *impossible*. But what, then, is the point of prohibiting the impossible?

This brings to the fore the *doubly normative* aspect of the inalienable right of conscience. On the one hand, agents can (in one sense) alienate this right. They can give consent (by saying certain words) and can always act according to the wishes of another *because* they have agreed to do so, and this they ought not to do. On the other hand, agents cannot alienate this right because such an agreement with others does not enable agents successfully to shift responsibility for their actions. So even if an agent were to cede to another the right to make decisions about how to worship, that agent would still be responsible for his actions in that area. That is why others should not act as if an agent has transferred this right.

Even if one is impressed with this Madisonian/Jeffersonian argument, it seems to be very limited. It may fit religious freedom well, but can it be extended? Unless one believes that all moral decisions are based on religious beliefs, this is a matter of concern. It is to this that I now turn.

The Madisonian/Jeffersonian Argument Generalized

The essence of Madison's argument is that duties that people have to God prohibit them from alienating rights necessary to discharge those duties. Can this be extended to all moral requirements, not just duties to God? The following argument suggests an affirmative answer to this question.

(i) Each agent is (trivially) required not to do what is, all things considered, wrong.
(ii) Suppose that S_1 has agreed always to obey S_2. S_1 has alienated his right of conscience and will obey S_2 no matter what.
(iii) So, for any action A, if S_2 orders S_1 to do A, then S_1 is not free not to do A.
(iv) But since A can have any content whatsoever, doing A might be wrong, all things considered.
(v) Therefore, S_1 should not agree always to obey S_2.

The idea underlying this argument is that an agent who abdicates his right of conscience to another may be instructed to do any act whatsoever, including an act that is, all things considered, wrong. But the *mere fact* that an agent has agreed to obey another cannot make an otherwise wrong act right.[24] So, such an agreement creates no obligation to obey.[25]

A variant of this argument can be developed based on the rights of innocent third parties.[26] Putting it briefly, S_2 might order S_1 to do something that violates the rights of S_3. Even though the rights of an innocent person may be overridden in extreme situations, they are not overridden simply because of an agreement between two *other* people. Therefore, S_1's agreement to obey S_2 does not create an obligation to do so.

One might object to the move from (ii) to (iii) in this argument. Agreements, such as promises and consent, create only prima facie obligations, the critic says. So while S_1 may have a prima facie obligation to do what S_2 orders, it is an obligation that can be defeated. And it will be defeated in those cases where what S_2 orders S_1 to do is morally heinous. So, we can affirm the alienability of the right of conscience without trouble. The problem with this objection, however, is that it misunderstands what it is to alienate the right of conscience. To give up one's right of conscience is to transfer *irrevocably* the right to act on one's own moral judgments. If S_1 retains the right to act on his own judgments, he simply has not alienated his right of conscience; for in such a scenario it is the agent's own conscience that is the final arbiter of what he ought to do. So unless (iii) follows from (ii), such alienation has not occurred. It is worth pointing out here that though a genuine act of alienation is irrevocable, it need not be for all time. One *can* agree to obey another for all time. But one can also agree to do so for a week, or a day, or an hour. Whether the alienation is permanent or for a limited period, the agent has *for that time* irrevocably surrendered the right to act on his own moral judgments and agreed to obey the orders of another. For that time, the agent is not free not to do whatever the person to whom he transferred the right orders him to do; the agreement cannot be revoked by the agent during that time. With respect to this particular right, anything short of this is not genuine alienation.

The generalization of Madison's (and Jefferson's) argument to cover all (all things considered) moral requirements suggests a broader underlying principle: If an agent has a moral requirement to do something, then he not only has a right to do it, but an inalienable right.[27] For if an agent ought (or ought not) to do something and he transfers irrevocably to another power over that matter, then he puts himself in a position of not being able to control whether that requirement is discharged. The burden of the above argument is to show that agents should not put themselves in such positions; and even if they do, they do not successfully avoid responsibility. One might suspect that a similar argument could be used to prohibit self-enslavement contracts. And, indeed, some legal scholars appeal to the preservation of personal integrity to ground such a prohibition.[28] Still, something seems amiss here. Two different objections readily come to mind.

For the first objection, consider a particular example. Parents (let us suppose) have a duty to see to it that their children are properly educated. But it is not wrong for parents to let others take over the task of educating their children. So haven't they properly alienated a right correlative with one of their duties? The answer is that they have not alienated the right. They retain responsibility for the education of their children, and if those to whom the task is delegated are not discharging it adequately, the parents have a duty to make changes (to the extent that it is within their power to do so). They have not alienated the right because they can (and should) continue to monitor the arrangement and retain the right to make changes. Suppose, though, that a set of parents have given up their only child for adoption. They certainly do not retain the right to monitor that child's education. The reason for this, however, is that they have also transferred (to the adopting parents) the duty in question. The above-stated principle must be qualified, then. If it holds, it holds only so long as the agent retains the moral requirement in question. What moral requirements can be transferred to another is a separate matter that I shall not pursue here.

The second objection concerns the nature of rights. As discussed earlier, some think that rights are such that their possessors may either exercise them or not exercise them as they choose.[29] Since individuals must make moral decisions in light of their own beliefs, it seems conceptually confused to talk about a right of conscience. But this need not be so. As explained in chapter 1, some rights may be *mandatory*; these are rights that must be exercised by their possessors. And as was mentioned there, an example of an allegedly mandatory right is the right to an education.[30] These rights involve "half-liberties" with respect to their objects, since the possessors have a duty (not merely a liberty) regarding the object. *Not all* inalienable rights are mandatory. The right to vote is a clear example.[31] A citizen may not transfer her right to vote to another; nor may she incur an obligation to another not to exercise that right. Nevertheless, a citizen of the United States is not (legally) required to exercise the right to vote. Perhaps only a few inalienable rights are mandatory. But one can readily see why the right of conscience must be mandatory. When a person confronts a moral situation, any decision that person makes has moral import. Since the person is responsible for making at least a permissible decision, the person must make some choice and so must exercise the right to do so; no agreement that the person has made absolves him of this responsibility.

There still seems to be something wrong, however. Let us suppose that S_1 agrees (always or for a fixed time) to obey S_2. And suppose that all of S_2's orders during this time are morally exemplary. S_1's conduct is in accord with S_2's orders, and so S_1's conduct is (apparently) morally exemplary. Moreover, S_1 behaves as he does because he believes that he is obligated to obey S_2. If the right of conscience is inalienable, something is wrong here. But what? The generalized version of the Madisonian/Jeffersonian argument hinges on the claim that agents cannot be obligated to do what is, all things considered, wrong. But this obviously requires further exploration. For in the imagined scenario not only did S_2 not issue any morally heinous orders, but also her orders were morally exemplary. If the wrongness of alienating one's right of conscience depends on how things actually turn out, then it is not always wrong to alienate this right. What, then, is the basis of the wrongness? It seems initially preposterous to say that the act of alienation is wrong because things *might* turn out badly. That is a very high standard by which to judge people. It also seems incorrect to say that the wrongness hinges on the probabilities associated with the transfer. If that were the case, then transferring one's right of conscience to a person of high moral character would not be prohibited. But if the right of conscience is inalienable, it may not be transferred to anyone. So the puzzle remains to explain the wrongness of the transfer in the case where S_2's orders are morally exemplary.

The Argument Clarified

If the inalienability of the right of conscience is not based on the wrongness of the orders and the subsequent actions performed, we must look elsewhere. Regardless of how things actually turn out and regardless of the moral character of the person to whom the transfer is made, it remains true that the agent might be ordered to perform wrong actions. In thereby undertaking this unusual moral obligation, then, the alienator incurs a certain kind of moral risk. Even if no actual harm ensues, morally risky behavior can be and often is wrong.

Consider Annie, who plays a significantly modified version of Russian roulette. Like the real game, a bullet is inserted in one chamber of Annie's gun, the cylinder is spun, and the trigger is pulled. There are, however, two major differences between Annie's game and the usual version. First, Annie does not aim the gun at herself; she aims it at her neighbor, Bill, without his knowledge, each evening as he returns home from work. Second, Annie's gun has many chambers—say, 100 (or 1000). Because Annie spins the cylinder anew each day, it is improbable that her perverse game will end in Bill's death, even though she is an excellent marksman. Whether Annie has been doing this for a month, or a week, or only a day, her behavior is wrong. Even though the probability of harming Bill is small, subjecting him to this risk is unacceptable. It is not necessarily true that imposing risk on another is always wrong.

But in this case there is no attendant moral gain. Whatever pleasure Annie gets from this perverse game does not count as a *moral* gain, I assume.

Just as the wrongness of Annie's risky behavior does not depend on the probability of Bill's actually being harmed, so too the wrongness of S_1's alienating his right of conscience to S_2 is not based on the probability of harm. S_1 subjects others—who, we cannot always determine—to risk without any attendant moral gain. But we should pause here. The last leap may be too quick. Perhaps S_1's ceding his right of conscience to S_2 *does* carry with it a moral gain. For suppose that S_1 correctly recognizes that his own moral judgments are highly fallible; the past demonstrates to him clearly that he makes many moral mistakes. Suppose too that S_1 knows that S_2 is a better moral judge than he himself is. In such a situation, it is true that there is a risk if S_1 agrees irrevocably to follow the orders of S_2; but there is an accompanying moral gain, a gain that may outweigh the risk. So what is wrong with cession of the right in this case?

The suppositions of this criticism are important. Critics attribute to S_1 a certain kind of knowledge of his own moral ignorance. We need to examine this. S_1 is cognizant of the fallibility of his own moral judgments and of the superiority of S_2's judgments. But of what does this knowledge consist?

To begin with the most far-ranging possibility, it seems that an agent can never sensibly transfer his right of conscience to another because he knows that his entire moral outlook is mistaken. For if he knew that his entire moral outlook were mistaken, he would presumably cease to hold those views. And if he had no moral outlook (or set of moral beliefs), he would have no basis for selecting someone to whom to cede his right of conscience. The purpose of ceding such a right is, after all, presumably to bring one's own conduct more in line with one's own moral convictions.[32] But to achieve this one must be able to identify a reliable person whom one should obey, and to do that one must have general moral beliefs to guide the process of selection.

Perhaps the agent does not question his general moral outlook, but doubts his judgments in particular cases. But again one can never believe in a particular case that one's current (specific) moral conviction is mistaken; for if one did hold this, one would presumably abandon the belief in question.[33] There is another possibility, however. In a particular case (or type of case), an agent may know that his judgments are apt to be clouded or biased; so, in such a case there will be a moral gain if the agent follows the orders of someone else whose judgments are more reliable. The agent is aware of his own weaknesses and fallibility and is taking steps to guard against them. Even here we must presuppose that the agent has moral knowledge. First, his retrospective judgments about his own past decisions must be correct in order to identify the weakness. And second, he needs moral knowledge in order to select a reliable person to obey. Granting this knowledge, however, doesn't the agent then have a good reason to alienate his right of conscience?

Recall that transferring this right puts the agent under an irrevocable obligation to obey the other. In the case hypothesized, the agent's clouded judgments concern a selected area, and so the agent has no good reason to alienate the right to make *all* moral decisions. (If we assume that the agent's judgments are clouded in all areas, we essentially return to the assumption that his entire moral outlook is mistaken.) Nevertheless, this seems to leave room for the agent to cede his right for a selected type of case, and that is still genuine (though selective) alienation. Can anything be said against this? Selective alienation carries with it unlimited moral risks and these risks are unnecessary to achieve the moral gain that the agent seeks. The risks are without limit because the alienator may be ordered to do anything whatsoever. And the same gain can be achieved without the risk of alienation. If the right of conscience is inalienable, it does not preclude an agent from seeking moral counsel and acting on that advice. Nor does it preclude acting on that advice *because* it is endorsed by a reliable authority. What it rules out is the agent *obligating* himself irrevocably to follow the orders of another. One can still obtain the moral advice of another without giving up the right to review that advice.[34] And if, as we are supposing, the agent is acutely aware of his own fallibility in a certain area, he may attach additional weight to the advice he receives regarding such matters. Since the gain can be obtained without incurring the risk, the argument above against alienation stands.

Even if the gains hypothesized here could not be obtained without incurring the risks in question, transfer of the right of conscience is not an option. For agents do not cease to be responsible for their own deeds by making agreements with others. And if agents have confidence that another is a reliable moral authority, they are responsible for that judgment and for the actions they take on the basis of it. John Rawls puts it this way:

> Each person must insist on an equal right to decide what his religious obligations are. He cannot give up this right to another person or institutional authority. In fact, a man exercises his liberty in deciding to accept another as an authority even when he regards this authority as infallible, since in doing so he in no way abandons his equal liberty of conscience as a matter of constitutional law.[35]

It is in this sense that agents *cannot* alienate their right of conscience.

It was argued earlier that an agent's consent to obey another does not create an obligation to do so and does not free the agent of his responsibilities. If this is correct, then in a sense one cannot alienate the right of conscience. So why also insist that saying the words (*seeming* to consent) is wrong? One reason for such a prohibition is that these words might deceive another, leading him to believe that the alienator is required to obey him. One wishes for firmer grounds here, however, because if the right of conscience is inalienable we should expect mature agents to know this (and thus not be deceived by the words). Appearing to alienate the right of conscience is to be unduly flippant about the claims of morality. Consider a different kind of case. Suppose that Annie is preparing to shoot Bill for no apparent reason. You say to her, "Go ahead and kill him." But Annie recognizes that you have no right to authorize such action, and she receives no additional motivation to act as a result of your words. Even if your words are neither morally nor causally efficacious, in uttering them you demonstrate a kind of contempt for morality.[36] This same contempt is present if you appear to alienate your right of conscience to another. And others who act as if you have alienated this right display contempt too.

One additional objection against this "moral risk" argument should be considered. It may seem that the argument is too far-reaching, and if successful will grossly overstock the realm of inalienable rights. The reason for the suspicion is that there seem to be moral risks associated with most transactions. Rights to property have been regarded as paradigmatically alienable; yet there may be moral risks associated with property transfers. Suppose that I sell my house to Celia. For all I know, Celia may be a member of a militia intent on destroying the government, and my property may provide her with a perfect opportunity to carry out her activities. Given this, if the moral risk argument works where I have employed it, it will also show that property rights are inalienable; but this is a conclusion that most will reject. This application of the argument can be resisted, however. Though both transactions may lead to bad outcomes, there is a difference between revoking the right to make moral decisions and revoking the right to a piece of property. When a person transfers his right of conscience, he is still the agent of any wrong that follows from this transfer.[37] But when a buyer uses property purchased from another for morally bad purposes (that the seller could not have been reasonably expected to foresee), the seller is neither the agent of nor a witting accomplice to the wrong that ensues.

Conscience and Political Obligations

When contemporary philosophers write about the right of conscience being alienated, they envision this right being transferred to another particular individual. It is hard to imagine realistic cases of this sort, cases in which one has morally enslaved oneself to another. As noted above, Madison, Jefferson, and Leland (and Thoreau too) argued against an individual transferring his right of conscience to the *state*. Richard Price, in a 1778 treatise, defended this same position. He argued that

> [N]o people can lawfully surrender or cede their liberty. This must appear to anyone who will consider that when a people make such a cession and the extensive powers of government are trusted to the discretion of any man or body of men, they part with the powers of life and death and give themselves a prey to oppression, that they make themselves the instruments of any injustice in which their rulers may chuse to employ them. . . .[38]

Here Price in effect invokes the moral risk argument as it applies to the relationship between an individual and the state. But if an individual may not alienate his right of conscience to the state, does that not wreak havoc with the notion of political obligations? If an individual retains his right of conscience, it seems to leave him free to act on his own moral judgments, regardless of the state's pronouncements. Indeed, no less an authority than Madison says that a person's duty to pay the homage to the Creator that he believes is acceptable "is precedent, both in order of time and in degree of obligation, to the claims of Civil Society," and that every person who becomes a member of a particular "Civil Society" must still preserve "his allegiance to the Universal Sovereign."[39] But far from wreaking havoc with the notion of political obligation, the inalienability of the right of conscience merely shows something about consent theory. Nor is this conclusion at odds with the tradition.

Note that a consent theorist as traditional as Locke attributed to people a similar sort of right. Locke held that people give their consent even to bad governments by residing within their territories, but people are not obligated to bad governments. This does not show that for Locke consent is not relevant to political obligations;

rather, it shows that consent alone is *not sufficient* to generate such requirements.[40] Rawls makes a similar point succinctly: "Acquiescence in, or even consent to, clearly unjust institutions does not give rise to obligations."[41] This means that all people, even those who have given consent, must (in some sense) retain the right to make and act on their own moral decisions. It is no accident that contractarians such as Hobbes, Locke, and Rousseau were especially interested in inalienable rights. For while they held that consent is necessary for political obligations, it was natural for them to wonder when, if ever, consent was also sufficient to obligate.

Even if people retain the right to make their own moral decisions, this, by itself, does not necessarily invite chaos. Indeed, Ronald Dworkin refers to what he calls a "great tradition of freedom of conscience in modern pluralistic democracies," and suggests that in such societies many hold that "government has no business dictating what its citizens should think about ethical and spiritual values, especially religious ones."[42] The fears of chaos are overblown for several reasons.

First, the inalienability of the right of conscience does not preclude one from obeying the commands of others. The "voice" of conscience tells agents to stay true to their own principles. But the orders of others may be perfectly compatible with those principles. Indeed, the content of many laws reflect widely accepted moral requirements—such as not to kill, not to steal, not to defraud, etc. It is only when the orders or laws are contrary to a person's moral principles that we can tell whether that person (wrongly believes that he) has alienated his right of conscience.[43] And we may not even be able to tell in this case since an agent may fail to act on his own moral principles and act instead on the orders of another due to (for example) weakness of will (rather than the fact that he so obligated himself).

Second, even if the right of conscience is inalienable, it is possible that grounds other than consent provide support for political obligations. For example, principles such as fair play or gratitude may do so.[44] If that is the case, agents may have to give due weight to the state's pronouncements in deciding what, in the final analysis, they ought to do, though for reasons other than the fact that they have consented.

And third, the very existence of laws creates in others expectations, and so agents must take into account that disobedience will sometimes adversely affect others. And in some cases, laws serve to coordinate the behavior of people in ways necessary for orderly living. Traffic regulations provide an obvious instance of this.[45]

This may appear to bring us back to a radically subjective view. For, as C. D. Broad remarks, it seems that in some sense of "ought" a person ought always to do that act that he believes at the time to be right.[46] I think, however, that this is best understood not as endorsing a radically subjective view about moral requirements, but rather as affirming a second-order precept about blame: an agent who acts against his conscience is always culpable.[47] How others should respond to the person acting from conscience is a different issue, however. The value of tolerance suggests that society should allow individuals the freedom to act (or refuse to act) on grounds of conscience when possible. But there will be times when society must prevent individuals from acting on their consciences. "Liberty of conscience is limited . . . by the common interest in public order and security."[48] The most conspicuous case here is to protect the rights of innocent persons. Even if members of certain religious sects regard themselves as morally required to abduct teenagers for the purposes of indoctrination, society is right to outlaw such behavior and to punish those who engage in it. It is more controversial to say that society may coerce members to perform services for the common good when those actions are in conflict with the consciences of some. Compulsory military service is the obvious example here.[49] Perhaps a tolerant society will allow conscientious objection in this case as long as the common good is not compromised. Even this allowance is controversial, though; for it may be unfair to those who are willing to serve.

So, though the inalienability of the right of conscience does imply that agents cannot obligate themselves irrevocably to obey the commands of the state (or a particular individual), such a result need not be lamented. What is morally important for the maintenance of an orderly society need not depend on such a strong obligation.

Conscience and the Practice of Medicine

Persons who enter any of the various fields of medicine have *role-related obligations*, obligations that agents have in virtue of their position, role, or job in society.[50] Role-related obligations are normally voluntarily incurred, and certainly persons enter the field of medicine voluntarily. One might say, then, that role-related obligations are typically the result of the agent's consent or something akin to consent. Here we are interested in whether agents can have role-related obligations that sometimes require them to violate their own consciences. We shall assume that the agents in question agree that they have the role-related obligations in question. Still, complying with such role-related obligations will require an agent to act against conscience in the case where some additional obligation conflicts with the role-related obligation, and the former obligation is judged by the agent to be stronger (or overridding). If in such a situation the agent is nevertheless required to comply with the role-related obligation, then this appears to be in conflict with the view that the right of conscience is inalienable; for the agent incurs the role-related obligation because of consent. In medicine, this sort of situation is apt to occur when the patient (or the patient's surrogate) wants the physician to do something that she regards as morally unacceptable. If the physician in such a case is required to comply with the patient's demand, it seems that she is required to act against conscience simply because of consent (or something akin to consent). Steven Miles says that the key issue faced by medical personnel in the well-known Helga Wanglie case (to be explained soon) was this: "We did not know whether providers were legally obliged to treat simply because the family demanded it."[51] They did not know if they were required to act against conscience simply because the patient's surrogate so demanded. If they were required to act against conscience, it would be because of the role-related obligations that they voluntarily incurred; for surely the Wanglie family could not make similar demands against just anyone. Putting the point more generally, this case raised the issue of whether patients have a right to regulate the conduct of their physicians, even when their doctors' moral judgments are in conflict with what the patients want.[52]

Legal recognition of a health care practitioner's right to decline to participate in some medical procedures on grounds of conscience was first recognized in the United States in the early 1970s. Following the influential abortion decisions,[53] a federal conscience clause was enacted protecting medical personnel in facilities receiving federal funds from being compelled to participate in abortion or sterilization procedures.[54] With the recent increase in the popularity of advance directives—legal documents enabling patients to limit medical treatment administered to them near the end of life—individual states have enacted conscience clauses designed to allow health care practitioners and institutions to refrain from implementing those directives to which they have moral objections. To avoid problems of abandonment, however, such conscience clauses usually require that institutions make their policies known to patients at or prior to admission, and they must provide continuing care until a transfer of the patient is effected or a court issues a final order.[55] A good example of this is a 1992 amendment to the Virginia Natural Death Act. The amendment said, in part, "Nothing in this article shall be construed to require a physician to prescribe or render medical treatment to a patient that the physician determines to be medically or ethically inappropriate."[56] It goes on to say that if the physician's decision is contrary to what the patient wants, then "the physician shall make a reasonable effort to transfer the patient to another physician."

There are two types of cases where physicians (and other health care practitioners) may be in conflict with the patient (or the patient's surrogate) about what ought to be done. One is where the patient (or surrogate) wants a certain treatment or intervention, but the physician believes that it would be wrong to provide such treatment or intervention. The other case is where the patient (or surrogate) wants a certain treatment or intervention stopped, but the physician believes that she is morally (or perhaps legally) required to continue such treatment. There are well-known examples of each of these types of situations.

Let us consider first the situation in which the patient (or surrogate) wants a medical intervention initiated or continued, but physicians and nurses believe that the intervention ought not to be initiated or ought to be stopped. Most common of cases like this are situations of "medical futility."[57] In such situations, one can ask about the health care practitioners' *moral* obligation and one can ask about their *legal* obligation. Here I shall assume (what has been argued elsewhere) that in at least some cases of this sort the health care practitioners *are not morally required* to comply with the patient's demand.[58] Let us examine some of the famous cases to see what the law has to say about this. One such case, alluded to earlier, is that of Helga Wanglie.[59] In December 1989, Helga Wanglie, an 87-year-old retired teacher, fractured her hip. Following surgery, she developed pneumonia and ventilatory failure. For the next five months, she could not be weaned from the ventilator. In May 1990, Mrs. Wanglie suffered cardiac arrest. She was resuscitated, but never regained consciousness. In June 1990, physicians judged that Mrs. Wanglie was in a persistent vegetative state and could not be weaned from the respirator. They judged that ventilator support was no longer medically indicated and recommended that it be discontinued. Mr. Wanglie, Helga's husband of 53 years, agreed to a do-not-resuscitate [DNR] order, an order specifying that certain medical interventions not be employed in the event that the patient's heart or breathing stops. But he would not consent to stopping ventilator support. He cited several reasons for this decision, including that Helga had told him that she wanted aggressive life support, even if she was in a coma, and that only God has the right to take life.

In February 1991, the hospital went to court. The hospital's ultimate goal was to discontinue the ventilator; but what it asked the court was that someone other than a family member be appointed Helga Wanglie's guardian. A Minnesota court rejected this request to appoint a new guardian. Mrs. Wanglie died, still on ventilator support, in July of 1991, a few days after the court's decision. During this conflict, the hospital, the Hennepin County Medical Center, had attempted to have Mrs. Wanglie transferred; but no other instituttion in the area would accept her. Thus, this institution and some of its employees were forced to act contrary to their moral beliefs and to administer treatment that they regarded as not indicated.

Cases like that of Helga Wanglie have prompted the American Medical Association (AMA) to issue a number of pronouncements about cases of medical futility. In the most recent such statement,[60] the AMA's Council on Ethical and Judicial Affairs said that patients and their surrogates should have the right to have the disagreement heard by others, including outside consultants and an institutional ethics committee. But if in the final analysis no agreement between the physician and the patient/surrogate can be worked out and if transfer to another physician or institution cannot be arranged, the physician is permitted to stop the futile intervention. Such a proposal gives priority to the physician's right of conscience.

Let us consider now the situation in which a patient (or surrogate) wants a treatment or intervention stopped, but the physician believes that she is morally obligated to continue the treatment. One legally contested case illustrating this conflict is that of Paul Brophy.[61] In March of 1983, Paul Brophy suffered a ruptured brain artery. Surgery was performed, but he never regained consciousness. He was transferred to New England Sinai Hospital, and his condition was diagnosed as a persistent vegetative state. Later that year, Brophy's wife gave physicians permission to insert a feeding tube into his stomach. Artificial feeding was continued throughout the next year, with Brophy's condition remaining unchanged.

Early in 1985, Mrs. Brophy asked physicians to discontinue artificial nutrition. She was Catholic and a nurse, and this was a difficult decision for her. But Mr. Brophy had often told family members that he did not want to be sustained if he were irreversibly comatose. In discussions of the Karen Quinlan case, Mr. Brophy had stated that he did not want to be sustained that way. And he had had such conversations with his wife, several siblings, and several of his children. Mrs. Brophy's decision to have artificial nutrition and hydration discontinued was supported by their five children, by Paul's seven siblings, and by his elderly mother.

In spite of this unanimity, the physician-in-chief at New England Sinai Hospital would not go along with the request. The hospital regarded the withdrawal of nutrition as killing, and so unethical. Mrs. Brophy sought court intervention. The case was typically drawn out, but in September 1986, the Supreme Court of Massachusetts ruled in a split decision (4 to 3) that Mr. Brophy's feeding tube was to be removed. They did not require the hospital to compromise its principles, however. Instead, they gave the hospital the option of transferring the patient to another institution. That is what the hospital did, and Paul Brophy died on October 23, 1986.

Let us consider one other situation in which a surrogate wants a medical intervention stopped, but the institution where the patient is housed is morally opposed to complying with the request. This is the well-known case of Nancy Cruzan.[62] On

January 11, 1983, 25-year-old Nancy Cruzan was in an automobile accident. She was thrown from her vehicle face-down in a ditch. By the time paramedics arrived, her brain had been without oxygen for at least twelve minutes, and possibly longer. She was resuscitated and taken to a hospital. She remained in a vegetative state until her death. In February 1983, a feeding tube was implanted in Nancy. In October of that same year, she was transferred to Missouri Rehabilitation Center in Mt. Vernon, Missouri, where she remained until death. By the fall of 1986, Nancy's parents, Joseph and Joyce Cruzan, reached the conclusion that she would never regain consciousness and that her feeding tube should be removed. But they did not act precipitously. Early in 1987, they sought legal assistance from the American Civil Liberties Union, and in May of that year they contacted William Colby, an attorney who would serve as their lawyer throughout the case. On May 28, 1987, more than four years after Nancy's accident, they hand-delivered a formal request to Missouri Rehabilitation Center (MRC) to stop all artificial nutrition and hydration. The request was opposed by MRC, regarding such action as killing.

In March of 1988, a hearing was held, and on July 27, 1988, a judge ruled in favor of the Cruzans. But the decision was appealed, and on November 16, 1988, the Missouri Supreme Court overturned the judge's decision and ruled against the Cruzans. Missouri law did not allow the withdrawal of nutrition or hydration from an incompetent patient, unless there was clear and compelling evidence that this is what the patient would have wanted. The Cruzans had testified about their daughter's general outlook on life but did not satisfy the standard of clear and compelling evidence. In July 1989, the Supreme Court of the United States agreed to hear the case. Oral arguments were presented on December 6, 1989, and on June 25, 1990, the Court upheld the Missouri Supreme Court ruling (in a 5–4 split decision).

In the meantime, two former coworkers of Nancy had come forward, claiming that in conversations Nancy had maintained that she would not want to be maintained in the way that Karen Quinlan had been. They explained various reasons why they had not come forward sooner. In any case, this was new evidence, and so the Cruzans renewed their request for a discontinuance of life-sustaining treatment on August 30, 1990. In September, the Missouri Attorney General withdrew from the case, thereby opening the door for the Cruzans. On December 14, 1990, the judge ruled that Nancy's feeding tubes should be removed in compliance with the family's request. That action was taken. On December 18, right-to-life protestors stormed MRC, but the family's wishes prevailed. On December 26, 1990, nearly eight years after the accident, Nancy Cruzan was pronounced dead.

In the case of Helga Wanglie, a health care facility was unable to transfer the patient and so was compelled to continue a treatment to which it objected morally. In the case of Paul Brophy, a hospital was not required to stop a treatment and thus perform what it regarded as murder; but it was required to permit the transference of that patient to an institution which agreed to comply with the family's wishes. And in the case of Nancy Cruzan, an institution was ordered to discontinue a treatment that it was morally opposed to stopping.

In each of these cases, there is a conflict between the wishes of the surrogates and the wishes of the health care practitioners. In some respects, the Brophy and Cruzan cases are easy. *If* there really is clear evidence that the patient would not want a given intervention continued under conditions that obtain, then that intervention should be stopped. The patient's right to self-determination must prevail in such a case. This is not to deny that there are a host of interesting questions about such cases. One important issue is what constitutes evidence of what the patient would want. Two other important questions concern who the appropriate surrogate is (when a patient cannot make his own decisions) and what principles that surrogate should employ.[63] Yet another important issue—one often overlooked—is who should be responsible for discontinuing the treatment (if transferring the patient to another institution is not feasible). Perhaps the institution has an obligation to look for a practitioner who does not object morally to stopping the intervention in question. This option would be akin to transferring the patient, though to another physician not another institution.

What is clear is that when conflicts of this sort exist, the preferred solution is to transfer the patient to another institution (or another provider). This option—which has been called dumping the "ethical hot potato"[64]—is preferred because it seems to respect both sides to the conflict: it allows the patient (or surrogate) to achieve her end, and it does not force the health care practitioner to act against conscience. But for those who take the right of conscience seriously, there are reasons to be troubled by this solution.

First, as many have observed, securing the transfer of a patient whose case raises troubling ethical questions is often difficult, if not impossible.[65] Second, requiring health care professionals or institutions to arrange a transfer may itself force them to act against conscience since it requires their participation in or facilitation of an activity that they regard as unethical.[66] And third, even if a health care professional (or institution) is not reticent to assist in transferring such a patient, perhaps he should be.[67] For it is far from clear why someone should take the commission of conduct that he regards as unethical to be untroubling so long as he is not the agent of the behavior. Viewed one way, this displays excessive concern for one's own purity and a disregard for the well-being of others. Even if one agrees with Judith Daar that "an action against one's conscience is more burdensome than any actions toward facilitation of a patient's transfer,"[68] it does not follow that providing such facilitation is permissible.

Stephen Wear and colleagues have suggested a compromise that would help to resolve some of these cases.[69] They suggest that physicians tell patients at the outset if they are in principle opposed to the withdrawal of life-sustaining medical treatment, thereby allowing the patient to choose another provider. And presumably this suggestion could be extended to cover cases like Wanglie: they could tell patients that they will not continue interventions that they regard as no longer indicated. But as the authors themselves acknowledge, this compromise is very limited and will not resolve all conflicts. In this context, the most important limitation is that in cases like Brophy and Cruzan, the patient presents unexpectedly and the physician is not one with whom the patient has had a previous relationship. Moreover, the nature of the situation dictates that treatment be initiated before the severity of the patient's condition or the prospects of recovery are known. Because of such limitations, this compromise will fail to eliminate many of the conflicts.

Given that conflicts between patients or surrogates and health care providers are all but inevitable, it appears that the right of conscience in medical contexts must be limited. But this does not show that the right of conscience is not inalienable. To the extent feasible, our society tries to respect a person's right of conscience. As Bernard Lo puts it, "Deeply held claims of conscience generally are honored. It would be dehumanizing to compel people to act in ways that violate their sense of integrity and responsibility."[70] But in cases where both patients or surrogates and physicians appeal to conscience and their views are at odds, someone must lose; and in some situations it is appropriate to resolve the conflict by favoring the patient or surrogate. As noted earlier, we do not always let religious fanatics do what they believe they ought to do if it interferes with others; the same is true of physicians. The physician can still hold that he *ought* to abide by his conscience and that he is *not morally obligated* to comply with the wishes of the surrogate. But in cases of conflict, society must enforce one view or the other. And to allow a physician's appeal to conscience *always* to trump the wishes of the patient or surrogate would be to endorse a medical imperialism of the most dangerous sort. This renders unsurprising the discoveries of Solomon and colleagues. In 1993, they surveyed 687 physicians and 759 nurses in five different hospitals. Nearly half the nurses and nearly three-quarters of the physicians acknowledged they had on occasion acted against their conscience in aggressive treatments provided to terminally ill patients.[71]

Contracts That Bind?

Arthur Caplan reports about the following case.[72] ProChoice of Minnesota, a non-profit organization that supports abortion rights, awarded a $1500 scholarship to a third-year medical student at the University of Minnesota. The scholarship came with a condition attached. To qualify for the award, recipients must pledge to be willing to perform abortions as one of the services they will provide when they become physicians. Caplan tells readers what many surely anticipated: pro-life leaders immediately spoke of creating a counterscholarship fund to educate young physicians about the evils of abortion. Some even spoke of creating a Joseph Mengele prize for physicians who perform abortions.

Regardless of the particulars of the situation in the Land of Ten Thousand Lakes, let us imagine a situation in which scholarships are offered to medical students in exchange for a contractual commitment. The "pro-choice" scholarship stipulates that the recipient agrees to perform abortions for the first five years of his or her medical practice; the "pro-life" award requires the recipient to agree not to perform any abortions for the first five years of his or her medical practice. Given what I have argued about the inalienable right of conscience, what is one to make of these agreements?

I suspect that I am not unusual in my response to each of these "contracts": they are at best inappropriate, and at worst disgusting. What I have said about the inalienable right of conscience gives some intellectual credence to such a response.

The argument of this chapter attempts to show that a promise to do what another tells one to do cannot be binding in the case where the content of what the agent is commanded to do is judged by that agent to be morally wrong, all things considered. Each of the contracts postulated here is morally inefficacious precisely because of what the main point of this chapter demonstrates; and this is so regardless of what either student's current beliefs about the morality of abortion are.

Consider first the promise (or contract) to perform abortions. Each time there is a request for an abortion, a physician may agree to provide that service only if she believes that abortion in this situation is not impermissible. But she cannot know in advance that she will believe this in every case (or even in any case). She may radically change her views about the morality of abortion; or there may be new facts revealed about the procedure or the fetus that prompt her to adopt a more complicated view; or she may regard a particular woman's reason for wanting an abortion to be heinous; or she may think that abortion in a particular situation is medically dangerous for the woman herself.

But the other promise fares no better. Any time there is a request for an abortion or an occasion for an abortion to be performed, in order for the physician to be allowed not to provide that service he must at least believe that not performing an abortion for this woman in her particular situation is not impermissible. Like our other doctor, however, he cannot know in advance that this will be the case. He too may radically change his beliefs about the morality of abortion. Or he may encounter an abortion for what he takes to be a compelling reason that he had not previously contemplated. It is true that a doctor who signed the "pro-life" contract would have one way off the hook not available to a physician bound by the "pro-choice" contract. For in the situation imagined—where it is morally mandatory for someone to perform the abortion—some other physician may be willing to do so, thus allowing our protagonist to adhere to his end of the bargain. But there is no way to assure that this will always be the case. There may be an emergency where there is no time for another physician to be contacted; or there may be no other doctor within close enough proximity to do the abortion, as is the case in some sparsely populated areas of the United States.

I have argued here that these contracts lack moral force. I am not prepared to say that those who make offers of this sort are engaged in wrongdoing; nor am I in a position to assess their characters negatively. My point is more modest: such contracts cannot bind the agent morally.

FOUR

The Right of Informed Consent and Inalienability

A patient's right of informed consent is well established. Bioethicists agree that this is a moral right, and in the United States and many other Western nations it is a legal right too. This right is grounded on the principle of autonomy (that agents should respect the freedom and choices of others), and that principle in turn is the basis for the right of self-determination.

There are several core components of informed consent.[1] The right applies only when patients possess decision-making capacity; competence is a presupposition of informed consent. When this condition is satisfied, a key element of informed consent is the *disclosure of information*. When securing a patient's permission to administer treatment, health care providers must convey to that patient the nature and duration of the treatment, the likelihood of success, the likely risks and benefits associated with the recommended treatment, the alternatives (if any) available to the recommended treatment, and the likely consequences if treatment is refused.[2] Another key element of informed consent is *understanding*. The patient must grasp or comprehend the information that is conveyed. Perhaps no health care provider can be sure that a patient has understood information that has been conveyed. But they can be aware of factors that impede understanding, such as immaturity, informational overload, and irrationality. Yet another element of informed consent is *voluntariness*. This means, minimally, that a patient's decision must not have been made because of pressure or coercion, or when under undue duress. Appropriate *authorization*, such as a patient's signature on a consent form, is an important formal aspect of informed consent.

As explained in chapter 1, rights have associated with them correlative duties. The most obvious duties associated with the right of informed consent are borne by health care providers. The two chief moral requirements generated by this right are the *duty to disclose* and the *duty to obtain consent*.[3] One might say, then, that there are two aspects of this right. The duty to disclose requires providers to convey to patients, among other things, appropriate information about risks and alternatives. The duty to obtain consent requires securing proper patient authorization. If the patient does not understand the pertinent information, that may indicate that the duty to disclose has not been adequately discharged. If pressure, coercion, or undue duress were present, that may undermine the voluntariness of the consent.

These two aspects of the right of informed consent evolved gradually in the legal system of the United States. The aspect of the right that generates the duty to obtain consent has its roots in the early part of the twentieth century. This aspect is connected to the right of bodily integrity and is really a right that others ask for consent before treatment is initiated and a right to refuse the recommendation. In one of the earliest and most commonly cited cases, Justice Benjamin Cardozo observed, "Every human being of adult years and sound mind has a right to determine what shall be done to his own body; and a surgeon who performs an operation without his patient's consent commits an assault, for which he is liable in damages."[4] The legal right to self-determination in the context of medicine has been reaffirmed many times since this decision. One of the most forceful statements of this right was made in an important Kansas case:

> Anglo-American law starts with the premise of thoroughgoing self-determination. It follows that each man is considered to be master of his own body, and he may, if he be of sound mind, expressly prohibit the performance of life-saving surgery, or other medical treatment. A doctor may well believe that an operation or form of treatment is desirable or necessary, but the law does not permit him to substitute his own judgment for that of the patient by any form of artifice or deception.[5]

Though it is a bit oversimplified, one might say that this path of the law established that when a competent patient says no, that means "no" and it must be respected. The requirements are not to begin treating a competent patient without consent and to stop the treatment if the patient so instructs.

During this same period of time, it is reasonable to say that if a patient said yes, that meant "yes" and health care providers were authorized to proceed. But in a series of cases in the latter part of the twentieth century, that changed; it was established that only an *informed* "yes" legally authorizes medical treatment.[6] It is here that the other aspect of the right, that which generates the duty to disclose information, emerged. And with that, we had the right of *informed consent* in full.

As one would expect, exceptions to informed consent have been identified.[7] These exceptions indicate that there are societal interests other than and in addition to self-determination. When an exception to the right of informed consent is legitimately invoked, one (or more) of the duties generated by that right is suspended. Two widely recognized exceptions involve the suspension of *both* the duty to disclose information and the duty to obtain patient consent. The first of these is when there is an *emergency*; treatment is needed immediately, the patient lacks decision-making capacity, and there is no surrogate available to act on the patient's behalf. The second of these is when the patient is *incompetent*. Ordinarily, however, when a patient is not competent, informed consent must be obtained from an authorized surrogate. In emergency cases, the duty to obtain consent is suspended because the patient's wishes are not known and patient well-being is a value (in addition to autonomy) that society may promote. And the duty to disclose information is suspended because doing so would serve no good purpose.

A third and more controversial exception is the *therapeutic privilege*. When this exception is invoked, the duty to disclose certain information is suspended if in the physician's judgment disclosure of that information would be harmful to the patient.[8] For example, if in the physician's judgment the patient is apt to become so distraught upon hearing certain information as to lose the ability to make decisions, then the physician may withhold that information when soliciting consent, even if that information is otherwise pertinent. This exception is controversial because it seems to authorize health care providers to treat certain patients in a strongly paternalistic manner; and it was precisely a rejection of such paternalism that served as the basis of the seminal judicial decisions regarding informed consent.

A fourth exception concerns cases in which the *well-being of innocent third parties* may be jeopardized. A patient with a contagious disease transmittable through casual contact fits the bill here; tuberculosis is a familiar example today. Precedent in this area goes back to the first decade of the twentieth century, in which a statute allowing for compulsory inoculation against smallpox was held to be constitutional.[9] In such cases the duty to disclose information is *not* what is suspended. But the duty to obtain consent—authorization from the patient—may be suspended if that is what is necessary to prevent the well-being of others from being put at risk; the freedom of patients is curtailed to the degree necessary to protect the public.[10]

A fifth exception, and the one that is the focus of this chapter, is *waiver*. This is when the patient voluntarily relinquishes the right of informed consent. Waiver was explicitly recognized as an exception to informed consent by the judiciary in the United States in *Cobbs v. Grant,* when the court asserted that "a medical doctor need not make disclosure of risks when the patient requests that he not be so informed."[11] To endorse this as a legitimate exception to the right of informed consent is to adopt a certain social policy, a policy with important normative implications. In this chapter we will explain these implications and will ask whether the policy that allows waiver of the right of informed consent is morally defensible.

Waiving and Alienating Rights

Let us now review some basic points developed in chapter 1. There are different ways of divesting oneself of one's rights. What is possible will vary, depending on the context and the nature of the right in question.

In some cases, one may simply choose not to exercise a right that one possesses. Examples cited earlier illustrate this. A citizen has the right to vote, but she (legally) may choose not to vote. If you are married, you have a right to sue your spouse for divorce if certain conditions are satisfied; but of course you need not exercise that right.

In some cases, one may *waive* a right that one possesses. Waiver involves the intentional or voluntary relinquishment of a right, or conduct that warrants the inference of relinquishment of that right. When valid waiver occurs, the possessor has by his consent suspended certain claims that he has against others. Others are permitted to do what would otherwise be impermissible because of the right-holder's consent. As previously explained, if the police properly inform me, I may give up my right to have legal counsel present when I am being questioned by authorities. In this type of case, such a waiver is formal, effected by the possessor of the right uttering certain words in an appropriate context. It is important to understand, however, that waiver may also be informal and inferential. To cite an example from the first chapter, suppose that last winter Mr. Kowalski specifically told the neighborhood children that they could go sledding on his nicely sloped driveway. He even shoveled a path along the side of the driveway so that they could easily retreat to the top after a successful run. This year, after the first snow, Mr. Kowalski again shovels a path on the side of the driveway. He does not explicitly give the children permission to use his driveway for sledding, but they take his behavior as evidence that he will allow them to do so. The inference is reasonable; such a waiver is informal.

An important difference between not exercising a right and waiving a right concerns what others may do. If I do not exercise my right to vote, I nonetheless retain it. I continue to have the choice to vote in any particular election until the polls close, and I retain the right to vote in subsequent elections if I choose. And even if I do not exercise my right to collect Social Security benefits when I reach the specified age, I retain the right to do so. But if I waive my right to legal counsel, police are now authorized to question me about my activities. In this case, of course, I may stop the interview at any time and *regain* my right to have counsel present if I choose. Similarly, Mr. Kowalski could announce—verbally or by a posted sign—to the neighborhood children that they were no longer authorized to use his driveway.

By contrast, some rights are said to be *mandatory*; they must be exercised by their possessors. Examples of allegedly mandatory rights include the right to education and a student's right to be vaccinated against certain contagious diseases.[12] Feinberg says that these rights involve "half-liberties" with respect to their objects, since the possessors have a duty (not just a liberty) regarding the object. If there are any mandatory rights, the possessor may neither waive nor refrain from exercising those rights.

Transfer is yet another way of divesting oneself of a right; it involves the voluntary and complete conveyance from one person to another. An alienable right is one that may be waived or transferred to another person by the possessor. Property rights are paradigmatically alienable. If I own a book, I may give or sell it to you. If I do, all claims and correlative obligations (based on property rights) regarding the book that were owed to me are now owed to you; you are now the possessor. Transfer effects significant normative changes; the individual to whom the correlative obligations are owed is different after the right has been transferred. By contrast, an *inalienable* right is one that may neither be waived nor transferred by the possessor.

It should be clear that an alienable right is nonmandatory; if the possessor may transfer the right to another, then she is not required to exercise that right. As was argued in chapter 1, however, an inalienable right may be mandatory but need not be. A person may not transfer to another her right to vote, but neither is she required to exercise that right; and the same is true of the right to collect Social Security benefits.

With this brief review, let us now see how these distinctions apply to the topic of informed consent. In one sense, it is clear that a person need not exercise her right of informed consent. For example, a person is not required to protest if a physician does not provide her with adequate information about her options or if the physician proceeds without her consent; nor must that person exercise the right to sue after the fact. But it is not clear if the *physician* is relieved of his duties to disclose information to the patient and secure permission from the patient before administering treatment *simply because* the patient does not exercise her rights. In short, whether a patient's nonexercise of his right of informed consent thereby *authorizes* a physician to administer treatment without that consent is not obvious.

Matters might seem otherwise if the patient *explicitly* waives her right. That is what we shall explore here. But to begin, we need to review at least two conditions that must be satisfied in order for waiver to be valid. First, the choice to waive the right must have been *voluntary*.[13] This means minimally that the choice was not due to coercion, pressure from others, or made under duress. In one case, a patient had signed a release from liability for future negligence as a condition of admission to a charitable research hospital.[14] Such a waiver was regarded as not voluntary (and so not valid) because the parties were vastly unequal and one was in an inferior bargaining position. Second, the person must *know* that she has the right in question. So, in the case of the right of informed consent, the patient must know that she has the right to receive relevant information *and* the right to decide.[15] Were the patient to lack knowledge of either of these, any apparent waiver would not be valid.

If a right is waivable and valid waiver occurs, then certain obligations correlative with that right are limited or suspended because of the possessor's consent (in the case of explicit waiver) or because the possessor's conduct warrants an inference of relinquishment. In the case of the right of informed consent, in principle waiver may limit or suspend either the health care professional's duty to disclose information to the patient or the duty to obtain consent before administering a specific treatment, or both.[16]

Waiver of the right of informed consent may be either limited or broad. A case of *limited* waiver discussed in one popular textbook involves a Jehovah's Witness who asks his physician to do everything possible to save his life, but not to inform him if a blood transfusion is employed.[17] If such a waiver is valid, then the physician is no longer under an obligation to provide this patient with information about the blood transfusion (such as benefits, risks, and alternatives), nor is she obliged to obtain the patient's consent for this particular procedure. Waiver is *broad* if the patient effectively gives the physician carte blanche. The patient might say, "You are the doctor. Do whatever you think is best."[18] If such a broad waiver is valid—and in one case[19] it was held to be so—then apparently the physician may administer any treatment that she regards as appropriate without further authorization from the patient. While acknowledging that such "blanket" consent may protect the physician from charges of battery, some scholars urge that this approach not be used.[20]

Whether waiver of the right of informed consent is limited or broad, *someone* must decide what treatments will be administered to the patient. In the cases just described—the case of the Jehovah's Witness and the case of the patient who gives the doctor carte blanche—it seems clear that the patient wants the physician to make the decision(s). In effect, the patient has delegated decision-making authority to the physician. And one suspects that this is typical in cases of waiver. In such cases waiver is *specific*; a selected individual (or individuals) is authorized by the possessor to disregard the duty correlative with his right. Waiver may also be *general*; in such cases multiple but not a definite number of individuals are authorized to disregard the duty correlative with the possessor's right. This is what is going on in the case of Mr. Kowalski and the neighborhood children.

We can easily imagine at least one type of case in which a competent patient divests himself of the right of informed consent without authorizing the *physician* to disregard the correlative duty. This is the case in which a patient designates another specific individual to make his decisions. Thus, an elderly father might say to his physician, "Doctor, just do whatever my daughter tells you to do. I don't want to be bothered." Of course, as long as the patient is competent, he may reclaim this right in full from his daughter. One scholar thinks that this sort of case is less problematic than when the patient wants the physician to make the decisions.[21]

As noted at the outset, the right of informed consent presupposes competence on the part of the possessor of that right. This suggests that waiver of that same right is relevant only so long as the patient is competent. If the patient is not competent, he cannot decide; and giving him information about the risks and alternatives serves no purpose. So there is no sense in which an incompetent patient can be said intelligently to have waived his right to informed consent. Once a patient is no longer competent, the issue is who is the appropriate surrogate for that patient. If the patient while competent has given the physician carte blanche, perhaps one can make a case that the physician is the most appropriate surrogate. And if the elderly father has said that his daughter may speak for him when he is competent, perhaps she should be the surrogate when he is incompetent. But in neither situation is it a case of waiver because the *patient's* right of informed consent is no longer relevant. Waiver of any right is operative only so long as the patient is capable of reclaiming that right in full.[22]

There is another area of health care ethics in which the issue of informed consent is pertinent and where the issue of waiver arises. Unfortunately, this creates some confusion. The area concerns using human subjects in medical research. It is now a well-established precept of research ethics that humans should not be used as subjects without their informed consent (or in the case of incompetent subjects, the consent of their surrogates). In the United States, regulations regarding the use of human subjects are issued by the Department of Health and Human Services (DHHS) and by the Food and Drug Administration (FDA). Hospitals, universities, and other institutions conducting research on human subjects must have an Institutional Review Board (IRB), which is responsible for reviewing, assessing, and monitoring research proposals involving human subjects and making sure that guidelines are followed. Occassionally, exceptions to the requirement of informed consent from research subjects are recognized, and one such exception is referred to as "waiver."[23] This is misleading, however, because waiver in these cases is granted by the national governing body or a local IRB. But in standard cases of waiver, it is only the *possessor* of the right who has the authority to waive that right. The duty is owed to the possessor of the right and so only that possessor's consent releases others from the requirement of informed consent. I am not disputing the exceptions identified by DHHS. Rather, I am saying that it is a mistake to say of these exceptions that the right of informed consent has been *waived*. It erroneously implies that the correlative duty is owed to the DHHS. It would be more accurate to say that in these cases the requirement to obtain the subjects' informed consent has been suspended.

The Case for Allowing Waiver

Examination of the extant literature suggests that there is a consensus in support of a policy that treats waiver as a legitimate exception to the right of informed consent. This means that if a patient voluntarily and knowingly relinquishes his claim against others, then the physician may either withhold pertinent information from that patient or administer a specific treatment without patient authorization, or both, without violating any duties or being liable for so acting. Before asking what reasons can be advanced in support of such a *social policy*, it is worth discussing reasons that an individual *patient* might have for wanting to waive his right of informed consent.

A number of considerations have been mentioned.[24] Some patients may find medical information and the accompanying decisions burdensome and overwhelming. These patients feel more comfortable letting the doctor decide. Some patients are very anxious about their illness and know that their anxiety affects their ability to understand medical information. Some patients may know that they become depressed when they think about the issues surrounding their own serious illness. Some may simply prefer to live their last days with hope, even if false hope. Moreover, some may know that they make poor decisions under duress; if such patients trust their physicians, it makes sense for them to let those physicians make the medical decisions. And one can see that these same considerations may prompt a patient to transfer his right of informed consent to a family member.

There are at least two general arguments in support of a social policy that allows competent patients to waive their right of informed consent (and thus relieve health care providers of one or both of the correlative duties). The first of these arguments is conceptual, based on analyzing the very notion of a right.[25] The idea is that rights arm their possessors with certain normative advantages, usually understood in terms of claims, liberties, immunities, and powers. Among other things, a person's rights impose certain obligations on others. But if the possessor consents, acts that would otherwise violate those rights are permissible. Thus, rights by their very nature may be waived by their possessors. This is one of the powers that is part and parcel of what it is to possess a right. This, of course, is an instantiation of the conceptual argument against inalienable rights discussed in chapter 2.

The second general argument begins with the observation that though waiver of the right of informed consent may seem inconsistent with the goal of self-determination, in fact it may be a manifestation of that goal. According to this argument, compelling patients to receive information that they do not want and to make decisions that they do not wish to make is a paternalistic denial of the right of self-determination. As one advocate of this position says, "Waiver is the patient's counterpart to the therapeutic privilege."[26] If the patient believes that participating in the decision-making process will be harmful and wishes to avoid doing so, it is appropriate to comply with such wishes. Refusal to do so is paternalistic.[27]

Neither of these arguments is without difficulties, however. The first argument seems to be based on the assumption that the function of rights is to protect individuals' choices; for only if this is assumed, can one say that it is a part of the *concept* of a right that its possessor may waive that right. But, as discussed in chapter 2, there is a serious controversy about the function of rights. And though many do hold that their function is to protect individual choices, many others argue that they serve their possessors' well-being.[28] In the absence of *establishing* that the function of rights is to protect choices, the conceptual argument is question-begging.

Even if the function of rights is to protect choices—and for the purpose of conceding to opponents of inalienable rights as many of their assumptions as possible, I have adopted this conception of rights—there is a point that counts against *both* of the arguments in support of recognizing waiver. The choices that right-holders have are not unlimited; there are moral constraints on how they may exercise their rights. And typically if exercising one's right in a certain way would significantly endanger the welfare of others, then one is not permitted so to act. For example, even though I have the right to vote, I may not exceed the speed limit in order to make it to the polls before they close. This shows that it is consistent both to attribute a right to an individual and to assert that there are certain acts apparently based on that right or designed to carry out that right that are prohibited. It also shows that restrictions on how persons may utilize or exercise their rights need not be based on paternalism. Of course, this puts a *burden* on opponents of these arguments; they must *show* that allowing waiver of the right of informed consent will put others at risk. But if they can show this, then each of the above arguments will have been undermined.

These considerations alone do not show that society should not allow the right of informed consent to be waived. For there may be better arguments, not considered here, in support of such a policy. But for now we turn to arguments against allowing waiver.

The Case Against Allowing Waiver

There might well be an argument for the contention that on the whole competent patients will be *better off* if they are not allowed to waive their right of informed consent. Such an argument could cite paternalistic considerations in favor of adopting a certain social policy, a policy that forbids health care providers from not seeking consent or from not disclosing all pertinent information *because of consent*. One might argue, for example, that informed patients are better able to cooperate with their treatment, can be on the lookout for complications, and are more likely to be compliant.[29] And if the function of rights is to protect the possessors' welfare, this may be a plausible argument. But here we are not assuming that the function of rights is to protect the possessors' welfare. And one of the ground rules we have adopted is to eschew paternalistic considerations in making a case for inalienable rights. Are there any other considerations to support a social policy that does *not* allow health care providers to be released from either the duty to inform or the duty to seek consent, even though the patient has authorized them to do so?

We are now in a position to apply one of the arguments in chapter 2 to this topic. The least controversial exercise of society's power over an individual is to prevent that individual from harming other nonconsenting parties. One might argue that adopting a social policy that allows physicians to administer treatment without the competent patient's informed consent, even if that patient has waived her right, will put other nonconsenting individuals at risk. If so, there is a credible, nonpaternalistic defense of not allowing waiver. It is usually acknowledged that the law as a social policy must be formulated in such a way as to limit well-intentioned misuse and must also be constructed to minimize abuses.[30] And if competent patients may waive their right of informed consent, it seems that the possibilities of abuse and misuse are great. Some physicians may subtly suggest to patients that they do not want them to participate in decision making.[31] Given that in medical contexts patients often feel intimidated and not the equal of physicians, this arrangement may lead to many cases of apparent waiver that are not genuine because waiver is not truly voluntary. But in any particular case, it may be difficult to determine if the patient has been moved by fear or intimidation. Patients may even feel that their care will be compromised if they do not waive their right as they believe the physician wants them to do. In addition, those physicians who find getting informed consent burdensome may welcome patients who waive their rights, thus creating an atmosphere that discourages all patients from seeking to be informed and participating in decision making.[32] Physicians may even falsely claim waivers in certain cases. These worries are compounded by the fact that recent studies suggest that patients want relevant information about their own medical condition and that clinicians underestimate patients' desire for such information.[33] If this is the case, then many patients who have no desire to waive their right to informed consent will nevertheless be depicted or perceived by physicians as having done so.

It might seem that these arguments do *not* apply when a patient has designated someone other than a physician to make his decisions. And, indeed, Marcia Angell has argued that "a competent adult may want someone else, usually a family member, to mediate in medical decisions" for various reasons, including that "he doesn't feel well enough to think clearly," that "he has particular faith in someone else's judgment," or that "he prefers not to know about his medical condition." When this occurs, Angell says, such a "desire should be respected."[34] But this may be too quick; for some of the same considerations cited when physicians are deciding will apply to the case where a family member is designated to do that job. If, for example, a patient is relatively passive but one of his family members is domineering, that dominant family member may take control of the situation, even when the patient really does not want this. And surrogates do not always want what is best for their family members. In such cases, then, both the autonomy and well-being of the patient may be compromised.[35]

The reasons just cited against allowing waiver of the right of informed consent assert that the rights of all persons are jeopardized if some are permitted to waive their rights. If there is adequate empirical evidence to support these assertions, this provides society with good reason not to recognize waiver as a legitimate exception to the doctrine of informed consent. Reasons more deontological in nature might also be advanced against allowing waiver. If these are convincing, they provide the patient herself with moral reasons not to waive or transfer the right. I have in mind here an instantiation of the Kantian defense of inalienable rights outlined in chapter 2. The principle underlying the right of informed consent is autonomy. And some have argued that dignity and respect for one's own autonomy requires one to remain an active participant in one's own medical decisions.[36] Allowing oneself to be treated like a child is undignified and shows a lack of self-respect; each has a duty not to allow herself to be treated in a servile manner.[37] Moreover, one might say that a patient who wishes to waive his right of informed consent is someone who refuses to take responsibility for his own life and health.[38] If this does not display objectionable servility, then it at least exhibits a kind of laziness that is incompatible with dignity and self-respect.

The first of these arguments against waiver depends on certain claims about what can happen if society permits competent patients to waive the right of informed consent. The second argument appeals to Kantian notions regarding self-respect and duties to oneself. When we are concerned about what *the law* and public policy should say about waiver of the right of informed consent, it is philosophically prudent to restrict ourselves to the first of these arguments. For preventing abuses and minimizing certain risks to innocent persons is uncontroversially a legitimate function of the law; there is far less consensus about whether there is a duty of self-respect, let alone a right to enforce such a duty. Nevertheless, the second argument is important when considering how to understand the *moral* rights involved. And though I do not develop the Kantian defense here, this should not be taken to indicate that I think it is without promise.

Duty to Inform, Duty to Obtain Consent

Rights have associated with them claims, which in turn form the basis of the correlative obligations and duties borne by others and owed to rights-possessors. As was discussed earlier, a patient's right of informed consent gives rise to two sorts of duties on health care providers: the duty to provide patients with information, especially about the expected risks and the available alternatives, and the duty to obtain patient authorization before administering treatment. When a right is waivable and is waived, the possessor's consent renders permissible behavior that is normally not allowed. If the right of informed consent is waivable and is waived, health care practitioners will be relieved either of the duty to provide information or of the duty to solicit authorization. When the right of informed consent is transferred to another, health care professionals owe these duties to that other rather than to the patient. Let us explore this further.

When waiver occurs, the possessor's consent authorizes behavior normally not allowed. If you walk across my land without my permission, it is trespassing; with my consent, it is not. Similarly, my consent makes it permissible for you to write in my book; normally, such behavior is not permitted. If a right *may not* be waived or transferred by its possessor, then the possessor's consent is not sufficient for suspending the correlative duties. To cite an obvious example, in many legal systems a person's consent does not justify killing that individual. When consent does authorize infringement, the waiver must be both voluntary and informed.

In one sense, a competent patient cannot waive the right to consent to medical treatment. This right, let us say, is *pragmatically* unwaivable. For when waiver seems to occur, the very thing that authorizes the physician not to solicit further authorization from the particular patient is that this particular patient *has given* her consent. In order for waiver to be valid, it must be voluntary and informed. If waiver of the right of informed consent were valid, then the patient would have to know that she had the right to make her own decisions. But then in appearing to waive the right to consent, the patient is actually giving consent. We can see this in particular examples. Return to the case of the Jehovah's Witness, who asked the physician to administer blood if necessary but not to tell him. In this case, what authorizes the physician to proceed (if he judges it to be necessary) is that the patient has so authorized him.[39] And the story is the same if the patient's apparent waiver is broad, authorizing the physician to do *whatever* he judges medically best. Again, this *is* to give consent, albeit not directly and not informed about the particulars of the situation.

There is another sense in which a competent patient cannot waive the right to consent. As long as the patient is competent, the physician will have to tell her certain things (for example, that he is about to commence treatment) because the patient's cooperation is typically necessary. And if at this point the patient refused or said no, that refusal would have to be honored. So, in spite of an apparent waiver, the patient retains the right to refuse as long as she is competent, just because of the nature of the situation.

There is an apparent paradox here. The very thing that determines whether a physician's actions are battery or medical treatment is whether the patient has consented. So the right to bodily integrity, upon which the right of informed consent is based, must be waivable since the possessor's consent or its absence is the very thing that determines whether the right has been impermissibly infringed. The apparent paradox disappears when we understand that if the patient has seemingly waived the right to consent, he is actually giving the physician permission to proceed. But, as we saw earlier, such permission retains its normative force only so long as the patient is competent. If the patient is competent and refuses, such refusal must be respected. Apparent waiver of the right to consent is actually an exercise of that right; in securing permission to proceed without further consent, the physician has fulfilled the duty to obtain consent. And in continuing to acquiesce, the patient is declining to exercise the right to refuse.

If apparently explicit waiver is actually exercising the right to consent, matters are more complicated when the competent patient will say nothing—will not consent, will not refuse, and will not appear to waive the right. If a patient's unwillingness to respond when a physician recommends treatment is to count as waiver—and therefore an exercise of the right to consent—it is informal and inferential at best. My account leaves it unclear how to handle such cases, but I think that it *is* unclear how these cases should be handled. Consider the situation of Willie Mae Powell.[40] On December 22, 1965, Mrs. Powell was in a hospital, critically ill and bleeding profusely. Because of her religious convictions, she would not consent to a blood transfusion; but she would not explicitly refuse or actively resist either. The hospital sought judicial intervention, and Judge Jacob Markowitz authorized the administration of blood. The judge said, "This woman wanted to live." He apparently construed her unwillingness either to consent or to refuse as informal waiver and therefore consent. I am not at all sure that this is correct; but neither am I sure that it is incorrect. Cases of this sort, I think, are among the most puzzling. I am cognizant that judges do not have the same luxury of suspending judgment that scholars have.

Let us turn now to the other aspect of the right of informed consent. It seems more promising to say that a competent patient's waiver relieves health care professionals of the duty to provide the patient with information; in particular, they need not provide the patient with information about the benefits and risks associated with the recommended treatment or about alternatives that might be available. Of course, allowing waiver of this sort has associated with it risks of the sort noted earlier. For example, physicians who find explaining matters to patients burdensome may subtly suggest to them that they waive their rights. And this may create an atmosphere in which all patients are discouraged from participating actively in their medical care. These risks might be minimized if patients who wish to waive their right to information were required to sign an *explicit form* to that effect. Such a requirement would better ensure, though not guarantee, that the patient understands that she has a right to the information and understands the normative implications of her waiver. There is a downside, too, however; requiring patients to read and sign yet another form may be onerous and create confusion.

There is one obvious sense in which a patient need not exercise her right to be informed. A patient can refuse to listen to the physician or simply tune out what the physician is saying. And it seems insensitive and inappropriate to force information on a patient against her will, even if the patient has a *duty* to know, as some have argued.[41] For the patient may have anxieties or fears about being informed, and even if it is a patient's duty to be informed, it is not a duty that can easily be enforced.

So how should a case be handled when a patient seems to waive her right to be informed about the nature, benefits, and risks of the recommended treatment and about the alternatives to it? Does the patient's voluntary and informed waiver relieve health care practitioners of the duty to provide such information? As was just noted, as a practical matter the information cannot be forced on the patient. So unless a physician is willing to wait until a patient agrees to listen to the information and try to understand it, treatment will have to proceed without the patient's being informed. Waiver—voluntary consent—authorizes the suspension of the duty to provide information.

Still, one suspects that the responsible physician will be uncomfortable about waiver of the right to be informed because it may discourage other patients from seeking needed information, because the treatment may be less successful (since patients will not know what side effects to expect), and because it may later invite legal problems. But there may be plausible ways to deal with these difficulties. Concerning the fear that patients will be discouraged or even pressured not to seek information, the appropriate policy in the face of apparent waiver is repeatedly to *offer* patients information or remind patients that they have a right to be informed.[42] Of course, if the waiver seems sincere, then the physician must be cautious about how these reminders are conveyed. Offers made too frequently or too aggressively will cross the line and become badgering.[43] But on occasions when the patient's cooperation is needed as treatment is initiated, the physician can remind that patient that there are risks and can ask the patient if there is anything he would like to know about what is happening. Conducted in the right manner, this will serve to remind patients that they retain both the right to be informed and the right to decide.

The concern that legal problems may later arise when patients seem to waive their right to be informed is understandable and not without foundation. For if medical interventions used in good faith produce bad results, patients may be disgruntled and sue on grounds that they were not adequately informed. This would seem to open physicians to liability in a way that is particularly unfair, since in not providing information they were simply trying to comply with patients' wishes. At the very least, that the patient has waived his right to information will have to be recorded in the medical record. But that may not afford sufficient legal protection. It may be that only a form *specifically* waiving the right to be informed will do the job. The reason for this signed form is that if a case is contested, health care professionals will be claiming, *not* that the patient was adequately informed about the specific treatment, but that he knowingly and voluntarily waived that right; the patient will presumably deny this. It would seem, then, that some more formal document is needed, just as is the case now with informed consent to specific treatments. And, just as in the case with informed consent *to* treatment, the existence of an appropriately signed form will create a *presumption* of valid waiver. The presumption, of course, is rebuttable, but the burden will be on the patient to rebut it. All of this is unfortunate since it may add to the burdens and confusions of patients; but it may be the price that must be paid if waiver of the right to information is allowed, and physicians are not put at an unfair risk. Similarly, the fact that patients will not be as able to monitor potential adverse side effects because they have chosen not to be informed about them is part of the price that individuals must pay for choosing this option.

When we are talking about "blanket" consent given for surgery—apparently authorizing the surgeon to do whatever he thinks is necessary—matters are slightly more complicated.[44] In such cases at the time the medical decisions are to be made, either the patient has the capacity to make his own decisions or lacks that capacity. If the patient has the capacity, then matters are as stated above: the patient can be reminded of his rights, and to the extent that the patient's cooperation is needed, his continued acquiescence is evidence that he does not wish to exercise those rights. On the other hand, if the patient lacks the capacity to decide at the time that decisions must be made, then two possibilities are present: either delaying the decision will put the patient in further danger (either because the problem must be dealt with immediately or dealing with it later imposes additional risks) or it will not do so. If delaying the decision does *not* put the patient at further risk, then it is hard to see why it should not be delayed until the patient again possesses decision-making capacity. If it cannot be delayed without imposing further risks, then in many cases the intervention would justifiably be done, even if the patient had not given blanket consent, on grounds that that is what the reasonable person would want; that this additional consent is present would seem to make the case for proceeding with the intervention even stronger.

Conclusion

With the emphasis during recent decades on the patient's right to informed consent, the case of waiver of this right seems puzzling. Physicians may appropriately wonder whether they are permitted, or indeed even obligated, to go along with the patient's desire in such cases. Physicians are certainly *not obligated* to comply with such a patient's wishes. For a physician may justifiably choose to enter into and maintain a professional relationship only with patients who are willing to be active and informed participants in their own medical care. Such is the nature of the contractual relation. The matter of permissibility is more complicated.

In the case of informed consent, apparent waiver is often by default specific. This is because someone must make treatment decisions, and when a patient seems to waive his own right to do so, it is appropriate to assume that the patient is transferring this right to the physician unless the patient has explicitly designated someone else. The upshot of this chapter is to suggest that our understanding of waiver of the right of informed consent is enhanced if we distinguish two duties correlative with that right: the duty to obtain consent and the duty to provide information. In an important sense, a competent patient's right to consent cannot be waived. This is because waiver is valid only if it is voluntary and informed, and so valid waiver *is* a form of consent; the very thing that authorizes treatment in the case of waiver is that the patient consented. In addition, a patient's cooperation is typically needed when treatment is administered, and so as a practical matter the patient always retains the right to say no or not acquiesce at that point. Thus, the right of competent patients not to have medical treatment administered without consent is pragmatically not waivable. So health care providers cannot be relieved of the duty to obtain a competent patient's consent (at least by waiver); but they may treat acquiescent patients who choose not to exercise their right to refuse. The right to be informed seems to be such that a patient need not exercise it; for a patient can be forced neither to listen to information nor to understand. Proceeding with treatment when the patient says that he does not want to be fully informed is no doubt the compassionate thing to do. But if patients are reminded that all treatment decisions are made on the basis of information and that they have a right to that information, then that is the best that health care providers can do to ensure that patients are aware that they may exercise their right to be informed if they so choose. Still, this aspect of the right—the right to be *informed*—is waivable.

By definition, if a right cannot be waived, then it cannot be transferred. But we might wonder about the aspect of transfer that is not a part of waiving—namely, obligating oneself to another because of one's consent. Though the case has not been made in this chapter, I would suggest that the right of a competent patient not to have medical treatment administered without consent also cannot be transferred because the possessor cannot be obligated (merely as the result of his consent) to allow another to make his medical decisions. It is difficult to fathom how one could be obligated not to refuse a medical intervention to which one objects simply because of a promise one has made to another. One could construct arguments analogous to those Hobbes makes about the right to self-defense; the content of the promise (not to resist) is not something that the agent can fulfill.[45] Moreover, the case of the Jehovah's Witness shows that such a promise might conflict with the inalienable right of conscience.[46]

FIVE

The Inalienable Right to Life

And Its Implications for Volutary Euthanasia

Whenever lists of putative inalienable rights are composed, the right to life usually is at the top. It was for Jefferson, and it is for most others. This chapter and the next will explore what it means to say that the right to life is inalienable and what the normative implications of such a claim are.

As we have already seen, if a right is inalienable, then the possessor's consent does not provide an adequate basis for suspending the duty or duties correlative with that right. With alienable rights, consent is a *permission-generating* activity; with inalienable rights, it is not. To see how this works with the right to life, we must begin by examining what duties such a right entails.

The Right to Life and Its Correlative Duties

As one might guess, there has been considerable dispute in the philosophical literature about how to characterize the right to life, about what duties that right implies, and about what sort of beings are capable of possessing such a right. One of the arenas in which this dispute plays out, of course, is in the debate about abortion.[1] Fortunately, the abortion debate need not distract us here; for the principal issue about putatively inalienable rights concerns whether the possessor's consent alters others' duties, and clearly human fetuses are not capable of giving consent.

What we must address directly is what duties are correlative with the right to life. And though it is too simplistic to say that there are only two competing interpretations of the right to life, there are at least two. On some construals, the right to life implies only duties to refrain from certain sorts of activities; we might think of this as a minimalist account. On other construals, it implies duties to provide services to the possessor; this is a more expansive account. Following terminology introduced earlier, we will call the former of these accounts the *negative interpretation* of the right to life and the latter the *positive interpretation*.

At the very least, the right to life imposes a duty on others not to kill beings who possess that right. Judith Thomson endorses such an account,[2] and according to Hugo

Bedau, Jefferson does too.[3] Defenders of the negative interpretation say that this is the only duty that the right to life imposes on others. That leaves it an open question how *strong* such a right is. Whether the duty not to kill can be suspended because the possessor has forfeited his right to life is open for debate, as is the issue of whether the duty can be overridden by more compelling moral considerations. But those questions aside, the minimal duty associated with the right to life is the duty not to kill individuals who possess that right.

Defenders of the positive interpretation agree that the right to life implies a duty on others not to kill possessors of that right; but they do not agree that that is the *only* duty implied by the right to life. They see the right to life as normatively more encompassing; it implies requirements on others to provide assistance too. In particular, the right to life, understood positively, implies duties on others not to allow a person to die, and a duty to save persons.[4] The duty not to allow others to die does not require one to work miracles. For P_1 can correctly be said to have allowed P_2 to die only if P_1 had the ability and the opportunity to prevent P_2 from dying and was aware that he was so positioned. How strong the duty to save others is may create a debate among proponents of the positive account. One would guess that no one holds that a person is normally required to sacrifice her own life to save the life of another. But how much of a sacrifice another's right to life may impose on one is still debatable. If all that is required to save another is tossing him a life preserver, presumably all defenders of the positive interpretation would agree that doing so is obligatory.[5] But how much sacrifice, short of putting one's own life at serious risk, can another's right to life require of one? Suppose that Chang has a fatal form of leukemia and his only chance for survival is to be given a bone marrow transplant. Though unrelated, it happens that Florio is the only person known to be a suitable donor for Chang. Florio can donate bone marrow to Chang without putting his own life at risk. Is Florio morally obligated to make such a donation? And if so, is that obligation based on Chang's right to life? It sounds odd to say that Florio *violates* Chang's right to life if he refuses to donate his bone marrow, though that would be the implication if we say that there is such a duty and that it is based on the right to life.

This case about Florio and Chang is not far-fetched. At least one such case has made its way to the *legal* system in the United States. This is a case involving cousins, Robert McFall and David Shimp.[6] In June 1978, McFall was diagnosed as having aplastic anemia, a usually fatal disease in which the patient's bone marrow fails to produce enough red and white blood cells and platelets. McFall's only hope of survival was to receive a bone marrow transplant. His six siblings were examined, but none was compatible to serve as a donor. Then McFall's first cousin, David Shimp, underwent preliminary tests, and he was determined to be a perfect match for tissue compatibility. At that point, however, Shimp refused to undergo further tests and withdrew as a potential donor. Reasons for his refusal were not entirely clear, though apparently the requests of his wife and mother and a longtime family feud were factors affecting the decision. Many people tried to persuade Shimp to change his mind, but he would not. McFall then filed suit to compel Shimp to serve as a bone marrow donor for him. Pennsylvania (Allegheny County) Judge John Flaherty ruled against McFall. Judge Flaherty said that although Shimp's refusal to donate was morally indefensible, nevertheless, there is *no legal duty* to take action to save another's life and certainly no duty to serve as a bone marrow donor for another. Robert McFall died on August 10, 1978.

A more recent case raised similar issues, though it involved minors.[7] Jean-Pierre Bosze was a boy dying of leukemia. His only hope was a bone marrow transplant. But his immediate family members were not suitable to be donors. The boy's father asked the mother of three-year-old twins, Allison and James Curran, whom he had fathered during an affair, to have them tested to determine if one of them might be compatible to serve as a bone marrow donor to their half-brother, Jean-Pierre. The mother refused to permit the testing. The father sued, but predictably the court ruled in favor of the mother. In this case, the court would have overridden the mother's judgment only if she had been acting contrary to the best interests of her children.

Cases like these present some difficulties for defenders of the positive interpretation of the right to life. It appears that this account implies a duty (moral or legal) the existence of which most people would deny. In reply, it seems that defenders of the positive account must argue for one of two claims: either there is after all a (moral) duty to serve as a donor in cases like this, or contrary to appearances the positive interpretation does not entail such duties.

What is common to the positive and negative interpretations of the right to life is that such a right imposes a duty on others not to kill the possessor. That provides one reason for restricting ourselves to the negative account when we ask whether the right to life is inalienable; for it endorses only what is common to both. But there is a second reason.

It is well established that competent individuals have the legal and moral right to refuse medical treatment, including life-saving interventions.[8] This is an extension of the right to self-determination, and the consensus is that this is both a moral and a legal right. This right imposes obligations on others: any medical intervention must be withheld or withdrawn if the individual for whom the intervention is intended is competent and so requests.[9] Given this, notice the implication. If the right to life is understood as positive, it implies duties on others to save lives and not to allow persons to die. But if a competent person declines life-saving treatment, that treatment must be withheld or withdrawn. So if the right to life implies a duty to save, then such a duty is suspended with the possessor's consent. Indeed, not only are others *permitted* to withhold or withdraw life-saving medical treatment at the patient's request, but they are also *required* (legally and morally) to do so. So, if the right to life is positive, the possessor's consent does alter the correlative obligations of others (assuming that defenders of the positive account are not willing to deny that competent persons have a right to refuse life-saving treatment).

Given the right to refuse medical treatment, this still leaves at least two options. One option is to say that this shows that the right to life is alienable. We must be careful, though. For it is possible that *only some* of the obligations correlative with the right to life are suspended because of the possessor's consent. Another option is to adopt the negative interpretation of the right to life. Here, for purposes of simplicity, I shall embrace the latter option. Doing this enables us to confine ourselves to one correlative duty—the duty not to kill—and to ask whether that moral requirement is suspended or altered by the possessor's consent. Defenders of both interpretations of the right to life have to answer this question; defenders of the positive construal have to answer additional questions. So by focusing on the negative account, we simplify our task. But doing this begs no questions. Whatever we say here is also relevant to at least one of the obligations endorsed by proponents of the positive interpretation; it is just that these theorists have a more complicated task to discharge.

The Inalienable Right to Life

If the right to life is alienable, then the consent of the possessor justifies killing that person. If the right to life is inalienable, then freely given, fully informed consent does not suspend the duty not to kill; the possessor's consent does not justify killing. It seems fair to say that proponents of the alienability of the right to life view this right as being a property right; or, to put it another way, property rights are the paradigm and other rights are like them. Lance Stell, who defends the alienability of the right to life, argues that "the right to life ought to be construed as a property right," and suggests that that means, in part, "that voluntary consent should be sufficient for alienating one's right to life."[10] Stell is aware that so conceiving the right to life has important normative implications, for he later concludes: "[I]f we acknowledge that the right to life is a property right, we acknowledge the right of persons to squander it, risk it foolishly, or trade it away too cheaply."[11]

Some are incredulous about conceiving the right to life as a mere property right. Daniel Callahan, without explicitly mentioning the inalienability of the right to life, expresses such doubts. Arguing against voluntary euthanasia, Callahan asks, "Is our right to life just like a piece of property, to be given away or alienated if the price (happiness, relief of suffering) is right? And then to be destroyed with our permission once alienated?"[12] And later, Callahan suggests that the burden of proof is on those who affirm the alienability of the right to life: "The idea that we can waive our right to life, and then give to another the power to take that life, requires a justification yet to be provided by anyone."[13] Whether no such justification has been given is doubtful; certainly several have been attempted. And where exactly in this debate the burden of proof lies is not at all clear. But since I propose here to defend a version of the inalienability of the right to life, I shall initially regard the burden of proof as falling on my side of the debate. We begin with observations about the legal system of the United States.

In the U.S. legal system, the mere fact that a person consents does not justify killing that person. If I asked you to kill me and you accommodate my request, that will not prevent you from being charged legally for my death. Nor will it help you if there were 50 witnesses who testify that I did indeed request that you kill me. Nor will your legal position be any better if there are a bevy of psychiatrists willing to testify that I was fully competent at the time I made the request of you, and that my request was not coerced or made under duress. In our legal system, consent does not justify killing. And this seems morally plausible too.

One obvious rationale to support the inalienability of the right to life is strongly paternalistic, one designed to protect people from their own foolishness. If consent justified killing, too many people in moments of weakness would request of another to kill them. To protect people from making such tragic choices, we do not allow the killer off the hook merely because the victim consented. This rationale provides people with a strong incentive not to comply with a person's request to kill him, thereby protecting that person from his own weakness and irrationality. And presumably this rationale could be used to justify both moral and legal inalienability.

As was noted in chapter 2, hard paternalism does seem to provide one normative foundation for inalienable rights. But as was also noted there, in this book we are looking for nonpaternalistic bases for inalienable rights. For if inalienable rights can be grounded only on a paternalistic foundation, then there is a danger that such rights will become "burdensome baggage" for their possessors—something that their possessors would like to dispose of but may not. Does a nonpaternalistic rationale exist for inalienability of the right to life? We shall begin first by examining whether a nonpaternalistic rationale exists for the right to life's having a *legal* status of inalienability.

Laws are a part of social policy. If a type of behavior is legally prohibited, society is committed to using the coercive apparatus of the law to prevent people from engaging in such behavior and to punish them if they do. From the mere fact that a type of behavior is legally permitted, it does not follow that society encourages it; for people may criticize behavior that violates norms of morality or etiquette, even though it is not legally proscribed. Still, in our society if behavior is not legally prohibited, then presumably people will not be forceably prevented from engaging in such conduct. To that (limited) extent, legally permitted behavior has society's stamp of approval.

If you kill me, as I requested, it seems that the conduct in question involves only consenting parties. And to proscribe behavior involving only consenting parties is often to engage in paternalism. But our behavior can affect others; or to put the point more accurately, the fact that society permits us to have such a relationship can affect others. Ronald Dworkin, writing in a different context, says, "Individual choices together create a moral environment that inevitably influences what others can do."[14] If society allows the possessor's consent always to count as a legal justification for killing that person, this may well increase the chances that harm to nonconsenting persons will occur.[15]

Certainly the cases of Susan Potempa and Sharon Lopatka, discussed in chapter 1, make vivid to us that allowing consent to serve as a legal justification for killing will create risks for nonconsenting persons. Even if we are convinced that in each of these cases the person who was killed did in fact consent, we cannot know if the person was competent; and it would be all too easy to make cases involving nonconsenting victims to look like one of these cases.

To explain the dangers, consider first these somewhat speculative points. Allowing a person to kill another simply because the latter consents may create a moral climate in which the lives of all persons will be less secure. People may become hardened and less outraged when someone's life is taken. Such a society may eventually take less seriously a genuine *violation* of a person's right to life. A legal system cannot, without great difficulty, both claim to place a high value on human life and allow some to kill human beings simply because those individuals have consented.

More important, however, and less speculatively too, the problems of proof that will arise if the possessor's consent justifies killing are potentially great. Almost any murderer can claim that his victim consented; and it will be difficult to prove otherwise. In this respect, the right to life is different from many other rights and so is reasonably assigned a special status. Consider the right of bodily integrity, a person's right to control what others do to his or her body.[16] It is this right that arms patients with the authority to refuse recommended medical interventions. As Justice Cardozo observed in 1914 in the well-known passage cited in chapter 4, "[E]very human being of adult years and sound mind has a right to determine what shall be done with his own body. . . ."[17] This right also renders it impermissible to force another to engage in sexual intercourse. If a person genuinely consents, however, having sexual intercourse with that person is not wrong.[18] And this immediately gives rise to a potential problem. Because consent justifies otherwise inappropriate conduct, there is a danger that one person will rape another and then falsely claim that she consented to the act. And, indeed, in many cases in which the charge of rape is contested by the alleged perpetrator, that individual claims that the activity was mutually consensual. In cases like this, however, at least the victim is able to bring charges against the rapist and to testify that she did not consent; and additional evidence can be adduced in support of her testimony. When a person's life is taken without consent, however, these options are unavailable. The point here is this. Given these inherent problems of proof, everyone's life will be less secure precisely *because* society permits one person to kill another with consent. This can be avoided only by not allowing consent to justify killing; thus, society is morally justified in designating the right to life as inalienable.

Another contrast between the rights of bodily integrity and life will demonstrate further why the latter appropriately has the legal status of inalienability. Some are suspicious of inalienable rights because they believe that the status of inalienability renders rights burdensome baggage that must be borne by their possessors regardless of their wants.[19] Inalienable rights, these critics believe, restrict the freedom of their possessors too much. But this need not be the case. That the right to life is inalienable does not compel a person to stay alive against his wishes. If a competent person refuses medical treatment—even life-sustaining treatment—his wishes must be respected.[20] The inalienability of the right to life limits the freedom only in a narrow way: it does not allow one person to take the life of another simply because the latter consents. By contrast, if the right of bodily integrity were inalienable, this would pose a considerable constraint on the freedom of its possessors. It would entail, for example, that informed consent alone would not justify a physician in providing medical treatment for a patient; unless there were *some other* justification, such an invasion would be unwarranted. Moreover, sexual intercourse between consenting adults would not be warranted merely because each consented. (And it is hard to see what other than mutual consent would justify such a relationship!) Such restrictions would be onerous indeed, far more so than in the case of the right to life. This suggests, but does not prove, that the right to life may have a different status.

Those who wish to argue for the alienability of the right to life may respond to the problem of proof by claiming that the harm in question can be prevented without endorsing the inalienability of the right to life. They might suggest the adoption of an official procedure in which a person can declare legally that he has consented to being killed. When and only when this procedure has been followed will the defense that the "victim" consented be accepted as a justification for killing. And this procedure will presumably include assurances that the right-holder *knows* that he has the right to life and is giving it up *freely*—conditions that must be satisfied in any case of genuine waiver. It must be admitted that adopting such a procedure is likely to reduce significantly the risk of harm to nonconsenting parties of the sort discussed above. This response, however, is still fraught with difficulties. Setting up the legal machinery necessary to determine whether consent is knowledgeable, uncoerced, and fully voluntary will be impractical and expensive.[21] First, it will likely be difficult in particular cases to ascertain whether an individual's consent is substantially voluntary. Second, professionals employed by the state to make these difficult judgments will undoubtedly command handsome fees. Given these factors, third, it is not at all obvious that prospective consenting individuals who are prohibited from engaging in the relationship in question have a legitimate complaint against the state for being so restricted. What they are deprived of is minimal. Since attempted suicide is not a crime, individuals who wish for their own deaths still have permissible options available to achieve their desired end. It is true that the state is prohibiting them from having a consensual relationship in which a second party brings about the first's death, but the state is justified in this restriction because of the cost it would have to incur to permit such relationships without endangering innocent third parties. The critic's retort, then, does not undermine the argument for inalienability.

It is important here to review a clarification made earlier (in the last section of chapter 2). When we reflect on the nature of the relationship between the consent of the possessor and the permissibility of infringing the right to life, there is still a problem to be resolved. If the right to life is inalienable, then the consent of the possessor is neither necessary nor sufficient to justify infringing that right, assuming that that right can be forfeited or overridden. But it does not follow that the possessor's consent is irrelevant to the issue of whether infringing his right to life is permissible. For it is at least not incoherent to suppose that consent *in combination with* some other relevant factor(s) may justify infringing the right to life. Indeed, to make sense of common intuitions, we must grant that consent has some relevance here (though the exact nature of that relevance will for the moment remain unexplored). The very thing that distinguishes voluntary from nonvoluntary euthanasia is whether the person whose death is hastened has given consent. Now there clearly seems to be a normatively relevant difference between voluntary euthanasia and nonvoluntary euthanasia. If there is such a difference, then either the right to life is not inalienable or inalienability does not entail that consent is irrelevant to the issue of justifiably infringing the right to life. When discussing the implications of the inalienability of the right to life for the practice of euthanasia, the second of these disjuncts will be defended.

Inalienable Rights and Duties to Oneself

Some reject inalienable rights, both in the moral and legal realms, because they believe that endorsement of such rights implies a commitment to duties to the self; that is, if a person's right R is inalienable, that entails that the person has duties to himself because of R. This raises an important question. What duties are associated with or entailed by inalienable rights, and on whom do those duties fall?

These questions can be addressed specifically with regard to the right to life. One obvious possibility here is that the inalienability of the right to life entails that suicide is always wrong and that the duty not to commit suicide is a duty owed to oneself. In this context, the first question to be asked is this: If the right to life is inalienable, does it follow that suicide is always wrong? Some have answered this question affirmatively. Stell, for example, writes, "The right to commit suicide is important because, if we have it, then the right to life is alienable. . . ."[22] This claim is logically equivalent to affirming that if the right to life is inalienable, then people do not have a right to commit suicide; and that certainly suggests that if the right to life is inalienable, then suicide is always wrong. On the account of inalienability that I have offered in this book, this question need not be answered in the affirmative; the inalienability of the right to life *need not* preclude the permissibility of suicide. If a right is inalienable, it prohibits a certain *relationship* between the possessor of that right and others. Such a right may not be waived or transferred to another; the possessor's consent is not sufficient to suspend the duty (duties) correlative with the inalienable right. Thus, what is proscribed by inalienable rights are certain *relationships* or *agreements* between two or more consenting parties. So understood, there is some reason to think that the inalienability of the right to life will have implications for the permissibility of voluntary euthanasia, since that practice involves a relationship between consenting parties. But whether the possessor of the right to life may kill himself is a separate issue not determined by the fact that the right to life has the status of being inalienable.[23]

Even if the inalienability of the right to life does not imply that suicide is always wrong, that still does not show whether inalienable rights imply duties to the self; for it is possible that the inalienable right to life implies some duties to the self, though not a duty not to commit suicide. To examine the conceptual issue of whether there is a necessary connection between inalienable rights and duties to the self, I shall discuss a well-known argument *against* the existence of duties to oneself presented by Marcus Singer. Singer's argument has three premises:[24]

(1) If *A* has a duty to *B*, then *B* has a right against *A*.
(2) If *B* has a right against *A*, then *B* can give it up and release *A* from the obligation.
(3) No one can release himself from an obligation.

From these three premises, one can conclude (by two operations of *modus tollens*) that no one has a duty to himself. Premises (1) and (2) are conceptual claims that are alleged to hold for *all* duties and for *all* rights. For our purposes, (2) is crucial. It says that the possessor of a right can always release others from the moral requirement generated by that right; in effect, it says that all rights are alienable. If there is *no necessary connection* between inalienable rights and duties to oneself, as I maintain, then there must be responses to this argument. And these responses should be such that they indicate that there is conceptual room for two possibilities (possibilities precluded by Singer's argument): (i) that some rights are inalienable, yet there are no duties to oneself; and (ii) that some rights are alienable, yet there are duties to oneself.

To defend claim (i), one must deny Singer's premise (2). And one can do this without presupposing that some rights are inalienable. Note, for example, that we can have obligations to individuals who are comatose, but those individuals cannot release us from those obligations.[25] But defenders of this position can still argue cogently against duties to oneself by affirming premise (1) and accepting an additional premise:

(4) No one can have a right against himself.[26]

From (1) and (4), one can conclude that there are no duties to oneself and not be committed to the claim that all rights are alienable. Assuming that (2) is not an obvious conceptual truth—and this book clearly assumes this—then this position is perfectly coherent.

To defend claim (ii), one must affirm that Singer's premise (2) is true of at least some rights, but deny either (1) or (3). The more likely strategy here would be to deny premise (1); to argue, that is, that it is not conceptually true that all duties imply rights. Obvious candidates spring to mind. Some hold that moral agents have duties to animals, but deny that animals have rights. Some contend that agents have duties to deceased individuals, but deny that the deceased have rights. If either of these examples—or some other one—is plausible, as I think, then premise (1) is not a conceptual truth.

In a sense, all that is needed here to respond to Singer are very weak claims; for, in effect, claims (i) and (ii) merely *deny* that the crucial premises of Singer's arguments are conceptually true. Surely, the burden of proof is on Singer at this point. And lest the reader be led astray by this somewhat tangential discussion, bear in mind that all I want to do is respond to the objection that inalienable rights are suspect because they imply (the presumably more suspect) duties to oneself. I need not deny that there are duties to the self; I need only deny that they are *implied* by inalienable rights.

Let us now turn to *relationships* governed by the inalienability of rights and their connection with the issue of duties to oneself. If the right to life is inalienable, then P_2 is not justified in killing P_1 simply because P_1 gave free and informed consent. But suppose that P_1 does give P_2 permission to kill him and P_2 does so. Who is guilty of wrongdoing in this case? P_2? P_1? Both? It at least initially seems that if P_1 is guilty of wrongdoing (because of the inalienability of the right to life), then inalienable rights do imply duties to the self. But such an inference is too quick and unwarranted. For the more important issue in this case concerns to whom the duties are owed. It is possible that both P_1 and P_2 are guilty of wrongdoing (legal or moral, depending on the context) if P_2 kills P_1 with P_1's freely given, fully informed consent, yet the duties violated by each are not owed to P_1. As was suggested earlier, the duty may be owed to the community at large. And the most plausible nonpaternalistic basis for designating selected legal rights as inalienable is to appeal to the interests of innocent third parties. If such a position can be adequately defended, then in the interaction between P_1 and P_2 the duties associated with P_1's inalienable right to life—whether those duties are borne only by P_2 or by both P_1 and P_2—are not owed to P_1. Such a defense would show that inalienable rights need not imply duties to oneself.

Although it is my contention that there is no conceptual connection between inalienable rights and duties to oneself, it may be that particular philosophical defenses of one imply a commitment to the other. As we saw in chapter 2 (the section on "Kantian Defense"), in Kantian moral philosophy there seems to be a close connection between inalienable rights and duties that possessors of such rights owe to themselves. We can see this clearly in the work of Thomas E. Hill, Jr. Hill argues, for example, that respect is owed to all agents, and each agent has a duty of self-respect. An agent might fail such a duty to himself by not taking his own rights seriously and allowing others to use him solely for their own means. Such an agent is said to be servile. And others' duties are no less stringent to this person simply because he is willing to let them use him. "No matter how willing a person is to submit to humiliation by others, they ought to show him some respect as a person."[27] So individuals have both a right to be respected by others and a duty to work for that end. Along these same lines, Hill suggests that an individual's rights to life and liberty are "like a trustee's rights to preserve something valuable entrusted to him: he has not only a right but a duty to preserve it."[28] The general principle at work here is something like this: If P_1 has a duty to P_1 regarding L, *and* P_2 also has a duty to P_1 regarding L, then P_1 cannot release P_2 from the duty to P_1 regarding L. So if an agent has a duty not to kill himself and others also have a duty not to kill that agent, then that agent cannot release others from their duty not to kill him.[29]

Within this theory, it is not clear to me whether duties to the self imply that some rights are inalienable, or whether it is inalienable rights that imply that there are duties to oneself. Or perhaps *both* duties to the self and inalienable rights follow from a more basic Kantian principle. Regardless of how this plays out, however, my point is simple: Inalienable rights need not imply that there are duties to oneself, though within certain moral frameworks there may be a close connection between the two (and perhaps within those frameworks duties to oneself imply inalienable rights).

Euthanasia

I argued above that though the inalienability of the right to life does proscribe certain relationships between consenting parties, these losses are minimal and necessary to prevent harm to nonconsenting parties; such prohibitions, therefore, represent good public policy. But the claim that the losses here are minimal may be disputed. The inalienability of the right to life does seriously restrict its possessors, opponents will argue, because it forbids voluntary euthanasia and assisted suicide. And if a person is afflicted with a painful, terminal illness, such restrictions are quite serious indeed. Here I shall argue that the inalienability of the right to life need not preclude the (legal) permissibility of voluntary euthanasia; in the next chapter I make a similar argument about assisted suicide.[30] We begin with some clarifications.

As one would expect, 'euthanasia' has been defined in different ways. Marcia Angell defines it as "purposely terminating the life of a patient to prevent further suffering."[31] And Ronald Dworkin characterizes it as "deliberately killing a person out of kindness."[32] Whatever else one might say, euthanasia involves at least these elements: (i) a person whose death is hastened; (ii) a second person who is involved in the hastening of the death; and (iii) the motive of kindness or the desire to relieve suffering on the part of the person doing the hastening.

It was at one time common to distinguish between passive euthanasia and active euthanasia. Each involved all three elements listed above; they differed with respect to the *means* by which death was brought about. So-called passive euthanasia involved letting a person die, typically by withholding or withdrawing medical treatment. Active euthanasia involved killing a patient, such as by a lethal injection. The definitions of 'euthanasia' advanced by Angell and Dworkin are limited to active euthanasia. Withholding or withdrawing life-sustaining medical treatment, once dubbed 'passive euthanasia', is seldom called that any more; and there is much less debate about its normative status. If a patient is competent and freely requests that life-sustaining treatment be withheld or withdrawn, it is now widely held that others are *legally and morally required* to comply with the patient's wishes. And if the patient is not competent and the patient's surrogate and physician are in agreement that the patient would not want the treatment in question or that such treatment is not in the patient's interests, it is agreed that it is at least *permissible* to withhold or withdraw such treatment.[33] Perhaps because there is now minimal controversy about it, what was once called 'passive euthanasia' is now no longer so called. 'Euthanasia' and 'active euthanasia' have practically become synonomous.

It is still common to distinguish between voluntary euthanasia and nonvoluntary euthanasia. *Voluntary euthanasia* is an act of euthanasia done at the request of or with the consent of the person whose death is hastened. *Nonvoluntary euthanasia* is an act of euthanasia done without the consent of the person whose death is hastened. *Involuntary euthanasia* is an act of euthanasia done against the will of the person whose death is hastened. So understood, involuntary euthanasia is a special case of nonvoluntary euthanasia. The more common cases of nonvoluntary euthanasia are ones in which the person whose death is hastened is not competent. Here we shall confine ourselves to cases of voluntary euthanasia; for it is only with such cases that issues concerning whether the right to life is alienable or inalienable arise.

Even confining ourselves to voluntary euthanasia does not eliminate all complexities. For one thing, we must address the issue of what counts as consenting to an act of euthanasia. Different accounts of *consent* are available. On a narrow account, one can only consent if one is competent at the time the act is to be performed. On a broader account, one can consent in advance by specifying, while competent, conditions under which one wants to have one's death hastened. The latter, were it legally recognized, would allow people to execute advance directives (such as "living wills") that arranged for their own euthanasia under specified conditions, conditions including that the person to be euthanized is not competent at the time the act will be carried out. Any proposal supporting the legalization of voluntary euthanasia will have to specify the account of *consent* on which it is based. For now, I will confine my discussion to voluntary euthanasia in the narrow sense; arranging for euthanasia in an advance directive will be touched on later.

The right to life is legally inalienable because if we allow consent alone to justify killing, this will put at serious risk the rights of nonconsenting parties. But, as was argued above, this does not preclude the possibility that consent in conjunction with other relevant conditions may justify killing. Society should allow killing in such selective cases, however, only if doing so promotes positive values *and* the risks to nonconsenting parties are reduced significantly. Can this sort of case be made for permitting voluntary active euthanasia?

Legally allowing voluntary active euthanasia can promote several important and widely shared values.[34] One such value is autonomy—respecting the freedom and choices of agents. If euthanasia is truly voluntary, then it is carrying out the choice of the person whose death is hastened. At the very least, autonomy imposes negative requirements on agents; they must refrain from interfering with the freedom and choices of others (in the absence of a moral justification for doing so). Not only is truly voluntary euthanasia not contrary to the person's choices, it actually promotes such choices. A second value promoted by allowing voluntary euthanasia is the prevention of suffering. As noted above, it seems that it is part of the concept of euthanasia that the act has as its aim the prevention of suffering for the person whose death is hastened. Persons afflicted with illnesses that are terminal, incurable, and painful, or illnesses that are incurable and debilitating, are the obvious candidates for euthanasia; for they may be individuals whose suffering can be prevented only by hastening death.[35] A third value that voluntary active euthanasia can promote is death with dignity. Some persons fear the way that they will die, independent of whether physical pain is involved. They fear helplessness, total dependency on others, slowly wasting away, and the sort of memory that others will have of their final days. When their death is imminent, they want to die on their own terms.[36] Timothy Quill, Christine Cassel, and Diane Meier claim that "the most frightening aspect of death for many is not physical pain, but the prospect of losing control and independence and of dying in an undignified, unesthetic, absurd, and existentially unacceptable condition."[37]

These are values worth pursuing, I shall assume. But can these values be promoted without seriously putting at risk the rights of nonconsenting persons? If euthanasia is to be legally permitted while avoiding the risks noted above, certain safeguards must be employed. These will be the additional relevant conditions which, when combined with consent, justify euthanasia. To be relevant, these conditions must be such that their satisfaction will make it unlikely that nonconsenting parties will be harmed. I shall suggest five such conditions. I will list them first and then briefly explain their relevance.[38] The conditions are the following: (i) the individual requesting that his death be hastened must have an illness that is terminal, incurable, and painful, *or* incurable and debilitating; (ii) the act of euthanasia must be performed by a physician; (iii) no fee is involved; (iv) the individual's diagnosis and prognosis must be confirmed by a second physician who is financially and professionally independent of the first;[39] and (v) the individual must undergo a psychological examination to establish that his consent was freely given.

If condition (i) is satisfied, the individual's request for euthanasia makes sense; for many of us can envision seeking such assistance were we similarly afflicted. Of course, not everyone who has a terminal, painful illness or an incurable, debilitating illness will request euthanasia; probably the vast majority will not. But that we can at least understand such a request when (i) holds is a step toward establishing the genuineness of the consent. In addition, requiring the satisfaction of (i) makes it more unlikely that persons who are not terminally or incurably ill will be killed under this policy. For if a dispute arises later, whether a person was in fact terminally or incurably ill can be verified with an autopsy. And if perpetrators are severely punished for killing individuals who consent but are not terminally or incurably ill, such actions will be discouraged.

If someone opts for an assisted death because he believes that he has an illness that is terminal, incurable, and painful, we want to ensure, to the degree possible, that these beliefs are accurate. Conditions (ii) and (iv) are designed to promote this end. If a person's suffering is due to a temporary, treatable illness, a physician is more likely to recognize this than are persons who have no medical expertise. And though physicians make mistakes, requiring that the diagnosis and prognosis be confirmed by a second, independent physician lends additional credence to the belief. Because human beings are involved, there is no way to eliminate the possibility of error; but these conditions at least make blatant errors far less likely.

Consent is not given unless it is freely given. And while it is very difficult to characterize *freely* given consent, it at least must be such that it was given in the absence of coercion and not under extreme duress. Coercion comes from others exerting pressure in various forms. If physicians could benefit monetarily from performing euthanasia, they would have some incentive to encourage patients to choose this option. The policy we want is one that patients whose symptoms can be treated (e.g., with pain medication) will be. Prohibiting fees is a small step toward promoting that end.

Requiring a psychological examination by a trained professional is designed to ensure, to the degree possible, that the patient's request for euthanasia is an autonomous choice.[40] One thing that the professional will want to know is whether the patient's request is due to pressure from others. For this reason, the psychologist should evaluate the patient alone, away from the influence of family members and others. The psychologist will also want to know whether the choice is due to depression. Matters are trickier here, however, for some depression is natural and appropriate for one afflicted with a terminal, painful illness or an incurable, debilitating illness. As Lonny Shavelson puts it, "[T]he depression of someone with a terminal illness is completely different from the classical psychological illness."[41] What the professional should be looking for here is evidence that the choice results from depression that is transient and treatable.

These conditions are not foolproof. But requiring their satisfaction will reduce significantly the likelihood that nonconsenting parties will be harmed *because* society permits one person to kill another when the latter consents. The *possibility* that the diagnosis or prognosis is mistaken is something that the patient himself should be aware of and can take into account in determining whether to request assisted death. Perhaps the greatest source of worry is associated with condition (v), the requirement that consent be freely given. Of course, if condition (v) is truly satisfied, then the individual is consenting and abuse to a nonconsenting person does not occur. The worrisome possibility is that conditions (i) to (iv) are satisfied, and (v) is said to be satisfied but is not. Such an error might occur due to incompetence, because the judgment is a very difficult one, or due to deliberate misrepresentation. All that we can do is be aware of these possibilities and try to guard against them. But even though mistakes and abuses are possible here, that is surely not sufficient grounds for banning the practice, as the following points show. First, relatively few are at risk (far fewer than if consent alone justified killing). For the only possible victims are persons who are terminally ill (or who can be falsely represented as such); and the perpetrator must be a physician or someone who is conspiring with a physician. Second, if the mere fact that a policy can be abused were sufficient grounds for outlawing that policy, then we would have to prohibit many things that we currently approve of. We allow killing in self-defense, even though it is possible that a sufficiently clever person may be able to make a cold-blooded murder appear to be self-defense.[42] Another example is provided by Ronald Dworkin:

> No one thinks, moreover, that the fact that doctors sometimes deliberately give dying patients large enough doses of pain-killing drugs to kill them—a covert decision much more open to abuse than a scheme of voluntary euthanasia would be—is a good reason for withholding all dangerous pain-killers from terminal patients in torment.[43]

And third, even if a few nonconsenting persons are harmed, adoption of the policy will allow many persons to benefit, and it is not clear that the mere possibility of abuse is sufficient to prevent those individuals from being helped. Again, Dworkin is clear on this point: "But it would be perverse to force competent people to die in great pain or drugged stupor for that reason, accepting a great and known evil to avoid the risk of a speculative one."[44]

My point here is a modest one: allowing voluntary active euthanasia is consistent with the inalienability of the right to life. My purpose has not been an overall defense of voluntary euthanasia. Nevertheless, certain objections that have been leveled against legalizing voluntary euthanasia should be addressed here (because they relate directly to the rationale that I employ).

Objections and Replies

In stating the positive values promoted by voluntary euthanasia, I (and many others) cited both autonomy and beneficence (in particular, prevention of suffering). The two together make a strong case. But the first objection, pressed by Daniel Callahan, says that there is no compelling reason to keep these considerations together. And if we do not keep them together, interesting and unacceptable consequences seem to result. Callahan puts it this way: "If we really believe in self-determination, then any competent person should have a right to be killed by a doctor for any reason that suits him. If we believe in the relief of suffering, then it seems cruel and capricious to deny it to the incompetent."[45] This suggests that if we are true to the values put forward, euthanasia cannot be confined to the small class defined above; and if it cannot be so confined, the problem of abuse is back in full force.

My argument above is based on the idea that autonomy (in the form of consent) and beneficence each is necessary but neither alone is sufficient to justify voluntary active euthanasia. Callahan is presumably willing to concede the *relevance* of these two values. But his challenge effectively asks defenders to show why it is not simply arbitrary to deny that autonomy alone or beneficence alone is sufficient to justify euthanasia. In responding to Callahan's challenge, we must bear in mind that we are working at the level of *social policy*, defending legally *permitting* voluntary euthanasia under specified conditions. The answer to why autonomy or self-determination alone is not sufficient to justify euthanasia has already been given: a social policy that allows consent alone to justify killing is fraught with too many risks for too many people, as was shown above.

The more difficult part of this challenge is to show why beneficence alone (in the form of preventing suffering) is not sufficient to justify euthanasia. Callahan asks whether it is not "cruel and capricious" to deny relief of suffering to the incompetent, individuals not capable of giving voluntary consent. Current policy allows giving such patients all the pain relief available, and so too would a system allowing for voluntary active euthanasia. But in requiring the voluntary consent of the person whose death is hastened, the modified system would not allow one kind of relief to the incompent person—namely, active euthanasia. Is this denial arbitrary? The justification for this sort of conservatism—if one dare call it that—is that there is a lack of consensus in our society about the appropriateness of deliberately hastening death. Following Ronald Dworkin, one could put it this way.[46] We all agree that preserving human life is important, but we disagree about the conditions under which it is permissible to hasten or bring about the death of a human. Some hold that euthanasia is consistent with the sanctity of human life; others deny that. When an individual is incompetent, in the absence of strong evidence we cannot presume to know what his views are regarding the sanctity of life. And in the face of this uncertainty we proscribe euthanasia, since opting for it effectively precludes all other choices. Moreover, given that opponents of voluntary euthanasia have warned us that those most likely to suffer from the abuses that may result from the legalization of that practice are society's most vulnerable,[47] we have additional reasons for requiring contemporaneous competence as a condition of permissible euthanasia.

Nevertheless, it should be acknowledged that there is a problem here. Those who oppose even voluntary euthanasia argue that permitting it will lead to permitting nonvoluntary euthanasia. And they might point to compelling analogies to make their point. As a *proponent* of voluntary euthanasia, Dan Brock, has acknowledged, something comparable has happened in allowing individuals to refuse medical treatment.[48] The primary value that justifies allowing patients to refuse medical treatment is self-determination. Yet we have rapidly moved to allowing surrogates to refuse treatment for incompetent patients. We think that this does not deviate from self-determination because we appeal to the principle of *substituted judgment*: a surrogate should make medical decisions for an incompetent patient based on what that patient would want were she competent and aware of the facts.[49] There are serious questions, however, about the ability of surrogates to determine reliably what incompetent patients would want. Studies suggest that proxy predictions are not very good.[50] It need not be inevitable that we will follow a similar path with respect to euthanasia; but it is a possibility.

We turn now to the second objection. Opponents argue that the legalization of voluntary euthanasia will force health care providers to act against their own consciences; for many will continue to disapprove of euthanasia, even if it is legalized. And health care providers, like the rest of us, have a right of conscience. Indeed, if I am right, they have an inalienable right of conscience, and so the mere fact that they have voluntarily entered the field of health care should not require them to hasten death deliberately when they believe that doing so is wrong. Fortunately, there is a short answer to this objection. The legalization of voluntary euthanasia does not require health care providers to act against their own consciences. Patients will *not* be entitled to *demand* that physicians and nurses perform euthanasia. Rather, euthanasia will be *permissible* if appropriate conditions are satisfied.[51] Just as now patients have no authority to demand that physicians write prescriptions or perform procedures which the physicians believe are unwarranted, so too would this hold with respect to euthanasia.

A third objection turns one of my own earlier arguments against me. I argued against allowing consent alone as a justification for killing partly on grounds that determining whether consent was genuine would require difficult judgments made by expensive professionals, and that those who want another to kill them have no claim to such societal resources. Why not say the same thing about those who wish to opt for euthanasia? The response to this objection, in part, is that the potential costs to society are far less if we allow only euthanasia than if we allow killing anytime a person consents. For in the latter arrangement, the size of those eligible to request society's permission is equal to the number of competent persons in that society. But if only voluntary *euthanasia* is allowed, the size is limited to those competent individuals who have a painful, terminal illness or an incurable, debilitating illness. Numbers alone suggest that the costs to a society that allows only voluntary euthanasia will be far less than a society that allows killing *whenever* genuine consent is present. But numbers are not all that is important here. In addition, even opponents of euthanasia at least understand why a person with a painful, terminal illness would request euthanasia; there is a broad consensus that minimizing suffering is a good thing (though opponents of euthanasia object to at least one means of doing so). But if consent alone justified killing, persons could request death for any reason. Given society's appropriate commitment to the preservation of life, if society must also provide (at least indirect) support for ending human life, that should occur only when doing so promotes other fundamental values for which there is wide support. Thus, the third objection can be handled.

Let us consider a fourth objection. Many have argued that proposed safeguards will be ineffective.[52] If "ineffective" means "will not reduce the risk of abuse at all," then surely the burden of proof is on those who make such a strong claim. But if "ineffective" means "not perfect," that must be acknowledged. Indeed, defenders of voluntary euthanasia have generally granted that "it is possible to substantially reduce, though not to eliminate, the potential for abuse of a policy permitting voluntary active euthanasia."[53] The issue, then, is whether the mere possibility of abuse is sufficient for prohibiting an activity. And, as noted above, we apparently do not think so with respect to many activities. So if the mere possibility of abuse is grounds for prohibiting voluntary euthanasia, again the burden is on those who advance this view.

To reiterate, my conclusion is modest. Legally permitting voluntary active euthanasia is compatible with the right to life having the legal status of inalienability.

SIX

Assisted Suicide and the Inalienable Right to Life

With an understanding of the inalienable right to life and its implications for voluntary active euthanasia in place, let us turn now to implications of this same right for assisted suicide and the use of advance directives in making decisions about medical treatment for incompetent patients.

Assisted Suicide

Assisted suicide occurs when one person aids another in bringing about her own death. Typically, the one rendering the assistance provides the would-be suicide with the knowledge and/or the means necessary to end her own life. In principle, anyone might provide another with such assistance. In our society, *physician*-assisted suicide is the practice most commonly debated. An example of this practice is when a physician writes a prescription for barbiturates and tells the patient what constitutes a fatal overdose. Dr. Jack Kevorkian, the best-known practitioner of physician-assisted suicide, provides individuals with a device that enables them to inhale carbon monoxide, thereby bringing about rapid death.

Voluntary euthanasia and physician-assisted suicide are alike in that the choice to hasten death rests solely with the patient. These practices differ in the nature of the causal role played by the physician (assuming, for now, that the agent of euthanasia is a physician). As Dan Brock says, "In physician-assisted suicide the patient acts last . . . whereas in euthanasia the physician acts last by performing the physical equivalent of pushing the button."[1] Quill et al. put it this way: "Physician-assisted suicide is distinguished from voluntary euthanasia, in which the physician not only makes the means available but, at the patient's request, also serves as the actual agent of death."[2] One way that a physician might perform active euthanasia is by administering a lethal dose of medication, such as morphine or potassium chloride. In that case, the "physician both supplies the means of death and is the final human agent in the events leading to the patient's death."[3] In November 1998, Dr. Kevorkian "advanced" from assisted suicide and performed euthanasia, showing the tape on the television program, *60 Minutes*. In both voluntary euthanasia and assisted suicide, the person whose death is hastened at least gives her consent. Here we shall ask whether assisted suicide is compatible with the inalienability of the right to life.

Since I have suggested above that suicide is not automatically precluded by the inalienability of the right to life, that might make the answer to our question seem easy. Of course, assisted suicide is compatible with the inalienable right to life! Those who make such a rapid inference seem to be relying on what I shall call "the permissibility-extension principle": If it is permissible for P_1 to do a certain act or bring about a situation, then it is permissible for P_1 to enlist the freely given aid of P_2 in doing the act or bringing about the situation.[4] Unless qualified, however, the permissibility-extension principle is dubious. To cite an obvious example, it may be permissible for marital partners to do things to each other but impermissible for either to enlist the assistance of a third party in such an act.[5]

Nevertheless, given that I argued in chapter 5 that voluntary euthanasia is compatible with the inalienability of the right to life, it would be extraordinary if assisted suicide too were not compatible. There are at least three reasons for this. First, on the face of it, assisted suicide seems to promote the same three values that I praised voluntary euthanasia for: self-determination, prevention of suffering, and death with dignity. Second, there are factors about assisted suicide that make it less problematic, morally and legally, than allowing P2 to take P_1's life with P_1's consent. An obvious difference concerns the likelihood of abuse. When a person takes his own life, questions about the genuineness of consent appear to be irrelevant. But if one person is allowed to take the life of another because that individual has given his consent, questions about the quality of the consent must be addressed.[6] Did the person in fact make the request? If so, was it freely given? If so, was it based on adequate information? And if the answer to any of these questions is negative, we arguably do not have *voluntary* euthanasia; we may even have a case of cold-blooded murder. Quill et al. put the difference between the two practices this way: "In assisted suicide, the final act is solely the patient's, and the risk of subtle coercion from doctors, family members, institutions, or other social forces is greatly reduced."[7]

The third reason that assisted suicide is compatible with the (legal) inalienability of the right to life is that the parties participating do not appear to be violating any special duties implied by the inalienable right to life. As was argued earlier (chapter 2), legally inalienable rights seem to entail no duties to oneself. If that is correct, then the possessor of the right to life who is taking his own life is violating no duty *entailed by that right*. As for the person doing the assisting, what he may not do is to infringe the right merely because of the possessor's consent. But when one person provides another with the means and/or the knowledge necessary for ending one's own life, that person is not infringing the right at all; for the possessor of the right kills himself. I assume here that providing a competent person with the means and/or knowledge to do something does not violate the rights of *that person*. On the face of it, it would seem that the only time that one who assists another in committing suicide might plausibly be open to the charge of either infringing or violating the right to life would be if the one lending assistance used pressure or coercion, or *caused* the other to commit suicide. In that sort of case, there are doubts that the person who committed suicide did so freely. Other than those cases, however, the one providing assistance appears to violate no duties implied by the right to life.

I grant, then, that if my argument for the compatibility of voluntary euthanasia and the inalienability of the right to life is sound, one can infer that assisted-suicide too is compatible with inalienability. It is interesting that available evidence suggests that the majority of Americans approve of physician-assisted suicide at least for terminally ill patients.[8] Yet in referenda in Washington State (in 1991) and California (in 1992), voters rejected initiatives that would have legally permitted such a practice. (As will be explained later, voters in Oregon decided in favor of assisted suicide.) Some explain this by claiming that the public fears that the practice will be abused.[9] If that is plausible, it suggests that assisted suicide needs to be regulated; without safeguards, the rights of nonconsenting individuals may be put at risk.

Safeguards

It is exactly the fear of abuse that has led an advocate of physician-assisted suicide, Timothy Quill, to propose safeguards that must be observed if physician-assisted suicide is to be allowed. Assisting in a suicide without following these regulations should result in a stiff penalty. As a former hospice physician, Quill supports comfort care and approves of assisted suicide only in cases where patients' suffering cannot be adequately controlled or when patients reasonably fear indignities and dependence likely to be associated with their terminal illness. Quill acknowledges that the possibility of abuse—often depicted in the so-called slippery slope argument—provides good reason to worry about allowing assisted suicide. But he claims that if strict safeguards are enforced, these worries can be minimized. Thus, Quill approves of assisted suicide only if the following conditions are satisfied:[10]

1. The patient must freely initiate and repeatedly request assistance in death.
2. Psychiatric evaluation must demonstrate that the patient's judgment is not distorted.
3. The patient's condition must be incurable and involve intolerable suffering.
4. The patient's suffering must not be the result of inadequate comfort care.
5. Assisted suicide should occur only when the physician has had a standing and meaningful relationship with the patient.
6. Consultation with another experienced physician is required to confirm the patient's diagnosis and prognosis and that the request is voluntary.
7. Documentation to support each of these six conditions is required.

In a well-known case in which Quill himself assisted a patient in death—the case of "Diane"—he provided her with a prescription for barbiturates and knowledge of what constitutes a lethal overdose; his description of the case indicates that he followed his own guidelines carefully.[11]

The purpose of these guidelines is to take seriously the preservation of human life and to ensure, to the degree possible, that abuse does not occur. Guideline (1) requires that the *patient*, not the physician, initiate the request, and do so on several occasions. The idea here is to make sure that the desire is the patient's own and is not merely transient. Guideline (2) is designed to ensure that the patient is competent and not suffering from treatable depression. Some have objected to specific legislative proposals because they do not require persons with psychiatric expertise to make such judgments.[12] Baron and colleagues, who have recently constructed a model statute for regulating physician-assisted suicide, have responded to this objection by requiring that this examination be performed "by a licensed psychiatrist, clinical psychologist, or psychiatric social worker."[13] Quill also insists that the patient's condition be hopeless; thus guideline (3) requires that the patient's illness be incurable and guideline (4) demands that the suffering not be the result of inadequate comfort care. Demonstrating that guidelines (3) and (4) have been satisfied will require documenting that standard medical interventions have been tried but have failed; only then is it appropriate to think in terms of hopelessness. This is important because some opponents of assisted death worry that legalization will eventually lead physicians to be less diligent in looking for ways of dealing with the patient's pain and other symptoms.[14] Quill believes that it is important for the physician to "understand why, from the patient's perspective, death is the best of a limited number of very unfortunate options."[15] Such understanding can be achieved only if the physician has a meaningful relationship with the patient, as guideline (5) requires.

Even well-meaning and competent physicians can make mistakes. To minimize errors—whether about the prognosis, the diagnosis, or the voluntariness or rationality of the request—guideline (6) requires consultation with another experienced physician. This, of course, will not eliminate errors; but presumably if the consulting physician is appropriately serious, it will reduce them.[16] And guideline (7), the requirement of documentation, provides a basis for developing a system of reporting and reviewing cases of physician-assisted death. Indeed, in the context of developing safeguards to minimize abuse of voluntary euthanasia, Margaret Pabst Battin argues that appropriate documentation and reporting will enable us to develop objective indices to check for abuses.[17] She has in mind doing retrospective examinations to determine who is opting for assisted death. One can utilize numerous categories, including race, gender, type of illness, income, insurance status, and the like. Certain outcomes, we can easily foresee, would raise red flags and suggest, if not abuse, the existence of serious social problems.[18]

Quill is quite concerned to assure that the person's request is freely given. If the request is not freely given—for example, because the patient was pressured or coerced, or the patient was deliberately given erroneous information about his prognosis or diagnosis—then this is precisely the sort of abuse that puts the rights of nonconsenting parties at risk. And this is why that, even if suicide is consistent with the inalienability of the right to life, assisted suicide may not be. In this context, many worry that the "choice" of assisted suicide will not be voluntary,[19] that if assisted suicide is legally permitted, family members may pressure a patient to choose such an option.[20] Such family members may be motivated by a desire to save money, acquire an inheritance, or simply spare themselves the emotional trauma of watching a loved one die. Whatever the motives, such pressure threatens to undermine the voluntariness of the patient's request. Indeed, Grisez and Boyle discuss a case involving an elderly woman and her adult daughter. The mother was 87 years old and in a nursing home. The daughter was in debt and stood to inherit a good sum of money upon her mother's death. The daughter brought 15 Nembutal tablets with her and urged her mother to take them with whiskey. The following rather frightening conversation is alleged to have occurred between the daughter and mother.

> "How many have you brought?" asks the mother.
> "Fifteen."
> "But does it take fifteen?"
> "For most ten are fatal, but if you take them with whiskey, five are enough."
> "It is a mortal sin."
> "People are doing it left, right, and center. It's not a sin anymore. It's nothing nowadays. But it's up to you."
> "But is it cowardly to do it?"
> "No, it isn't cowardly. If you had a dog in this state, you would take it to the vet, wouldn't you?"
> "A dog hasn't got a soul."[21]

One response to this problem, articulated by Peter Singer, is that the very same considerations apply to withholding and withdrawing life-sustaining treatment.[22] One can raise doubts about the voluntariness of consent in those cases too, but few are willing to say that life-sustaining medical interventions should never be withheld or withdrawn, even with patient consent, because of the possibility of pressure from others. Indeed, we are often willing to withhold or withdraw treatment at a surrogate's request, even without firm evidence that that is what the patient would have wanted. In addition, as Marcia Angell has pointed out, assisted suicide has a built-in safeguard missing not only from euthanasia but also from cases where life-support is withheld or withdrawn: only in assisted suicide must the patient himself play an *active* role.[23]

There is a more positive response to this problem, however. The attending physician and the psychiatrist or psychologist who independently examine the patient must be alert to the possibility of such outside pressure. That is why there is considerable wisdom in requiring that such evaluations be conducted in private, away from family members and others, as Battin recommends.[24] Such a requirement enhances the likelihood that assisted suicides that are carried out genuinely reflect the wishes of the person whose life is ended.

It would seem to be a truism to say that if assisted suicide were legally permitted, more people will die sooner than if that practice is proscribed. But some have challenged this truism, claiming that the legalization of assisted suicide will actually extend lives. Shavelson refers to this as the "paradox" of assisted suicide. Some persons who end their own lives now, either with or without assistance, do so because they fear they will become so disabled that performing such an act will be impossible for them (without assistance that is currently proscribed). And if at that point others are legally prohibited from helping them, they will be unable to achieve the desired end. Discussing a particular case, Shavelson says, "With my guarantee to help her if her agony became too severe, Renee could live on. Without this promise of aid, if she desired to avoid future *possible* suffering, she must die now, while still mentally and physically capable of taking the overdose."[25]

Shavelson's point is illustrated concretely by Sherwin Nuland, in his excellent book *How We Die*.[26] Nuland recounts the story of Percy Bridgman, a Harvard professor of physics who won the Nobel Prize in 1946. At the age of 79 and in the final stages of painful cancer, Bridgman shot himself on August 20, 1961. He continued to work until his death, and on the very day of his suicide he completed the index to a seven-volume collection of his scientific works. Bridgman left a suicide note which said in part, "It is not decent for Society to make a man do this to himself. Probably, this is the last day I will be able to do it myself."

There is a second reason why the legalization of assisted suicide may prevent more suicides than it facilitates. If Quill's requirements are followed, some patients comtemplating suicide may find out that pain relief is possible or that they are afflicted with treatable depression. But these discoveries are less likely in a society that prohibits assisted suicide because such patients are less likely to tell physicians that they are considering such an act.[27]

Objections and Replies

Many objections have been leveled against those who advocate the legalization of assisted suicide. Only two will be considered here because only they seem pertinent to the inalienability of the right to life. The first objection says that we should not criminalize attempted suicide but should criminalize assisted suicide because of the possibilities of pressure, coercion, and abuse. The idea is this: just let the person commit suicide herself, but do not allow others to be involved. Unfortunately, there are two serious problems with this proposal. First, some patients are simply physically unable to take their own lives without assistance because of the presence of severe disabilities.[28] And second, successfully committing suicide is not as easy as many think. Suicide is easy to botch, easy even for those genuinely intent on ending their lives,[29] and various improvements and safety measures have rendered previously reliable methods of suicide far less reliable.[30]

The second objection concedes that *if* self-determination and prevention of suffering could be promoted only by legalizing assisted suicide, then there would be good reason to do so. But the critic claims that intentionally hastening death is never necessary to prevent suffering. This line of argument is most commonly advanced by those associated with the hospice movement. They claim that pain relief and control of symptoms can be achieved by using available medications. They admit that physicians in the past have been inadequately trained in these areas. But if doctors are properly educated, no one needs to suffer.[31] Assisted suicide is thus rendered unnecessary. One might therefore call this the "nonnecessity argument" (against both euthanasia and assisted suicide).[32] Defenders of assisted suicide have retorted that the critics' main premise is simply false. These advocates acknowledge that pain relief is often possible, and they credit the hospice movement with enabling many patients to have comfortable deaths. But they deny that this can be achieved in every case.[33] Examples might include patients with cancer of the stomach who are unable to swallow their secretions and patients with AIDS who develop the wasting syndrome, intractable diarrhea, and incontinence.[34] Some critics of assisted suicide do acknowledge that in a few cases pain relief seems unachievable; but in these cases physicians can induce a coma or provide continuous anesthetic levels of pain-relieving medication,[35] thus ensuring that the patients do not suffer; some call this "terminal sedation." It is certainly true that such an action will prevent suffering. But the appropriate response to this suggestion is provided by Shavelson:

> It is certain that placing dying patients under prolonged and deep anesthesia would relieve their symptoms. But many experts claim that this practice, increasingly being used by hospice physicians today, is virtually the same as killing the patient. Residing in a deep, drug-induced coma while awaiting death can be, from the patient's point of view, no different from death itself.[36]

It seems that one can hold that inducing a comatose state in a person is morally superior to killing that person, only if one is an absolutist about the prohibition against killing or assisted suicide. Such a claim seems implausible. Inducing a coma rather than hastening death may make some health care professionals feel better; but it does nothing positive for the patient.

In concluding this section, a difficulty with formulating a defensible public policy that allows for assisted suicide and/or voluntary euthanasia should be mentioned. As noted earlier, most who defend a policy that permits either or both of these practices urge that the class of individuals whose deaths may be assisted be restricted. And the restriction is usually limited to those who have a terminal, painful illness; many add to this, those who are afflicted with an incurable, debilitating illness.[37] But a serious question arises about how extensive this class should be. The difficulty is one of "drawing the line." Indeed, some critics of legalized assisted suicide have argued that no constitutional basis exists for limiting assisted suicide to the terminally ill or any other narrowly defined class.[38] The issue emerges clearly in Shavelson's discussion of the case of Kelly Niles.[39] Kelly was a quadriplegic. As an 11-year-old youngster, he had had a fight and received a blow to the head. He experienced severe pain and was taken to a hospital. Doctors reassured Kelly's father that he had merely sustained a concussion. Doctors did not discover that Kelly's agony was being caused by an expanding blood clot pushing on his brain. Later, Kelly became unconscious and was returned to the hospital for emergency neurosurgery. But permanent brain damage had already been done, leaving Kelly unable to control the movement of his arms and legs; and he was mute. The only good thing for Kelly was winning four million dollars in a malpractice suit; this enabled him to have around-the-clock care and whatever equipment was available to aid persons in his state. Kelly lived this way for more than 20 years! But he finally reached a point of no return and wanted to commit suicide. He was physically unable to do so, however, without assistance. Kelly is quoted as communicating, "I have the right to kill myself, like anybody else does. I just can't do it."[40] He became quite angry about his plight and came to see his inability to kill himself as the final insult of his disability.

Quadriplegia is currently incurable. Should a social policy permitting assisted suicide include persons in Kelly Niles's situation? It is here that one begins to feel the bite of slippery slope considerations. Shavelson puts his finger on the difficulty. "People with disabilities fear that judges, lawyers and physicians too easily see disabled people's lives as not worth living—and would agree to their suicides instead of working to improve their lives."[41]

This same consideration was raised in the well-known case of Elizabeth Bouvia, a (near) quadriplegic who checked herself into the psychiatric ward of a hospital and then wanted to starve herself to death.[42] Other disabled persons held vigils at the hospital, trying to convince Ms. Bouvia to change her mind; they feared that this would convey the message that any disabled person's life is not worth living. Indeed, some commentators argue that it is disingenuous to deny this; for if Ms. Bouvia were permitted to carry out her wishes, it would be *because* of her quadriplegia.[43] But again one wonders about drawing the line. As Shavelson puts it:

> It seemed intuitively right, when people saw Kelly's tortured body, to "understand" his wish to die. But a law that would permit a physician to assist in Kelly's death would have to draw the line at some level of disability—or it would eventually allow physicians to assist in the death of virtually anyone who claimed it was simply too difficult to go on living. . . . But should a law that grants assistance in dying to patients who suffer from a terminal illness be extended to *all* people with disabilities?[44]

As one might guess, there is not unanimity among disabled persons themselves on this issue. Shavelson quotes Paul Longmore, a severely disabled history professor, as saying that it is the ignorance and bias of nondisabled persons that lead them to support suicides such as that of Kelly Niles.[45] Andrew Batavia, a quadriplegic attorney, retorts that competent, disabled persons should have the same rights as any competent person. More recently, Batavia has expanded on this point. He argues:

> We do not believe that the right to assisted suicide is premised on our society's widespread misperception that people with disabilities have a diminished quality of life. It is based on respect for the autonomy of terminally ill persons in determining the quality of their lives during their final days. Moreover, the right to assisted suicide does not deprive people with disabilities of anything and therefore does not violate the Americans with Disabilities Act or the equal-protection clause of the Constitution. The right does not deny them suicide-prevention services, protection against murder, or protection from other abuses.[46]

I acknowledge the seriousness and importance of this issue, but here do not attempt to resolve it.

Withholding/Withdrawing Treatment versus Assisted Death: The Conventional View and the Behavior of Health Care Providers

What I shall call the conventional view, embedded both in the law and in official pronouncements by medical organizations, is that there is an important moral distinction between withholding or withdrawing life-sustaining medical treatment, on the one hand, and assisting suicide or performing active euthanasia, on the other. It is morally and legally acceptable to withhold or to withdraw life-sustaining medical treatment at the request of the patient, or at the request of the surrogate, when the patient lacks decision-making capacity and the burdens of treatment outweigh the benefits. But it is neither morally nor legally proper to assist suicide or to participate in active euthanasia.[47] The line must be drawn here.

The conventional view is widely preached; yet there is evidence that the attitudes, beliefs, and conduct of many health care professionals fail to comport with it. Here I shall discuss briefly a few of the recent studies that suggest this.

In 1991, Robyn Shapiro and colleagues sent a survey to physicians soliciting, in addition to demographic information, their responses to three hypothetical cases in which patients request euthanasia, and soliciting their opinions about euthanasia and how its legalization might affect them.[48] Surveys were returned by 740 physicians. Of those who responded, 28 percent were willing to perform euthanasia in one of the hypothetical scenarios and 17 percent were willing to do so in another of the scenarios. Religious affiliation was the demographic characteristic most influential in physicians' willingness to perform euthanasia. Of the respondents, 96 percent who identified themselves as Christian fundamentalists and 85 percent who identified themselves as Catholic were not willing to perform euthanasia at any stage of the cases.

A 1993 survey of oncology nurses reported that 47 percent of the respondents support legalizing physician-aid in dying.[49] Moreover, 16 percent said that with a physician's order they would perform voluntary euthanasia on a competent, terminally ill patient.

In a 1996 survey of selected Washington State physicians, Anthony Back and associates report that 26 percent of the respondents indicated that they had received requests for actively hastening death.[50] Of those receiving such requests, 24 percent acknowledged that they had assisted some patients with suicide and 24 percent said that they had on occasion performed active euthanasia.

David Asch recently surveyed 1600 critical care nurses in the United States.[51] Assured of anonymity, these nurses were asked to describe any requests from patients, family members, or physicians to perform euthanasia or assist in suicide. They were also asked about their own practices. Of 852 nurses who responded, 141 (17 percent) said that they had received requests from patients or family members to assist in suicide or perform euthanasia; and 129 (15 percent) indicated that they had on occasion engaged in such practices. An additional 35 (4 percent) reported that they had hastened patients' deaths by only pretending to provide life-sustaining treatment ordered by a physician.

And in a 1997 survey of physicians in the San Francisco area who saw AIDS patients frequently, Lee Slome and colleagues solicited responses to a case vignette.[52] Of the respondents, 48 percent said that they would be likely or very likely to comply with the request of a patient with AIDS for assistance in committing suicide. More significant, 53 percent of responding physicians reported that they had on occasion assisted AIDS patients in committing suicide.

What all of this suggests is that the behavior of a significant number of health care practitioners caring for patients near the end of life is in violation of the prohibitions set forth in the conventional view.[53]

Perhaps even more significant, however, there is a second problem. The moral assumptions underlying the conventional view make little sense to many health care practitioners. Physicians and other medical professionals routinely engage in certain behavior that hastens patients' deaths; yet such behavior is allowed by the conventional view. Withholding and withdrawing life-sustaining medical treatment are supposed to be permissible and on a moral par, while assisting in suicide and killing are absolutely forbidden. Yet this seems confusing to some health care providers.[54] And no wonder! Consider this. Withdrawing respiratory support from a patient with COPD (chronic obstructive pulmonary disease) occurs even when it is known that this will result in the patient's death. In a similar vein, providing high doses of narcotics and sedatives to relieve suffering in patients with terminal illnesses is common, even when it is known that doing so will suppress respiration and thereby hasten death.[55] And when mechanical ventilation is discontinued at the request of a competent patient, it is common to provide sedation to relieve feelings of suffocation; yet the sedative reduces respiratory drive, thus hastening death.[56] How can these activities be permitted by the conventional view when assisted suicide and active euthanasia are absolutely forbidden by it? Several answers have been proposed.

The first answer given to this question by proponents usually appeals to the cause of death. They say that when life-sustaining medical treatment is withdrawn, the cause of death is the underlying disease, not the actions of the health care practitioners. So when ventilator support is withdrawn from the patient suffering from lung disease, it is the lung disease that causes the death. If this supports the permissibility of such actions, then apparently the normatively important factor is whether one's act causes death. And the underlying assumption is that it is wrong to cause death. But this defense of the conventional view is problematic. For defenders of the conventional view approve of actions by medical practitioners that are surely properly described as causing the patient's death. One example, just cited above, is providing pain medication that one knows will cause respiratory distress. Another type of case that fits here is withdrawing artificial nutrition and hydration from patients in a persistent vegetative state. The landmark legal cases regarding such decisions are those of Paul Brophy[57] and Nancy Cruzan.[58] In each of these cases, the patient had been in a persistent vegetative state for several years and received nutrition and hydration through a feeding tube. In each case, the surrogate sought permission to have the tube removed. And in each case, the surrogate eventually won the right to do so, predictably resulting in the patient's death. Neither Paul Brophy nor Nancy Cruzan was terminally ill. Perhaps in these cases it is misleading to talk about *the* cause of death; but it is surely disingenuous to deny that removing the feeding tube was a significant *causal factor* in those deaths.

The second answer given by proponents of the conventional view appeals to the *intent* of the health care practitioner. In the case of providing pain medication that triggers respiratory distress, defenders of the view say that even if this action does cause the patient's death, that was not the physician's intent.[59] Her intention was to relieve the suffering; the patient's death was a foreseen but unintended consequence. But again this response appears to be fraught with difficulties; for again there are legally allowed actions that most approve of that appear to be cases of intending to bring about the patient's death. One such case involves Kenneth Bergstedt, a 31-year-old competent quadriplegic.[60] At the age of 10, Mr. Bergstedt became quadriplegic as the result of a swimming accident. He existed in that state, dependent on a respirator, for 21 years. Much of what sustained him was the absolute devotion of his father. But when his father became seriously ill and his death was imminent, Kenneth decided that he wanted to stop respirator support. Kenneth's quadriplegia was irreversible; he was examined by a psychiatrist and judged to be competent to make his own decisions. He thus won the right to stop respirator support. There can be no doubt that Kenneth's intent was to bring about his own death; and in cases like this, if a health care practitioner voluntarily complies with the patient's request, surely, she at least foresees the patient's death, and it is not obvious that one is not responsible for such a foreseen consequence.

Another illustration of this same point is clear in the well-known case of Clarence Herbert.[61] Mr. Herbert was a 55-year-old man who had an intestinal obstruction that required an ileostomy. After the surgery, he suffered a cardiopulmonary arrest and never regained consciousness. Three days after the arrest, his physicians, Drs. Barber and Nejdl, told Mrs. Herbert and their eight children that his condition was hopeless. The family unanimously said that Mr. Herbert would not want to be kept alive by machines, and they asked that life support be stopped. At this point, the physicians and family decided to discontinue the ventilator. But surprisingly, Mr. Herbert continued to breathe, though remaining comatose. Two days later, the family requested that intravenous fluids be stopped. The physicians complied, and Mr. Herbert died six days later. A nurse, distraught about withholding fluids, brought this case to the attention of the district attorney, who in turn filed charges of murder against the physicians. The charges were dismissed, however, for various reasons, including that physicians are not obligated to continue interventions that have proved to be ineffective. Given the sequence of events in this case, it stretches credibility to deny that the family and physician intended the death of Mr. Herbert. They might claim that their intent is to honor what they take to be Mr. Herbert's own wishes—the discontinuance of life-sustaining treatment. But if that is the intent, why stop ventilator support, and then *only later* withdraw fluids?

When defenders of the conventional view make this second move, appealing to intent, they are tacitly invoking what philosophers call *the doctrine of double effect*.[62] Put too simply, this is a doctrine which holds that it is permissible for an agent to bring about evil (a bad state of affairs) knowingly only if he does so unintentionally and doing so is necessary to produce a greater good. This view has struck many philosophers as suspicious, and one problem is with the understanding of intent that is employed. On this view, an agent intends what she seeks as an end or a direct means to that end. Something that she knows will happen but is neither the end sought nor a direct means to that end is said to be foreseen but unintended. But as Tom Beauchamp and James Childress point out, this is a very narrow understanding of intention.[63] In a sense, this narrow account limits intention to what the agent *wants*. But if the agent knows that something will occur as a result of her voluntary act, one might say that she *wills* it to occur; it is an effect that is *tolerated*. And it seems quite plausible to say that such effects are intended, in a broader sense of that term.

I do not want to claim, however, that the distinction between what an agent intends and what she merely foresees is not legitimate. Indeed, I believe that there is a genuine distinction.[64] The real issue for defenders of the doctrine of double effect is whether the distinction between what an agent intends and what she foresees will bear the moral weight that is placed on it by defenders of the conventional view. Several points suggest that the doctrine cannot be successfully employed to sustain the conventional view.

First, it seems that defenders of the doctrine of double effect are committed to a kind of absolutism the plausibility of which is not obvious. The way that the doctrine of double effect is employed to defend the conventional view requires that its advocates hold that it is *always wrong* to intend to hasten the death of another person, and that euthanasia and assisted suicide always include the intent so to hasten death. But each of these claims is doubtful. Is it really always wrong to intend to hasten another's death? This seems to assume that an individual's death is always a bad thing. As Judith Thomson puts it, "Isn't it likely that in the case of at least some of those patients, their condition is such as to make it better for them to die? Indeed, such as to make it good for them to die?"[65] And it is not obvious that a physician who writes a lethal prescription for a patient always intends that patient's death. It is possible that the physician intends only to give the patient the peace of mind that comes from knowing that he has the option to end his own life if the pain becomes unbearable.[66]

Second, as intimated earlier, the mere fact that consequences are foreseen but unintended does not seem to absolve agents of responsibility for them. Advocates of the doctrine of double effect *themselves* require agents to take account of foreseen but unintended consequences; for when such effects do not meet the proportionality test—when more good does not come about as a result—then agents are *not permitted* to bring them about. Why are they morally relevant in some cases but not others? As Quill and colleagues have pointed out, in most social and legal realms people are responsible for all reasonably foreseeable consequences of their actions. It is hard to see why physicians should be exempt from this.[67]

And third, when death is a certainty, such as when Mr. Herbert's fluids were discontinued, it seems artificial to say that the permissibility of acting on that decision hinges only on the intentions of the agent. It should not surprise us when physicians readily acknowledge that discontinuing life-sustaining medical treatment feels like causing the patient's death.[68]

The Conventional View Under Philosophical and Judicial Attack

The conventional view has been embraced by many in the medical and legal communities. And most of these same people approve of giving pain medication even if it triggers respiratory distress, of stopping respiratory support in certain cases even when this will result in the patient's death, and of discontinuing nutrition and hydration in selected situations, which will certainly lead to death. All of this has produced a strain. Do these particular actions square with the conventional view? To make them consistent, various distinctions have been appealed to: the distinction between ordinary and extraordinary treatment; the distinction between commission and omission; the distinction between intended and foreseen but unintended. But for these distinctions to do their work—rendering consistent the conventional view with particular acts most approve of—they must have moral relevance. And the attacks on them have, for the most part, been designed to show that what they distinguish is not morally important, or not important enough to bear the weight that they must. All of this has come to the fore in two recent court cases.

Statutes prohibiting physician-assisted suicide were challenged in both Washington State and New York State. And in each case, in the spring of 1996, a United States Court of Appeals ruled the statute unconstitutional. Each ruling, in part, challenged the relevance of the traditional distinctions employed to justify particular acts while retaining the conventional view. Without explaining these cases in detail, let us look at part of the courts' reasoning.

In the Washington case,[69] the Ninth Circuit Court of Appeals held that persons who are terminally ill and suffering have a liberty interest in determining the time and manner of their deaths. The scope of liberty guaranteed by the Due Process Clause of the Fourteenth Amendment is not limited to specific guarantees, but rather is a freedom from all substantial arbitrary restraints. Choices central to personal dignity are certainly protected. The effect of the Due Process Clause, the Ninth Circuit Court held, is to limit the ability of the state to intrude into the most important matters of people's lives. Not all liberty interests are equally weighty. But when a liberty interest is important, the burden is on the state to justify any limits it imposes. Judge Stephen Reinhardt, author of the opinion, explains the important liberty interest people have at the end of their lives.

> A competent terminally ill adult, having lived nearly the full measure of his life, has a strong liberty interest in choosing a dignified and humane death rather than being reduced at the end of his existence to a childlike state of helplessness, diapered, sedated, incontinent. How a person dies not only determines the nature of the final period of his existence, but in many cases, the enduring memories held by those who love him.

Judge Reinhardt does not deny, however, that the state has legitimate interests too. Among these state interests are a general interest in preserving life and a specific interest in preventing suicide. The individual's interests must be weighed against these interests of the state. The Ninth Circuit ruled that the state's interest in preserving life does *not* outweigh the terminally ill person's interest in determining the time and manner of his death.

According to Reinhardt, there have been various breakthroughs (in medical contexts) recognizing individual liberty. First, terminally ill persons were permitted to refuse medical treatment. The line was drawn between ordinary treatment (which was never to be withheld) and extraordinary treatment (which patients/surrogates could reject). But that distinction proved unworkable, and soon terminally ill patients were permitted to reject any medical treatment. Next, there was a distinction between commission and omission; patients could refuse treatment but not stop treatment. But again that proved to be an unfounded distinction. Today patients/surrogates may withdraw life support and even refuse or stop life-sustaining nutrition and hydration. In light of all this, "opponents of physician-assisted suicide must now explain precisely what it is about the physician's conduct in assisted suicide cases that distinguishes it from the conduct that the state has explicitly authorized." We cannot even draw the line at causing death, Reinhardt says, because physicians are permitted to administer pain medication that does just that; this is, as he says, "another bridge crossed."

Some may think that this creates a positive right that patients can assert against physicians.[70] But it does not create a claim-right on the basis of which a patient can *demand* assistance. Judge Reinhardt specifically says that access to assisted suicide "would not require doctors to do anything contrary to their individual principles." Assisted suicide is permissible; but no physician can be required to provide such assistance.

Though states may not proscribe physician-assisted suicide, they may regulate it for the purpose of preventing abuse and advancing legitimate state interests. Among permissible regulations, the Court specifically mentions requiring that patients be competent when they make the request and when they carry out the decision, that witnesses ensure the voluntariness of the request, that a second medical opinion confirms the existence of a terminal illness, and that a psychological examination be required to ensure that the patient is not suffering from treatable depression. In terms discussed earlier, these are safeguards to prevent a slide down the slippery slope.

In the New York case,[71] the Second Circuit Court of Appeals ruled that the New York statute prohibiting physician-assisted suicide was unconstitutional. The opinion was written by Judge Roger Miner. Judge Miner cited the Equal Protection Clause of the Fourteenth Amendment as the key to his decision. This clause directs that all persons similarly circumstanced shall be treated alike. The court ruled that New York State does not treat equally all persons who are in the final stages of fatal illnesses and wish to hasten their deaths. The state has for a long time recognized the right to refuse medical treatment, and so a terminally ill person may hasten his death in this manner. The state has also recognized that this right extends to the withdrawal of life-support systems, and so a terminally ill person being so maintained may end his life. More recently, the state has even given a patient the right to hasten her death by appointing a health care agent, who may thereby be empowered to require the physician to withdraw life-sustaining medical treatment. And the state allows physicians to administer pain-killing drugs that hasten patients' deaths. According to Judge Miner, "The ending of life by these means is nothing more nor less than assisted suicide." Terminally ill persons not hooked up to life-sustaining treatment and for whom pain medication that will hasten death is not indicated have no legal means of achieving what other terminally ill patients can; thus, the unequal treatment.

In reply to the Second Circuit Court, one might be tempted to say that there is a principled basis underlying the New York statute: New York allows only *natural* deaths. But Judge Miner anticipates such a retort, and says, "By ordering the discontinuance of these artificial life-sustaining processes or refusing to accept them in the first place, a patient hastens his death by means that are not natural in any sense." One might object that unless assisted suicide is prohibited, physicians will be allowed to take on the role of killer. But Judge Miner says that "[p]hysicians do not fulfill the role of 'killer' by prescribing drugs to hasten death any more than they do by disconnecting life-support systems." Indeed, Miner says, a physician writing a prescription so that a patient can hasten her own death "involves a far less active role for the physician than is required in bringing about death through asphyxiation, starvation and/or dehydration."

Some have objected to allowing physician-assisted suicide on grounds that it is very difficult to distinguish between psychiatrically qualified and disqualified suicidal requests.[72] Obviously aware of such a criticism, Miner contends that physicians currently make comparable judgments when patients request that life-sustaining treatments be discontinued. So again the Equal Protection Clause is invoked: if physician-assisted suicide is prohibited because it is difficult to determine competence, then so too we should prohibit ceasing life-support at the patient's request.

These two circuit courts came to the same conclusion by way of different reasoning. The Ninth Circuit Court appealed to the Due Process Clause of the Fourteenth Amendment; the Second Circuit Court, to the Equal Protection Clause. One major difference between the two concerns the way the conclusion was established. The Ninth Circuit Court, in effect, gave a positive argument. It claimed that terminally ill persons have a liberty interest in determining the time and manner of their death, and no state interest is sufficiently weighty to override this. One could only counter this argument either by denying that there is such a liberty interest, disputing its specific content, or pointing to a conflicting state interest of sufficient weight to take precedence over it. Some suspect that the key here concerns the scope of the liberty interest. Some critics think that this court's account was too broad; the interest is better understood narrowly as a right to be free of unwanted bodily intrusions.[73] The Second Circuit Court, by contrast, gave a negative argument. It simply held that New York was being inconsistent in denying terminally ill persons access to assisted suicide while permitting activities like the withdrawal of life support and the administration of narcotics strong enough to induce respiratory distress. A state could satisfy this criticism either by permitting assisted suicide or forbidding activities like the withdrawal of life support and the administration of strong pain medication. *Unless* one assumes that the right to withdraw life support is fixed—and perhaps the Second Circuit Court does assume this—a state is not forced by this argument to allow assisted suicide. There is at least one common thread running through these two opinions. Each court agrees that traditional distinctions that have been invoked to distinguish between legally *permissible* conduct that hastens death and legally *forbidden* conduct that does the same are without rational justification. In this, the courts have echoed the philosophical challenges.

The opinions of these two courts are consistent with the inalienability of the right to life. For as I have gone to great lengths to show (perhaps too great!), what that doctrine prohibits is killing someone merely because she has consented; to allow this is to approve of a policy that potentially puts many at risk. But this need not be the case if voluntary euthanasia and assisted suicide are allowed. The class of persons eligible for either of these options is quite small and appropriate safeguards diligently enforced make the chances of abuse much smaller.

The Supreme Court's Ruling

On June 26, 1997, the Supreme Court of the United States unanimously overturned the decisions of the Second and Ninth Circuit Courts.[74] Since those circuit courts had argued that state statutes prohibiting physician-assisted suicide are unconstitutional, the effect of the Supreme Court's ruling is that such laws are *not unconstitutional*. This does *not* mean that the practice of assisted suicide is itself unconstitutional. Rather, it means that individual states are permitted to proscribe that practice if they choose—and all states but one have done so. But nothing in this ruling precludes individual states from *permitting* that same practice if they choose. And voters in Oregon did just that in 1994, and again in 1997, approving a measure that allows physician-assisted suicide under regulated conditions.

In one way, supporters of assisted suicide may have done themselves in. In their most enthusiastic moments, supporters often say that assisted suicide (and some say euthanasia too) is *no different normatively* from withholding or withdrawing life-sustaining medical treatment. But surely there are normative differences between assisted suicide and withholding or withdrawing life-sustaining medical treatment. Withholding or withdrawing at a competent patient's request is morally (and usually legally) *required*; providing assistance with death at a competent patient's request is at best *permissible*, not required. This suggests that there are normative differences. Something that comes to mind immediately is that the requirement to withhold or withdraw treatment at the patient's request is based on a negative right, the right not to be interfered with (or the right of bodily integrity). But it is certainly not obvious that there is a corresponding positive right to be assisted, and even if there were such a right, it would not be as strong as the right not to be interfered with. It is for this reason that proponents of assisted suicide themselves insist that no physician will be required to participate in this practice if it is contrary to her own moral beliefs. So these proponents themselves are committed to *denying* that withholding or withdrawing life-sustaining treatment is normatively equivalent to assisted suicide.

Chief Justice Rehnquist was the author of the Supreme Court's opinions in these two cases. In *Washington v. Glucksberg*, Rehnquist emphasizes that the statute in question relates rationally to many legitimate state interests: the preservation of human life, preventing the mentally ill from committing suicide, protecting the integrity of the medical profession, protecting vulnerable groups, and avoiding a slippery slope that leads to euthanasia.[75] Even if citizens have a liberty interest in determining the time and manner of their deaths—a proposition that the Court regards as doubtful—the case is an easy one. Justice Rehnquist concludes: "We need not weigh exactingly the relative strengths of these various interests. They are unquestionably important and legitimate, and Washington's ban on assisted suicide is at least reasonably related to their promotion and protection."[76] Thus, the Ninth Circuit Court was reversed.

Chief Justice Rehnquist emphasized in *Vacco v. Quill* that the right to refuse life-saving medical treatment is based on "traditional rights to bodily integrity and freedom from unwanted touching," and that these had no distinct implications for assisted suicide.[77]

Instead of claiming no normative difference, supporters of assisted suicide should (and sometimes) do one of two things: either challenge the plausibility of the normative principles underlying the conventional view; or argue that if these principles show that assisted suicide must be prohibited, they also show that withholding or withdrawing life-sustaining treatment should be prohibited (even though neither of these is equivalent with assisted suicide). As a moral argument, either of these moves is superior to claiming no normative difference. It should be admitted, however, that such a strategy probably would have fared no better with the Court. For several things that Justice Rehnquist says suggest that he finds the normative principles underlying the conventional view plausible (or at least that states are constitutionally permitted to enact them), and that he thinks they do not have the same implications for withholding or withdrawing life-sustaining medical treatment as they have for assisted suicide. At one point he argues that "when a patient refuses life-sustaining medical treatment, he dies from an underlying fatal disease or pathology; but if a patient ingests lethal medication prescribed by a physician, he is killed by that medication."[78] And later he says that "in some cases, painkilling drugs may hasten a patient's death, but the physician's purpose and intent is, or may be, only to ease his patient's pain. A doctor who assists a suicide, however, 'must, necessarily and indubitably, intend primarily that the patient be dead.'"[79]

In the first of these passages, Justice Rehnquist agrees with advocates of the conventional view that since in cases of withdrawing or withholding life-sustaining medical treatment the disease is the cause of the patient's death, this absolves the physician of responsibility. And in the second passage, the Chief Justice acknowledges that in some acts allowed by the conventional view death is caused by medication administered by the physician; but in these situations the physician's intent is to relieve pain, not to hasten death. Here Rehnquist is giving credence to the doctrine of double effect, a view rejected by most supporters of assisted suicide.

Though the Court's decision was unanimous, this may not be the final word on physician-assisted suicide. For in these cases five other justices penned concurring opinions, suggesting that they do not fully support the *rationale* developed by the Chief Justice.

Assisted Suicide in Oregon

In 1994, voters in Oregon approved a measure permitting physician-assisted suicide in some cases if appropriate safeguards were followed. Various legal challenges, however, prevented anyone from acting under the auspices of that act. On October 27, 1997, Oregon citizens again voted to legalize physician-assisted suicide, this time by a wider margin than in 1994. The Oregon Death with Dignity Act permits terminally ill state residents to receive prescriptions from physicians for lethal medications to be administered by the patients themselves. The Act includes most of the safeguards discussed earlier in this chapter.[80] It was in March 1998 that the first terminally ill Oregonian exercised this newly available legal option.

Given concerns that have been expressed about vulnerable groups of patients, pressure to end one's life, and fears that financial considerations will prompt many to opt for assisted suicide, many eyes will be fixed on Oregon for the next few years. Already we have a study from Arthur Chin and colleagues dealing with the first year of physician-assisted suicide in Oregon.[81]

The study reports that 23 individuals received prescriptions for lethal medications in 1998. Of these patients, 15 died after taking the medication. Six died from the underlying illnesses, not having taken the medication. And as of January 1, 1999, two were still alive. The median age of the 15 patients who died after taking the lethal medication was 69-years-old. Eight of these patients were male; seven were female. All 15 were Caucasian. No patient indicated that financial concerns motivated the decision. Nor, surprisingly, was fear of pain a significant factor. Instead, the most salient reasons for choosing physician-assisted suicide were fear of loss of autonomy, inability to participate in activities, and loss of control of bodily functions.[82]

One study in one state over a period of one year is clearly not definitive. More evidence is needed. But two things reported in the study bear watching in the future. One is how prominently the fear of losing bodily control figured in people's choice for assisted suicide. This confirms a claim made by Quill, Cassel, and Meier, cited in the previous chapter, that the most frightening aspect of dying for many people is the "prospect of losing control and independence."[83] The second is the fact that six patients received a prescription for lethal medication but died of natural causes. Maybe having the option will indeed render some suicides unnecessary.

Advance Directives and the Right to Life

Advance directives are legally recognized documents that enable persons, while competent, to make decisions now that will have some impact on the sort of medical treatment they will receive should they no longer have the capacity to make their own decisions. A *living will* is a document through which one (typically) communicates to others that one does not want certain medical interventions employed in the event that one is terminally ill or in a persistent vegetative state. A properly executed living will does *not guarantee* that a patient's wishes will be followed, but it makes it more likely. For if health care professionals and family members act in accord with a patient's living will and the conditions under which it takes effect are satisfied, they are not subject to legal liability for that patient's ensuing death. A *health care power of attorney* is a document in which one designates another specific individual to make one's medical decisions if and when one no longer has the capacity to do so oneself. The sort of health care decisions that a health care agent may make for the person for whom she is a proxy varies from state to state. In a few states, once the patient lacks decision-making capacity the agent may make *any* decision that the patient could make (while he was competent); in other states, the agent may decide for the patient only when the patient lacks decision-making capacity *and* is either terminally ill or in a persistent vegetative state; and in some of these cases, the proxy must decide as the patient would have decided, when there is evidence about that.[84]

Neither a living will nor a health care power of attorney has the legal power to authorize a health care agent (or someone designated by the agent) to euthanize the patient; the patient's advance consent on this matter is not permission-generating. What a living will and a health care power of attorney do is to authorize others to *withhold or withdraw* life-sustaining medical treatment under certain statutorily specified conditions. As argued above, the principal duty correlative with the right to life is the duty not to kill the possessor of that right. If the right to life is inalienable, then consent alone does not suspend the duty not to kill. To see whether advance directives are compatible with the inalienability of the right to life, we have to ask whether what advance directives authorize—namely, withholding or withdrawing medical treatment under certain conditions—infringes the right to life.

As was noted, typically living wills apply only when the patient lacks decision-making capacity and is either terminally ill or in a persistent vegetative state. If those conditions obtain, health care practitioners and surrogates are specifically protected from liability. This is not a case where *consent alone* authorizes withholding or withdrawing life support; for other relevant conditions must obtain. And one could surely make an argument like the one sketched earlier (in the section on "Euthanasia" in chapter 5) to justify such a policy. Similarly, when health care agents are authorized to withhold or withdraw life support on behalf of the incompetent patient only under specified conditions—such as when the patient is terminally ill or in a persistent vegetative state—it is not consent alone that authorizes the decision. But there is one case where it does seem that consent alone authorizes the withholding or withdrawal of life support. This is in states whose statutes confer very broad powers on health care agents. In some cases, statutes authorize "the proxy to make decisions to the *same extent* that the principal could if the principal possessed decisionmaking capacity."[85] Here other conditions widely recognized to be relevant need not obtain. This is the troubling case, given the inalienability of the right to life. Throughout the remainder of this section, I confine my discussion to health care agents whose power is the same as that of the patient when the patient possesses decision-making capacity.

When such agents authorize *withholding* life-sustaining medical treatment from an incompetent patient, this does not infringe the right to life. The reason for this is that withholding life-sustaining treatment does not violate the patient's right to life because that right does not place demands on others to save another. This is not to deny that there may be a moral requirement to save others; but if there is (as I believe), that requirement is based on something other than the right to life.

Whether *withdrawing* life-sustaining medical treatment from an incompetent patient at the direction of a health care agent infringes the right to life is a more complex issue. It depends on whether stopping life support is a prima facie violation of the duty not to kill. Current legal opinions make it clear that termination of life-sustaining medical treatment is considered neither murder, suicide, nor assisted suicide.[86] On the basis of this consideration, one could say that extant legal doctrine renders the powers accorded to health care agents consistent with the inalienability of the right to life (because it does not authorize *killing* on grounds of consent alone). The trouble with this is that it is not obvious that extant legal doctrine is rationally based; for as we saw in the previous section, it is not clear that there is a principled foundation for distinguishing normatively among withdrawing treatment, assisted suicide, and euthanasia. It certainly appears that one cannot make the distinction on the basis of traditional ideas such as cause of death (medical condition vs. human acts) or the intent of the agent; as we saw, these seem not to be normatively relevant.[87] Of course, one would be on treacherous philosophical grounds to assert that no such basis exists for drawing the normatively relevant distinction. But until one is produced, there is a problem. And, I should add, *if* one is produced, it will show one of two things: *either* the judicial challenges coming from the Second and Ninth Circuit Courts can be answered, *or* those challenges show only that assisted suicide may not be consistently prohibited but have no applicability to euthananasia.

To take the difficult route, then, let us suppose that we can find no normatively relevant difference between withdrawing treatment when we know that death will follow (as when nutrition and hydration are withdrawn) and killing. This suggests that there is a problem with statutes that give unrestricted power to health care agents when the principal lacks decision-making capacity (assuming the inalienability of the right to life). Such statutes allow the agent to authorize the withdrawal of life support from a patient based on (previously given) consent alone. If, as argued above, the inalienability of the right to life implies that consent is sometimes relevant but never alone sufficient to justify killing a person, and if withdrawing life support is normatively equivalent to killing, then statutes should restrict the powers of health care agents.

At least two kinds of cases will be troubling and should be addressed. The first is when the designated health care agent makes a decision that is known to be contrary to what the patient himself would have wanted. The other is when the agent makes a decision that is blatantly contrary to the patient's best interests and not known to be that which the patient himself would have wanted. Qualifications on the powers of health care agents to avoid these two types of situations seem desirable.

I remind readers that I am examining these issues from a limited perspective, namely, consistency with the inalienability of the right to life. I want to end this section by acknowledging a problem in this area not directly bearing on inalienability. The issues surrounding surrogate decision making are complex.[88] But there is a consensus on certain issues. When a patient who currently lacks decision-making capacity has a properly executed advance directive, or when there is clear and convincing evidence of what that patient would want, the proxy acting for that patient should act in accord with that patient's wishes. If there is no advance directive and no evidence of what the patient would want, then the surrogate should decide based on the patient's best interests. Based on best interests alone, the law has allowed surrogates to withdraw life support from patients.[89] But given that and *assuming* that there is no normatively relevant difference between withdrawing and killing, then why not allow a surrogate to choose euthanasia for an incompetent patient who is suffering? The challenge could be put this way: If it is not incompatible with a patient's best interests to withdraw life-sustaining treatment when we know that will lead to death, why is it also not incompatible with that patient's interests to allow euthanasia? This is not relevant to the inalienability of the right to life because consent, which by hypothesis is not present, has no justificatory role. But it is an important question, especially in light of the opinions of the Second and Ninth Circuit Courts discussed above.

Suicide, Euthanasia, and Moral Inalienability

Throughout this chapter I have focused on questions of law and public policy. And I have assumed that a legitimate function of law and public policy is to prevent harm to innocent persons. It is on the basis of this principle, I claim, that the behavior of consenting parties may be restricted, as happens when a right is legally inalienable. I have also tacitly assumed that *unless* the rights or well-being of innocent parties are adversely affected, the law should not restrict the behavior of consenting parties.[90] One of my concerns, then, has been to examine whether there is a plausible normative basis for designating the right to life as inalienable, and then asking whether that precludes allowing voluntary euthanasia and assisted suicide. But there may be moral principles, ones associated with what is roughly known as the Kantian tradition (briefly discussed in the section on "Kantian Defense" in chapter 2), that entail that actions affecting only consenting parties are nevertheless wrong. And such principles may proscribe suicide and voluntary euthanasia. This would render the right to life *morally* inalienable, even if the law should not enforce such a prohibition. In this context, the issue is whether the right to life *is* inalienable, not whether there are adequate normative grounds for so designating it.[91] It is to this possibility that I now turn.

As we saw in chapter 2, Kantians might argue that a possessor of the right to life cannot release others from the obligation to refrain from killing him; consent is not a defense for murder. As Thomas E. Hill, Jr. puts it, to accept a principle of this sort is to hold that the right to life is "like a trustee's rights to preserve something valuable entrusted to him: he has not only a right but a duty to preserve it."[92] As is well known, Kant himself was adamantly opposed to suicide. This suggests, according to Hill, that a Kantian is committed to the following principle: "A morally ideal person will value life as a rational, autonomous agent for its own sake, at least provided that the life does not fall below a certain threshold of gross, irremediable, and uncompensated pain and suffering."[93] As Hill explains, this principle expresses an ideal rather than a duty, and it may conflict with and sometimes be overridden by duties or other ideals. The purpose of the qualification ("provided that . . .") is "to reflect the idea that although the value of rational, autonomous living is not a function of the pleasure and pain it brings, a sufficiently gross level of suffering can undermine that value, making the sufferer incapable of finding that life meaningful or even tolerable."[94] Hill thinks that, in spite of Kant's pronouncements to the contrary, most of us think that suicide is permissible in selected circumstances. Included in these are (1) suicide when human life is no longer possible because (for example) one has a progressive disease inevitably destroying one's ability to function and (2) suicide to end gross and irremediable pain.[95] And the principle Hill articulates would seem to allow suicide in at least these two cases. If Hill's account is a plausible rendition of Kantian ethics, as I think it is, this suggests that the Kantian can hold both that the right to life is inalienable and that suicide is sometimes permissible. One suspects that the permissibility of assisted suicide could be easily derived from this too. But whether the permissibility of voluntary euthanasia would also follow is perhaps less clear.

Ronald Dworkin writes in a similar vein. He believes that all of us are committed to what he calls the sanctity of human life. This implies a commitment to certain attitudes and values. And such a commitment is incompatible with ending human life for frivolous reasons. Deliberately ending human life is a serious matter and requires justification. Dworkin thinks, in fact, that what divides people on certain important moral issues is the way they interpret what a commitment to the sanctity of human life requires of them. This manifests itself most obviously in debates about abortion and euthanasia. "The disagreement that actually divides people [on abortion and euthanasia] is a markedly less polar disagreement about how best to respect a fundamental idea we almost all share in some form: that individual human life is sacred."[96]

Dworkin suggests that there are two controversies about euthanasia.[97] One is whether it is always in the best interests of a patient to keep him alive. It seems that there might be certain cases—for example, when the patient is irreversibly comatose—when the best interests principle does not demand that the patient be kept alive.[98] The other controversy is whether it is wrong to let such a patient die, even if dying is not contrary to his best interests. Some think that it is wrong because respect for the sanctity of human life requires that every effort be made to prolong life. Persons who have taken such a view have been labeled *conservatives*. Because of the value of human life, they think that euthanasia is wrong in all circumstances. People suffering should bear the pain and the unconscious should be cared for until life ends naturally.[99] Opponents of this interpretation think that human contributions are important to the value of human life. When such contributions are no longer possible, for example, because of an irreversible coma, euthanasia is not an insult to the sanctity of human life. Similarly, the life of a patient who is suffering and is riddled with disease does nothing to help realize the wonder of human life.[100] The conservative interpretation of the sanctity of human life holds that life must be preserved no matter what; the opposing view takes account of the "quality of lives."[101]

My point here is not to defend either Hill's or Dworkin's views on these matters. Rather, I want to show that this broadly Kantian tradition can, under certain construals, allow that the inalienability of the right to life is compatible with the permissibility of suicide, assisted suicide, and voluntary euthanasia, though in each case only in selected circumstances. Ending human life for frivolous reasons is, on this account, impermissible; consent alone does not justify killing. The quality of human life must be severely compromised before these life-ending actions are permissible. And whether either account would allow for cases of nonvoluntary euthanasia is an issue that I shall not pursue here. It is worth noting here that the account of rights implicit in this modified Kantian approach is neither the interests conception nor the protected choices conception (discussed in the third section of chapter 2). It appears to be closer to the protected choices account, but when a right is inalienable some choices with respect to that right are not permissible, even for the possessor herself. But the normative point is not to protect the possessor; rather, it is to demonstrate the proper attitude toward the value in question.

SEVEN

Human Organs and Inalienability

There are some things that the law allows one to give away but does not permit one to sell. I know, you're thinking of sex. And, indeed, that is an apt example given the law in many states in the United States. But in this chapter the focus will be on a different case, that of human organs for transplatation—organs that are procured from one human and transplanted into another. Section 274e of the U.S. Public Health Code makes it illegal for anyone to acquire, receive, or otherwise transfer human organs for valuable consideration. Anyone who violates this statute may be fined up to $50,000 and incarcerated for as long as five years. And the National Organ Transplant Act of 1984 makes it a federal crime "for any person to knowingly acquire, receive, or otherwise transfer any human organ for valuable consideration for use in human transplantation if the transfer affects interstate commerce."[1] But, of course, individuals are permitted to donate organs to others. One legal scholar has called this combination of prohibitions and permissions "market inalienability."[2] One type of alienation, *sale*, is forbidden; but another type, *gift*, is allowed.

Introduction

A decade ago, within a period of four months, two popular news magazines published stories concerning the purchase of human organs, stories that created a furor.

The first concerns a man known as Count Ranier Rene Adelmann von Adelmannsfelden, from the former West Germany.[3] Adelmann circulated letters to West Germans whose names he found on public bankruptcy notices. The letter said, in part, "You're broke. You're a social leper, tainted with the legal and social equivalent of AIDS. . . . I offer you a solution founded on logic. Donate your kidney." Adelmann's company, the Association of Organ Donations and Mutual Human Substitution, offered to pay up to $45,000 for a healthy human kidney. The plan was to resell these kidneys to patients in need for $85,000. Adelmann was aware that many people regarded him as a coldhearted businessman. But, he protested, "I'm doing good." The good he professed to be doing was attempting to eliminate, or at least improve, the shortage of available kidneys for transplantation. At the time of his statement (1988), Eurotransplant, Central Europe's official transplant-clearing center, reported that nearly 8000 renal patients each year were placed on a waiting list for a transplant; but typically the center was able to help only 2500.

If the only problem you have with this story is Adelmann's asking price, $85,000, do not despair. Apparently the free market was at work in West Germany. Another individual, Ranier Scherer, described as a Frankfurt businessman, offered an "Asia transplant" package that included round-trip airfare to India, a new kidney, and recovery care, all for the price of $45,000. Scherer planned to buy kidneys from healthy individuals in India, where he would have to pay far less than Adelmann was offering West Germans. Scherer too argued that he was helping people. "Which is better: for me to give a poor guy 20,000 marks, or for him and his two healthy kidneys to be thrown onto the corpse cart after he starves?" Everyone benefits: the person with renal problems who will be free from the rigors of dialysis, the poor person who sells one of his healthy kidneys, and the entrepreneur who makes a profit for arranging the transaction.

The second story was based in England.[4] Among several cases reported in British newspapers was that of a Turkish peasant who sold a kidney to an Englishman for $4400, allegedly because he needed the money to pay for an operation for his daughter. Isn't this what the free market is all about? One man had $4400 and needed a kidney; another man had two healthy kidneys while only one is necessary, and he needed the money. But upon publication of this story, the outcry was loud. One of the most tenacious defenders of the free market, (then) Prime Minister Margaret Thatcher, declared that the sale of any organs of the human body is repugnant. And the World Health Organization has consistently condemned the buying and selling of human organs.[5]

The response to each of these stories in the United States (and throughout the world) was the same: moral outrage at anyone who would either arrange the sale of human organs or attempt to purchase the same. But such outrage is at least initially puzzling. What wrong is done when a voluntary transaction between two parties occurs? And what wrong is done if a third party is compensated for arranging such a transaction? We shall begin by considering the position that such transactions are not wrong and should not be legally prohibited.

The Body, Property Rights, and Alienation

The simplest view on this issue is that people have property rights in their bodies, that property rights are paradigmatically alienable, and therefore people are morally allowed (and should be legally permitted) to alienate body parts. Such freedom would include the right to sell body parts while living, to give them away, to arrange for their sale or donation after death, and perhaps even to sell a life-sustaining body part (such as a heart) thereby bringing about one's own death.

To sustain this view—one that is at home in the libertarian tradition—one might appeal to the work of John Locke. Locke held that a person acquires property rights in that with which he mixes his labor.[6] There are superficial objections to this Lockean account that might be leveled. We might deny that people have property rights in their bodies because they do not mix their labor with their bodies. But on the face of it, it seems silly to debate whether people mix their labor with their own bodies. And in any case, if the appeal is to Locke, it is not relevant whether people mix their labor with their own bodies. For though Locke does indeed hold that an individual has a right in his own person, this is *not* because of his labor. On Locke's view, people have property rights in that with which they mix their labor precisely because they first have rights in their own person. Whether rights in one's own person and rights regarding one's own body are the same is perhaps debatable. But since it is rights in one's own person that Locke writes about, it does not appear that the simple view gains any additional credibility by appealing to the authority of Locke.

Of course, one need not appeal to authority to support the simple view. A defender might argue instead that (1) it is a conceptual truth that property rights are alienable; (2) that rights to and regarding one's own body are property rights; and so therefore (3) rights to and regarding one's own body are alienable. For purposes of clarity regarding (1), we should note that while particular property rights are alienable, the very right to hold property is plausibly regarded as inalienable;[7] perhaps this is because the right to acquire property is based on rights in one's own person. A critic of the simple view may be most inclined to attack premise (2), and it is obviously controversial. But we can, I believe, sidestep the difficult issue of whether rights to and regarding one's own body are best understood as property rights; for even if these rights are so understood, the conclusion, (3), follows only if we endorse (1) as well. And there are good reasons, I think, for denying (1).

Several legal scholars scholars have demonstrated clearly that property rights are not purely alienable. Susan Rose-Ackerman points out, for example, that *gifts* of one's own property are condemned as "fraudulent conveyances" if they are made just before filing for bankruptcy.[8] The rationale for such a restriction is not paternalistic; the aim is to protect the legitimate interests of creditors. Similarly, Stephen Munzer indicates that even if a person owns outright her Victorian house in a city's historic district, regulations may prohibit certain alterations to the facade of that structure.[9] Again the restrictions are not paternalistic; it is the interests of others (most directly, other owners of houses in the historic district) that are protected by such regulations. A defender of the simple view might retort that the human body is not like Victorian houses or gifts one is giving just prior to filing for bankruptcy. But that is not the point. It is rather to deny the truth of premise (1); it is not a conceptual truth that property rights are purely alienable. How the human body should be regarded remains open to debate. And in our society that debate is ongoing. A committee report to the American Medical Association seems to put it correctly when it says that there is "no consensus on the exact nature of an individual's property interest in his . . . own body."[10] All of this suggests that if we can address the issues in this chapter without attempting to resolve whether rights to and regarding one's own body are best understood as property rights, we would be well advised to do so.

Lest I be misunderstood, let me say that in denying the truth of premise (1), I am not suggesting that property rights are inalienable. The categories are more numerous and more complex than just alienable and inalienable. Rose-Ackerman usefully calls attention to several other categories, including what she calls "modified inalienability" and "modified property."[11]

Even if the simplest case for defending the sale of human organs among consenting parties fails, it does not follow that prohibiting such transactions is justifiable. And in a country that prizes freedom, it is not unreasonable to hold that the burden of proof is on those who advocate such a prohibition. Let us turn, then, to defenses of the legal prohibition of organ sales.

Harm and the Sale of Organs

The least controversial use of the power of the state to restrict the freedom of its citizens appeals to the harm principle: the state may restrict a person's freedom in order to prevent that person from harming others. Applying this principle to the issue under consideration, some may argue that prohibiting the sale of human organs is justifiable because such a practice would harm some, namely, those who sold their organs.

But what harm comes to someone who sells an organ? The organ most likely to be sold by a living human being is a kidney. People have two kidneys but can function well with only one. The first transplant of a kidney from one living person to another occurred in 1954 between identical twins. Harm done to living kidney donors must be understood in terms of *risks* to which they are exposed. Though it is not uncommon for health care practitioners to subject consenting persons to risky procedures, normally they do so only when the parties themselves are apt to receive therapeutic benefits from the intervention. And a living kidney donor is not expected to receive any direct medical benefits from such a donation. What are the risks that a living kidney donor undergoes? Such a person undergoes major surgery—the removal of a kidney—and is thereby subjected to the risks therein. These include postoperative complications, including death in rare cases. In addition, living kidney donors are less able to cope with kidney disease should it occur; they are at increased risk of hypertension; and they may experience negative psychological reactions.[12] These risks are certainly not insignificant; and when one adds that those undergoing the risks will receive no therapeutic benefits in return, it is at least understandable why the harm principle might be invoked to prohibit such exchanges.

There are, however, apparently insurmountable problems with justifying the prohibition of organ sales by an appeal to the harm principle. First, we should note that this would not prohibit all sales of body parts. Males can contribute semen to sperm banks for compensation without any risks; and females can contribute eggs with minimal risks. The U.S. Public Health Code does not consider semen or eggs to be human organs for the purposes of section 274e. But one wonders if this is not merely ad hoc. Moreover, some hold that there is a normatively important distinction between human products that are replaceable through regeneration (such as blood, bone marrow, and skin) and those that are not (such as a kidney), and that only removal of the latter is harmful to the contributor.[13] To place such normative weight on this distinction, however, seems strained; for in varying degrees contributors of blood, bone marrow, and skin do experience discomfort and are put at some minimal risk.

A second problem with the argument is that prohibiting organ sales will likely cause harm, and may well cause more harm than it prevents. *If* allowing the sale of organs would increase the available supply, then prohibiting such sales would presumably mean that some who would have secured a kidney will not.[14] In addition, some have argued that would-be sellers will be harmed by such a prohibition. Many say that if the sale of human organs is allowed, then the overwhelming majority of those who will contribute an organ for pay will be the poor and impoverished. And while this strikes some as undesirable, others have pointed out that banning payments to contributors who desperately need money deprives them of options, options they would prefer to have.[15] If being deprived of such an option is harmful to those who might choose to exercise it, then prohibiting organ sales damages both potential recipients and potential contributors.

Third, banning organ sales because of the harm to contributors seems inconsistent with both *judgments* we make about other cases and with *behavior* that we allow. If someone not merely risks her own life for others but rather gives her own life to save others, we do not condemn her; on the contrary, she is admirable and worthy of our greatest praise. An example of such a person would be someone who gave up her place on a overcrowded life raft so that others could live.[16] And many professions that society allows—and even encourages—are very risky for those who enter them, including law enforcement, the military, and mining.[17] It seems odd, at best, to prohibit the sale of organs because of the risks to would-be sellers, while at the same time allowing cities, countries, and companies to conduct advertisement campaigns that actually encourage people to enter the risky professions noted above. And this is to say nothing of campaigns designed to encourage people to smoke. Of course, these examples are not from medicine, a field historically committed to beneficence and the well-being of patients. So defenders of the ban against organ sales might say that it is especially important not to allow health care professionals to subject persons to risks when it is neither likely nor intended that they will receive a therapeutic benefit in return. But even here society does not consistently prohibit such activity. Phase I clinical trials of chemotherapeutic drugs are designed ultimately to determine when such agents are toxic to humans. Yet society allows people to subject themselves freely and knowingly to these risks and allows researchers to recruit subjects.[18] Indeed, any nontherapeutic research on human subjects may place persons at risk with no expectation of therapeutic benefit.

There is a fourth problem with prohiting organ sales because of the harm that it might do to contributors, and it is by far the most obvious and most telling. If harm does come to a living organ contributor, it is *not the payment* to the contributor that causes the harm; rather, it is the removal of the organ from the body. So if risk or harm to the contributor justifies prohibiting the sale of human organs, it will also justify the free donation of the same.[19] Yet, not only does our society not prohibit such donation, but it also overtly encourages it. And this brings us back to the original oddity: Why is it permissible (legally and morally) to donate organs to another, but it is impermissible to be paid for such a contribution? Is market inalienability defensible?

Before continuing this discussion of these normative issues, let us pause and provide a context for this debate. Why, today, are we debating whether it is permissible for persons to sell their own organs?

The Policy of the United States and Its Problems

As noted earlier, in the United States it is illegal to buy or sell human organs. The punishment—imprisonment for as many as five years and a fine for as much as $50,000—is aptly described as severe.

Some human organs for transplantation may be acquired from *living* contributors without causing them excessive harm. These include a kidney, bone marrow, skin, blood, and in rare cases a portion of an adult liver to be given to a child.[20] Human organs required for living are obtained only from cadavers. These include the heart, pancreas, lungs, whole livers, and others. In the United States, whether organs are obtained from living contributors or cadavers, the *sole source* is from voluntary contribution; we may refer to this as "the giving policy."[21]

Restricting ourselves for now to cadaver organs, the main tenets of the giving policy are contained in the Uniform Anatomical Gift Act (1968).[22] This act mandates that the sole source of cadaver organs for transplantation is from persons who, prior to their deaths, agreed to contribute, or from the next-of-kin who agree to contribute the newly deceased's organs. Today people can communicate their desire to be organ donors by signing a donor card and by indicating this on the driver's license. Two positive features of the giving policy are that it respects individual autonomy and that it gives people an opportunity to perform significant acts of generosity. In the United States, however, the giving policy is not working well; too few cadaver organs are obtained. As of early 1999, the waiting list for organs (in the United States) had reached 65,000. And it is estimated that as many as 4000 people per year die, waiting for organs to become available.

There are no doubt many reasons why there is a shortage of cadaver organs for transplantation in the United States. One limiting factor is that the pool of potential donors is small. Although there are more than two million deaths in the United States every year, with few exceptions cadaver organs are obtained only from individuals who who have been declared dead by the criterion of whole brain death.[23] And less than 1 percent of the total deaths in the United States are deaths by the standard of whole brain death alone. Moreover, not all individuals declared brain dead are suitable donors; some are disqualified because their organs have deteriorated or may transmit a fatal disease to recipients.

Another factor that contributes to the shortage of cadaver organs for transplantation is the family of potential contributors.[24] Though an individual may have specified the desire that any of his usable organs be procured upon his death, in fact, organs will not be procured without the permission of the next-of-kin. The reasons for this are principally practical: if organs were procured against the wishes of the next-of-kin, the harm done (to the cause of organ transplantation in general) by the resulting negative publicity would likely outweigh the good that might come from procurement of those organs.

But why might families refuse to donate organs if the newly deceased had specified a desire to donate? One important factor here is that the giving policy requires society to approach families at the worst possible time. The best source of cadaver organs is relatively young, healthy individuals who have received serious head injuries, often in automobile accidents. Since such deaths are quite unexpected, families are likely to be far more distraught than they would be when death is more predictable. A second factor that may adversely affect organ donation is the general attitude that people have about the practice of transplantation. A recent study[25] to try to determine why some people will not donate organs revealed the following: many (especially members of minority groups) *mistrust* the medical establishment; there is much *cynicism* about how organs are allocated (many believing that celeberties and persons of wealth get preferential treatment); some surprisingly have doubts about whether organ transplants even work; and some have misconceptions (such as whether contributing families must pay and whether a conventional funeral is still possible). Perhaps public education can diminish the mistrust, cynicism, and misconceptions. That, indeed, was one of the purposes of the so-called required request law that went into effect in 1991. This legislation directs any hospital receiving federal funds to inform family members of seriously ill patients that they have the option of donating organs upon death. It was hoped that if trained professionals approached families in a sensitive way, organ donations would increase significantly. It is not clear, however, that this hope is being realized.

If the supply of available cadaver organs cannot be sufficiently increased by tinkering with the giving policy, then it would appear that society has only two other ways of attacking the problem. One option is to expand the pool of potential contributors by allowing the procurement of organs from some who do not meet the criterion of whole brain death. The second option is to adopt a policy for procuring cadaver organs that is different from the giving policy.

Concerning the first option, we have already mentioned one way of expanding the pool of potential contributors that has been debated, namely, using persons who have died a "cardiac death," where the time of death is predictable (such as when life-support is removed from a patient). Another way of expanding the pool is to alter the definition of "death."[26] According to the accepted definition, an individual is dead who has sustained irreversible cessation of circulatory and respiratory functions *or* who has sustained irreversible cessation of all functions of the entire brain, including both the higher brain and the brain stem. Death declared by the latter criterion is called "whole brain death." Some individuals have permanently lost or never had higher brain functioning but still have an active brain stem. Included here are individuals in a persistent vegetative state and anencephalic infants. Neither is dead by the accepted account, but neither will ever again be conscious. Thus, some have held that either state is experientially equivalent to death and so expanding the definition is appropriate.

Here we shall not discuss further the first option—that of expanding the pool of potential contributors by procuring organs from individuals other than the brain dead. It is not that this option is unimportant; it clearly is significant. But only the second option—looking at alternatives to the giving policy—is relevant to concerns about inalienable rights. To that option we now turn.

Alternatives to the Giving Policy

Some have characterized the giving policy as one in which a person must "opt in." The presumption is that a person is not a donor unless she specifically opts in. There are two key features to this policy: one assumption is that it is the individual herself who has the right to determine what shall be done with her body after death; the other is the presumption against donation unless the individual specifies otherwise. Altering either of these features would create a substantially different social policy for procuring cadaver organs.

We could alter the first feature of the giving policy by denying that individuals have the right to determine what shall be done with their bodies after death; instead, it is the state that has this power. The state could then approve of the routine salvaging of any useful organs from the newly deceased. Such a position might appropriately be dubbed *the taking policy*. In effect, such a policy restricts the autonomy of individuals more severely than any other alternative. I am not aware of any country that officially has such a policy, and it seems clear that such a policy is neither normatively desirable nor feasible in the United States.

We could alter the second feature by reversing the presumption; we could presume that the individual wants to donate her organs unless she has told us otherwise; the individual must "opt out." This position has been dubbed *the policy of presumed consent.*[27] It is also referred to as "escheatage"; the idea is that "if the decedent has not specified his desires to the contrary his body will escheat to the state."[28] As many scholars have pointed out, a number of European countries have adopted a policy of presumed consent.[29] And such a policy has a number of advantages: it will increase the supply of cadaver organs more than any alternative, except the taking policy; the system can be efficient and not too costly; and it still respects individual autonomy in that it allows individuals to opt out. (And presumably such a policy will allow parents to decide for children under the age of 18.) But in spite of these advantages, one suspects that the policy of presumed consent is not politically feasible in the United States. There is some indication that this policy is not working as well as expected in some of the countries in which it has been adopted because hosptial personnel are unwilling to harvest the organs of the newly deceased (even though they have the right to do so) without the consent of relatives.[30] In any case, this policy is not pertinent to the alienation of rights and so will not be discussed further here.

There is one other feature of the giving policy that is addressed by neither the taking policy nor the policy of presumed consent. The giving policy seems to assume that providing incentives to potential contributors is either unnecessary or morally inappropriate. Given the current shortage of cadaver organs in the United States, we might here put aside the possibility that incentives are unnecessary.[31] Apparently, defenders of the giving policy hold that the provision of incentives—or at least certain types of incentives—is morally inappropriate. In order to uncover and discuss this assumption, it will be helpful if we first discuss some policies for obtaining cadaver organs that do provide incentives to potential contributors (and/or their families).

Let us call any policy that assumes that the supply of cadaver organs will be adequate (or will be as good as we can do while still respecting autonomy) only if potential contributors are provided with incentives *the trading policy*. Cadaver organs are something with value, and society must be willing to exchange something else of value if it is to generate an adequate supply of such organs. But what might society exchange for access to usable organs upon death? Two possibilities spring to mind.[32]

One version of the trading policy might be called *trade for access*. With the implementation of this policy, society pools all cadaver organs for transplantation and allows individuals to have access to these organs (when medical need dictates) only if they have themselves previously agreed to be contributors. Given that access to cadaver organs for transplantation is valuable, possibly life-saving, this policy provides individuals with a self-interested incentive to agree to contribute any usable organs upon death.[33] This policy has an intuitive appeal to our sense of fairness. Why should individuals receive the benefits of a system if they are unwilling to bear their share of the burdens? But not only is it likely that people of the United States lack the political will to institute such a system; in addition, there seem to be serious practical problems. When, in such a system, must individuals declare their willingness to be organ contributors? If we say that people may declare their wishes any time, this will defeat the purpose of increasing the supply of healthy, usable organs. For individuals can wait until they have been diagnosed with a medical problem for which organ transplantation is an effective therapy before declaring their willingness to be contributors. This suggests, then, that we must set a cut off point. But where? We could say that each individual must decide whether to be an organ contributor when he or she turns 18-years-old. But this seems unwise. Many of us are not sufficiently mature at that age, and most of us made decisions at that age that we are glad did not have a lasting impact on our lives. But then at what age does one require an irrevocable decision? Twenty? Thirty? This practical problem seems difficult to resolve.

Another version of the trading policy might be called *trade for pay*. As the name implies, this policy provides potential contributors with a monetary incentive to contribute organs. For now, we will ignore the issue of paying living contributors; our focus will continue to be on the acquisition of cadaver organs. At least two versions of the trade for pay policy are possible. According to one version, we pay the potential contributor *now* in exchange for the right to procure any useful organs upon her death. On this version of the policy, society has a contract with the potential donor that overrides any rights that her family might have regarding the disposition of her body at death. According to the other version of the trade for pay policy, an individual signs a document indicating her desire to donate any useful organs at death. The document identifies a beneficiary—possibly the individual's estate—to whom a modest payment will be made *after* that individual's death *if* any organs are procured. This arrangement is usually referred to as a "futures contract."

Of these two versions of the trade for pay policy, it should be clear that only the futures contract is at all practical. The former policy—paying potential contributors now—would be far too costly. Adopting this policy would result in paying many people from whom organs would never be procured because most will not be brain dead only with support systems being continued, and many will have medical conditions at the time of their deaths which preclude them from being organ donors. Here, then, we will discuss only the policy of futures contracts; for it authorizes payments to relatives only when organs are actually procured from the newly deceased. We will begin by discussing some of the considerations cited by defenders of this policy.

The Case for Futures Contracts

Defenders of a policy permitting futures contracts begin with the failure of the giving policy in the United States. In a country of great wealth, many people are dying or suffering needlessly. The giving policy, which relies exclusively on altruism, provides prospective donors no incentive to give. And the policy of presumed consent is criticized because it too provides no positive incentives to people to permit either their own or their loved one's organs to be harvested, and because it fails to respect personal autonomy.[34]

What we can learn from the other systems, defenders of futures contracts argue, is that human beings require economic incentives to perform significant tasks. As Gregory Crespi puts it, opponents of commercialization "fail to concede the brute fact that human behavior is much more responsive to prospects for financial gain than it is to appeals to altruism."[35] Lloyd Cohen is even more forceful, claiming that *all* parties involved need financial incentives in order for the system to be maximally beneficial. He writes:

> Wherever the blockage, now or in the future, the financial incentive will flush it out. Whether the problem is people's reluctance to confront their own mortality, relatives' reluctance to authorize the dismemberment of their loved ones, doctors' reluctance to harvest organs without the approval of relatives, or hospitals' reluctance to establish appropriate procedures, the creation and legal enforcement of property rights in the decedent's body will bring all incentives into line.[36]

The claims made here are a bit confusing because they seem to presuppose different policies. If doctors are provided financial incentives to harvest organs without the approval of relatives, this suggests that the contract signed by the contributor is binding and the next of kin need not be consulted. But if financial incentives are supplied so that relatives will overcome their reluctance to allow body parts to be extracted from a loved one, then this suggests that loved ones must be consulted. Which is it?

Making a contract to allow the harvesting of any usable organs binding regardless of the wishes of the next of kin has an obvious advantage. People believe that they have the right to determine the ultimate fate of their body parts after they die, just as they have the right to disperse their property through a will. It is upsetting to learn that someone else can exercise veto power, thereby preventing one from being a cadaver organ donor. Here I shall not understand a futures contract as being binding regardless of the wishes of the next of kin. There are two reasons for this. First, if such a contract were binding, then it is not obvious that financial incentives are needed at all. We could simply take the Uniform Anatomical Gift Act and enforce the provision that the wishes of an invididual who has signed appropriate documents cannot be overridden by relatives. It is certainly not obvious—though of course it is possible—that *many* more individuals will agree to be organ contributors upon death simply because their estate will be enhanced modestly by their doing so. If we assume that such a program would significantly increase the number of organ contributors, we must assume that most individuals are *strongly* motivated by a desire to improve modestly the financial prospects of their next of kin but motivated very little, if at all, to provide lifesaving benefits for strangers. It is not obvious that such an assumption is warranted. Second, as noted earlier, even in countries with a policy of presumed consent, health care practitioners are reluctant to harvest organs against the wishes of the next of kin. It is a brute fact—demonstrated dramatically in Sophocles' play, *Antigone*—that many people believe that they have an obligation to dispose of the body of a newly deceased loved one. Actively preventing relatives from disposing of their loved ones' bodies as they see fit is something that most societies are just not willing to do. And a signed contract is not likely to change that.

I restrict myself, then, to a futures contract that allows the next of kin to decide what shall be done with the newly deceased's body, but provides two types of incentives for allowing the harvesting of any usable organs: (i) evidence (in the form of a validly signed contract) that the newly deceased wanted to contribute his organs; and (ii) a modest financial incentive not to override the wishes of the deceased. How much money will be provided is a detail that need not be considered here, though I note that Cohen suggested $5000 for each major organ used.[37]

Are there any other factors in addition to the provision of incentives that support the adoption of a futures market? Defenders of this policy are quick to point out that some of the usual objections leveled against it can be answered. One criticism is that allowing a market in cadaver organs will drive out altruism. If some are paid for their contributions, the critics say, no one will donate freely. The retort, however, is that altruism and the free market can exist side by side.[38] Permitting the sale of organs (or anything else) does not mandate it. Though many people sell their old automobiles when they are ready for a new one, some donate theirs to a charity. And though hospitals employ many people, volunteers still work many hours in those institutions.

Another reputed advantage of the policy of futures contracts concerns the likely behavior of contributors. In the area of human reproduction, when persons sell sperm or eggs for artificial insemination, they are less likely to have an interest in what becomes of the offspring than are those who have donated reproductive cells.[39] It is reasonable, then, to suspect that those who contribute organs for money rather than from love will be less likely to try to identify and contact the recipients of the organs. And such contact can create problems, even harassment. The problem in citing this as an advantage of a market system, however, is that it seems most plausible when we are talking about *living* contributors. Indeed, the person making this point, Cohen, cites as an example a living contributor of a kidney. But the policy in question applies only to cadaver organs. So if the point holds, it must be the case that relatives of organ contributors will be less likely to contact recipients if they have received payment for those organs. Perhaps this is true. But the analogy with contributing reproductive cells is too far removed to be convincing.

Many fear that once payments for cadaver organs are introduced, those same organs will be allocated based on the ability to pay. Some defenders of the policy of futures contracts also favor *distributing* organs according to free market principles;[40] but such a position is atypical. By far the more common claim is that the methods of acquisition and allocation can be kept separate, and that a futures contract policy need not lead to allocating cadaver organs according to the ability to pay.[41]

It is interesting that recently the Council on Ethical and Judicial Affairs of the American Medical Association approved of financial incentives (in the form of a futures contract) for the acquisition of cadaver organs for transplantation. But the Council added these five qualifications:[42] (i) it is not ethical to pay living contributors for organs; (ii) only the potential contributor, and not his or her family, may make the contract to secure payment for cadaveric organs; (iii) any financial incentive should be of moderate value; (iv) payment to relatives should occur only after organs have been retrieved and judged medically suitable for transplantation; and (v) financial incentives should play no part in the allocation of organs for transplantation. It seems fair to say that the canonical form of the policy of futures contracts includes these qualifications.

Factors Relevant in Assessing the Policy of Futures Contracts

The motivation for adopting a policy of futures contracts is to increase the supply of cadaver organs available for transplantation. To achieve this goal, defenders of the policy believe that incentives must be provided. The policy is designed to influence two groups. First, it is hoped that society's adoption of this policy will increase the number of families who agree to allow organs to be retrieved from the newly deceased; these individuals will have a financial incentive to abide by the wishes of their loved ones. And second, it is hoped that this policy will prompt more people to agree to be organ contributors by signing a contract; the incentives for doing so are to increase the chances that one's wishes will be honored posthumously and to leave one's family slightly better off. Will this policy accomplish these ends?

Determining what consequences are likely to ensue if the United States were to honor futures contracts is clearly a complex empirical issue. The best that we can do here is to indicate what questions must be addressed in order to reach a reasonable conclusion. I suggest that the following four sets of questions are especially pertinent.

1. How common is it today to have cases in which a person has agreed to be an organ donor (on his driver's license and/or a donor card) and has usable organs but his next of kin refuses to allow those organs to be retrieved? Since futures contracts are aimed primarily at influencing the behavior of the newly deceased's relatives, we need to know to what extent that behavior is the source of the problem.

2. Of all the cases where the next of kin refuses to allow organs to be harvested in spite of the wishes of the deceased, how many will be altered because of the monetary reward? Even if this does have a major impact, some worry that we will be producing good results for bad reasons. If people will allow the wishes of their loved ones to be honored only if there is money in it for them, this is disconcerting. On the other hand, if a principal reason that relatives do not allow organs to be harvested from their loved ones is the emotional trauma triggered by an unexpected death, then we should not expect financial incentives to have much efficacy.

3. How many who have agreed to donate their organs in the current (giving) system will sign a futures contract? Defenders of futures contracts seem to assume that everyone who agreed to donate will also sign a futures contract. And perhaps that is true. But it is possible that some will be put off by the commercialization and the thought that their relatives need a monetary incentive to abide by their wishes.

4. How many who have not and will not agree to donate their organs in the current system will decide to contribute by signing a futures contract? Presumably, individuals motivated by the desire to help the seriously ill will have agreed to donate in the current system. So any additional contributors will be those prompted by a desire to help their families. But if the monetary reward to the family is modest, as most propose, it makes one doubtful that many more individuals will be prompted to become

organ contributors. Moreover, if people are aware that for any given individual the probability is very low that she will die in a way that will allow her organs to be procured for transplantation, then the efficacy of the additional incentive will be minimal.

Experience alone can enable us to answer these questions. This suggests that if we are to have a social policy based on accurate information, it would be desirable if we had the requisite empirical knowledge to answer the set of questions listed above. In the United States, this would be best achieved if some state or states adopted the policy of futures contracts. And it appears that this is likely to happen. Columnist Ellen Goodman has written recently about plans in the state of Pennsylvania to pay families $300 toward funeral expenses when organs of a loved one have been donated.[43] (I note in passing that this sum is considerably less than the $5000 per organ mentioned by Cohen.) If Pennsylvania adopts the qualifications recommended by the American Medical Association, then we will indeed have a state that has implemented the canonical form of the futures contract policy. One hopes that with guidance from the social sciences, careful empirical studies will be carried out in Pennsylvania to determine answers to the above questions, just as one hopes that much can be learned from the impact of legalizing assisted suicide by studying the effects of doing so in Oregon.

One other issue might be worth exploring in this context. Even if, as defenders of futures contracts suppose, incentives for prospective contributors and/or the next of kin are needed to increase the supply of organs for transplantation, it does not follow that *financial* incentives are either necessary or the most effective. It is at least possible that some other type of incentive would be equally or more efficacious. Perhaps public recognition or a public show of gratitude would be a potent incentive. Exactly what form this might take is difficult to say. One occasionally sees inspiring stories in newspapers about organ donation, but we cannot count on this as a source of public recognition; for as organ donation becomes more common, journalists are apt to regard the story as an "old" one not worth pursuing. Perhaps some kind of "wall of fame" in hospitals or something of this sort would do the job. Regardless of the form, the idea seems worth exploring.

One thing should be clear. Adopting a policy of futures contracts does not involve alienation in the usual sense. The possessor of the relevant rights, the newly deceased, is not the person who is paid for the organs. Payment is made to the next of kin, and in all likelihood many who agree to this do so only to increase the chances that their wishes regarding the disposal of their bodies after death will be followed. They are simply trying to make it more likely that what is permitted to happen and what they want to happen *will* in fact happen.

Alienation and Living Organ Contributors

One objection to allowing futures contracts has not been discussed yet: if a society adopts the policy of futures contracts, this will lead to paying *living* contributors for their organs; and the latter is wrong. This is an objection that is apparently taken seriously; for two prominent proponents of futures markets have gone out of their way to emphasize that their proposals do not allow the sale of organs from living contributors.[44] But why prohibit the sale of human organs from one living person to another? It is commonly said that such a practice will lead to the exploitation of the poor. It is clear that this is the point that Lloyd Cohen has in mind when he stipulates that his proposal will disallow sales between living persons. He says that "because there will be no acquisition of organs from live donors, it does not raise the spectre of exploiting the poor."[45] We will discuss the point about exploitation soon. First, though, let us examine the general structure of the objection.

Permitting futures contracts will *lead to* permitting sales of organs between living persons, the objection goes. Implicit in this objection are two claims: (i) that permitting one practice will lead to permitting a second and significantly different practice; and (ii) that it is normatively undesirable for society to allow the second practice.

Claim (i) invokes the well-known slippery-slope (or wedge) argument. But there are at least two different ways to understand this argument,[46] differing concerning how to understand 'lead to.' According to the *logical version* of the slippery-slope argument, "X leads to Y" means that Y follows logically from X; that is, if we accept X, then logically we must accept Y. According to the *empirical version* of the slippery-slope argument, "X leads to Y" means that Y follows X as a likely causal consequence; as a matter of empirical fact, people's adopting (or approving of) X will cause people to adopt (or approve of) Y. For now, I shall put aside the logical version of this argument; I return to it later. Understanding claim (i) in terms of the empirical version of the argument, then, we can see that one way to respond to the objection is to question the relevant empirical claim. What evidence is there to show that adopting a policy of futures contracts will lead society to adopt a policy allowing living individuals to sell their organs? Indeed, in the absence of any other society going through this process, it is hard to know what sort of evidence could be adduced in support of claim (i).

Claim (ii) asserts that it is morally undesirable for one living person to sell an organ to another for transplantation. One could challenge this claim too; one could assert that such exchanges, if engaged in by parties who are free and adequately informed, should be permitted. That is the position taken by one defender of futures contracts, Richard Epstein.[47] But, as noted earlier, two proponents of futures contracts, Cohen and Crespi, cite as an advantage of their proposals that they do not allow organ sales between living persons.[48] Cohen and Crespi, then, effectively concede the truth of claim (ii). Why is there this disagreement between Epstein, on the one hand, and Cohen and Crespi, on the other?

One suspects that one of the reasons that Epstein approves of organ sales between living persons is that he endorses the logical version of the slippery-slope argument. Think of the *positive* features associated with futures contracts: they (allegedly) provide people with an incentive to contribute their organs; they provide relatives with an incentive not to override the wishes of the newly deceased; they will increase the supply of organs for transplantation; and they promote autonomy by allowing freedom of exchange. These same positive features seem to be true of the practice of permitting organ sales between living persons (except for the second feature, which concerns only organs procured from the deceased). So if those features provide a strong case for allowing futures contracts, consistency suggests that sales between living persons must be permitted too. There are only two ways to avoid this conclusion.

One is to deny that all of the positive features that characterize futures contracts are also associated with a policy that permits sales between living persons; the other is to grant that the positive features are present, but to argue that allowing organ sales between living persons has additional, *negative* features associated with it, ones powerful enough to justify prohibition. It is apparently this latter line of argument that Cohen and Crespi endorse. But why? What are the additional, negative factors?

Cohen and Crespi hold that permitting organ sales between living persons has a significant moral risk associated with it that is not present in a policy that allows only futures contracts. One possibility is this: they may hold that in all sales of organs between living persons, necessarily one of the parties (presumably, the seller) has a defect in voluntariness or has inadequate information. Either of these conditions would render the consent of the seller inadequate, less than genuine. But how could one credibly establish that *all* such transactions necessarily have one of these defects? It is hard to imagine what sort of evidence could be proffered to support such a claim. Let us remind ourselves that with respect to *living* organ contributors, Cohen and Crespi are defending the status quo: living persons may donate some of their organs, but they may not sell them. As noted earlier, this is what is called "market inalienability." How might this be defended? Given that it seems implausible to say that all such sales but not gifts involve a defect in the voluntariness or information of the seller, what can be said? Three possible strategies come to mind.

The first strategy concedes that while *some* sales of organs between living persons are such that both the seller and the buyer have entered into the relationship voluntarily and with adequate knowledge, for *many* such exchanges this will not be the case. And often when the relationship is not entered into voluntarily and with adequate information, one of the parties will be affected adversely. If society could determine in advance which proposed sales involved defective consent, it could prohibit only those. But this cannot be determined in advance; society has no reliable criteria for picking out this subset of cases. Prohibiting all such exchanges is justified, then, because of the prevalence of cases involving defective consent.

The second strategy grants that organ sales between living persons can be entered into voluntarily and with adequate knowledge, and allows that when there are defects in consent society may be able to identify these in advance. But this strategy says that while some such exchanges are mutually advantageous, many are not. And society cannot easily determine in advance which exchanges will be mutually advantageous and which will not. So to prevent exchanges that are disadvantageous to one of the parties, all such exchanges may be prohibited.

The first strategy is committed to *soft* paternalism; it prohibits certain types of exchanges because a substantial number of those exchanges adversely affects one of the parties and that party's consent to participate in the exchange is defective either in voluntariness or knowledge. This strategy seems promising in providing a defense of market inalienability (regarding human organs) that does not rest on hard paternalism; but it faces one major challenge. Defenders of this strategy must explain why problems with consent arise only when organs are sold but not when they are donated. For if the same problems arise with donation, consistency requires that it too should be proscribed. And if proponents of this strategy say that the "lure" of money is what makes the seller's consent defective, then they must explain why other sales that one may later come to regret are not prohibited too (such as the sale of the family homestead, one's collection of baseball cards, or semen or eggs). It is not clear how these problems will be addressed.

The second strategy is not one that can be endorsed in this book because it appears to be committed to *hard* paternalism. If exchanges that are not (always? typically?) mutually advantageous are prohibited, even though both parties to the exchange are participating freely and with adequate knowledge, then the goal apparently is to protect one of the parties from making a decision that is contrary to his best interests. Since I wish to find a ground for inalienable rights that is not based on hard paternalism, I do not consider this strategy here.

That brings us to the third strategy. According to this view, even if the exchanges involved in the sale of human organs are voluntary, knowledgeable, and mutually advantageous, they ought to be prohibited to avoid the moral risk that is incurred if they are permitted. But what is this risk? The moral risk that Cohen and Crespi have in mind is the potential exploitation of the poor. Cohen specifically says that one of the strengths of his defense of futures contracts is that it avoids certain ethical pitfalls associated with other proposals; for example, because his proposal does not allow sales of organs between living persons, "it does not raise the spectre of exploiting the poor."[49] But if an exchange is advantageous to both parties and has been entered into voluntarily and is knowledgeable by both parties, can it still be exploitative? Here one suspects that Epstein will answer in the negative, but that Cohen and Crespi will answer in the affirmative. This tells us that defenders of this third strategy need to accomplish at least two tasks: first, they need to develop an account of exploitation that allows for the possibility of consensual, mutually advantageous exploitation; and second, they need to show that society is justified in legally prohibiting mutually advantageous, consensual exchanges *because* they are exploitative. These tasks will not be easy to complete.

Here I shall not attempt to complete the two tasks needed to make the third strategy work; that would take us too far afield. Instead, I simply note that recent work of Alan Wertheimer is pertinent here. He has developed an extensive account of exploitation, and one that allows for the possibility of mutually advantageous, consensual exploitation.[50] Wertheimer distinguishes among many different types of exploitation, but the unifying idea is that one party takes *unfair advantage* of another. This requires an extensive account of what makes a transaction unfair and what makes an exchange consensual, and Wertheimer has done this hard work.[51] But even having done all of this work, Wertheimer acknowledges that serious questions remain about the moral weight and moral force of exploitation.[52] Even if a relationship is exploitative, that does not automatically tell us how society should respond to it. For if we invoke the coercive apparatus of the law only reluctantly, we may have to acknowledge that some relationships are exploitative but still should be *legally* permitted. Wertheimer himself, for example, when discussing contracts between surrogate mothers and infertile couples, suggests that even if such relationships are exploitative, it is not clear that society is justified in prohibiting them.[53] Successfully completing this third strategy, then, is a daunting assignment. But we are not without rich intellectual resources needed to complete it.

Conclusion

The United States relies on donation as the source of human organs for transplantation. But given the current shortage of organs for transplantation in the United States, a reexamination of this policy and alternatives is called for. Recent attempts to increase the quantity of organs obtained within the giving policy do not appear to be achieving great results. And if, as I assume, the policy of presumed consent is not politically feasible in the United States, then it is natural to wonder if the introduction of incentives is necessary to increase the supply of organs.

A policy of futures contracts allows living, competent individuals to sign a document indicating their desire to contribute organs upon death. While the individuals themselves receive no monetary reward, this policy specifies that their designated beneficiary will receive a modest sum *if* any organs are procured and used for transplantation. This policy, it is hoped, will make it more likely that the autonomous wishes of the newly deceased will be honored because her family has a financial incentive not to override them. And this will then increase the supply of cadaver organs available for transplantation.

A significant objection to the policy of futures contracts is that this is the first step of a journey that will lead to allowing organ sales between living persons. There are two versions of this objection. One version holds that organ sales between living persons will follow causally because the adoption of futures contracts overcomes a significant psychological barrier which, when hurdled, makes other barriers much easier to clear. But unless empirical evidence is offered in support of these claims, this objection should not stop society from trying futures contracts. The other version of the objection says that permitting organ sales between living persons follows logically from permitting futures contracts; the positive values promoted by the latter are promoted by the former as well. If we are to allow futures contracts while still agreeing with the current laws in the United States concerning *living* organ contributors—namely, that gifts are permitted but sales are not—then we must be able to answer the logical version of this objection.

The most obvious way to defeat the logical version of the objection is to show that there are negative moral features associated with the sale of organs between living persons that are not present when *only* futures contracts are allowed, and that these features may warrant prohibiting sales between living persons. We identified three different strategies for responding to the logical version of the objection in this way. The most promising of these strategies held that permitting organ sales between living persons will allow for the exploitation of the poor; but no such risk is present if monetary incentives are permitted only in futures contracts. In order to execute this strategy successfully, defenders of market inalienability must do at least three things: they must develop an account of exploitation that allows for the possibility that mutually advantageous, fully consensual exchanges are nevertheless exploitative; they must show that organ sales between living persons are likely to be exploitative in this way; and they must show that society is justified in legally prohibiting exploitative exchanges. I am hopeful that this complex line of argument can be developed.

If this strategy for blocking the logical version of the objection does not work—and if no other strategy is available—then the peculiar idea of "market inalienability" (regarding human organs) appears to be indefensible. In that event, consistency would require society either to *prohibit* both gifts and sales or to *permit* each.

I do not know if allowing futures contracts will significantly increase the supply of cadaver organs for transplantation in the United States. I am somewhat skeptical that it will; but it is worth a try. If the impact of introducing such a market does not prove to be great, then we may have to deal with the problem in a less systematic, piecemeal approach. Increasing the number of people who agree to contribute and decreasing the number of relatives who refuse to honor the wishes of the newly deceased are but two things to be done. Perhaps we should also look at providing individuals and families with incentives other than financial ones, such as public recognition and gratitude. Perhaps we will be able to overcome the ethical risks associated with procuring organs from nonheart-beating cadavers. Improvement in immunosuppressive drugs may decrease organ rejection and thus decrease the need for multiple transplants in the same person. And maybe the recently developed cloning technology can be used to "grow" human organs in other species, assuming that there are no decisive ethical objections to doing so. However all this plays out, I doubt that markets in cadaver organs alone will solve the problem.

EIGHT

Concluding Remarks

No exhaustive list of inalienable rights has been provided here. Instead, I have tried to show why it is plausible to say that within a morally justified legal system, some rights are inalienable.

Inalienable rights may not be waived or transferred by their possessors. According to my analysis, the consent of the possessor alone is not sufficient to justify others in infringing inalienable rights. Some philosophers have given a broader account of inalienable rights, holding that if it is ever morally justifiable to deny another X, then the right to X is not inalienable.[1] But this is to confuse inalienable rights with absolute rights. For even if the consent of the possessor does not justify others in infringing that right, other considerations may provide such a justification. For example, if the right is forfeitable, the possessor's wrongdoing may justifiy infringement. And though anyone is free to stipulate how various terms will be used, I have tried to show (especially in chapter 3) that our prominent founding fathers, Madison and Jefferson, understood the concept of an inalienable right along the lines of my analysis. It seems quite clear that Madison, Jefferson, and their contemporaries did not hold that society is never justified in infringing a person's inalienable rights; for they held that under some circumstances justifiable punishment may involve depriving persons of inalienable rights.[2]

Two Types of Arguments for Inalienable Rights

In this book I have given two different kinds of arguments to show that some rights within a morally justified legal system are inalienable.

The first of these arguments demonstrated that some rights cannot be alienated. The right of conscience (discussed in chapter 3) is an example. Even if a person makes what he takes to be an irrevocably binding promise to obey the moral pronouncements of another and even if this person in fact obeys the commander, the right of conscience has not been alienated. For the person remains an agent responsible for his actions; the promise and subsequent obedience to another does not remove his own responsibility. Of course, if an individual ceases to be an agent, he is no longer responsible; but this cannot be achieved by making a promise to another.

The right of a competent patient not to be subjected to medical treatment without her consent is a second example of a right that cannot be alienated (discussed in chapter 4). This is ususally referred to as the right to informed consent, and it has associated with it at least two correlative duties. One of these duties is to provide the patient with information about the benefits and risks associated with the recommended treatment, about the alternative treatments available, and about the likely consequences of declining treatment. The other duty is that of securing the patient's permission before administering treatment. Since patients can be forced neither to listen to or to grasp information presented to them, the right to be informed need not be exercised. And if a competent patient insists on *not* being informed, it seems fruitless, and perhaps heartless too, for health care practitioners to persist in trying to foist information on that patient. But it is not permissible to proceed without giving patients information, unless those patients have consented to this; and their consent is genuine only if it is freely given and they know that they have the right to the information in question. Thus, a competent patient's right not to have treatment administered without her consent cannot be alienated; for health care professionals are permitted to proceed (and to withhold information) only if they have received the patient's consent.

The other argument for the inalienability of some rights appeals to the interests of third parties. This argument maintains that if certain rights within a legal system are alienable—that is, if consent alone justifies another in infringing that right—then the rights and interests of others will be inappropriately placed in jeopardy. The right to life (discussed in chapters 5 and 6) provides an example. If consent alone justified one person in killing another, then the right to life of each person would be far less secure (than if consent alone did not justify killing). For if one person kills another and his defense is that the second person consented, it will be very difficult to prove that the deceased did not give consent. As was noted earlier, whether a crime was committed depends on whether consent was given (as is the case with rape), and it is sometimes difficult to convict the perpetrator even when the victim's testimony is available. Problems of proof will be greatly exacerbated if the victim is not available to testify. This is why, I argued, that it is perfectly reasonable for a legal system not to allow consent alone to justify killing. But I also argued that, contrary to what most have maintained, the inalienability of the right to life need not preclude the permissibility of voluntary active euthanasia or assisted suicide. Each of these practices may be restricted in such a way that the consent of the person whose death is hastened is necessary but not alone sufficient to justify killing; the additional conditions that must be satisfied, if reasonably specified, can protect the rights and interests of innocent third parties without depriving terminally ill, suffering patients the reprieve they seek.

This same argument for inalienability was discussed, though more tentatively, in the context of so-called market inalienability. With the advent of transplantation, the organs of one person can be a life-saving resource for another person. Most organs for transplantation are obtained from the newly deceased. But some organs may be safely procured from the living. Kidneys provide an example. Normal human beings have two kidneys but can function well with just one. So for some renal transplantations, living donors are used. Law in the United States allows a person to donate a kidney to another but does not permit the sale of organs. Thus, it is permissible to give away one's kidney but not to sell it. Markets in human organs are legally prohibited; thus, what consenting parties may do is restricted. As with the right to life, such a restriction may be defensible (without appealing to paternalism) if one can show that it protects the rights and interests of innocent third parties. But how does this restriction do that? The argument presented here (in chapter 7) was conditional: if a plausible account of exploitation (in terms of one party having unfair advantage over another) can be developed, and if it can be shown that preventing such exploitation is a legitimate function of government, and if allowing the sale of human organs will likely lead to the exploitation of poor people, then the prohibition of a market in human organs can be justifed in a way that does not revert to paternalism. The argument must be stated in a conditional form because of the enormity of the tasks required to establish the antecedents.

An argument appealing to the rights and interests of third parties was also given to defend the inalienability of the right of conscience. It was argued that even if a person could through consent bind herself irrevocably to obey the commands of another, doing so would be morally unacceptable because whatever benefits such an arrangement might generate could be obtained in a way that is less risky to the integrity of the agent and to the well-being of third parties. Thus, versions of both arguments defending the inalienability of selected rights apply to the right of conscience.

Possible Extensions of the Arguments

It is natural to wonder whether either or both of the general arguments given can be extended to defend the inalienability of other rights. Again, I do not aim to produce an exhaustive list here; but some brief speculative remarks might suggest other areas of inquiry.

One of the arguments in defense of the inalienability of the right of conscience claimed that one cannot successfully alienate such a right. One cannot create for oneself an obligation to obey the pronouncements of another; for in many circumstances, obeying the commands of another to do certain actions may in fact be wrong, even if one has promised to obey. No agent can rid herself of moral responsibility in this way. It seems clear that this argument can be extended to prohibit self-enslavement contracts, given that such contracts include everything (and more) that alienation of the right of conscience includes. As Anthony Kronman explains, normally a contract creates an enforceable obligation, either to perform (as the terms of the contract specify) or to pay damages. But contracts of self-enslavement are different. "The distinguishing mark of a contract of self-enslavement is that it purports to take away the latter alternative [the option of paying damages rather than performing]."[3] Allowing a person the option of paying damages instead of performing the act or acts specified in the contract enables that person to avoid doing something that she may regard as morally wrong. But since self-enslavement contracts can have no such escape mechanism, at the very least they should not be enforced. "The prohibition against such [self-enslavement] contracts is best explained, in my view, by the special threat they pose to the promisor's integrity or self-respect."[4] Of course, circumstances may develop with permissible contracts in such a way that one of the contractors regards either performing or paying damages as compromising her integrity. If society's only value were protecting integrity, then paying damages would not be required in such a case. But Kronman shows why this sort of protection goes too far: "We might, of course, protect the employee's moral integrity by relieving him of any duty either to perform or pay damages, but a remedy with such extreme consequences would lend itself to exploitation and tend to undermine the stability of contractual relations generally."[5] Since permissible contracts allow the option of paying damages rather than performing the specified acts, they at least permit agents to choose what they regard as the lesser of two evils in cases where things go awry.

The second type of argument for inalienable rights holds that if allowing one person to infringe right R of a second person with that person's consent puts the rights or well-being of third parties at serious risk, then one has a legitimate, nonpaternalistic reason for saying that R is an inalienable right. One instantiation of this argument holds that if permitting a certain relationship between two consenting parties is likely to lead to the exploitation of a significant number of other persons, then it is justifiable not to allow even consenting parties to enter the relationship in question. One obvious instance where this type of argument is worthy of serious investigation is in the area of surrogate mothers. In such cases, a woman agrees to carry a child which, upon birth, will be given to another woman and man. In some cases, the egg that is fertilized may be that of the surrogate mother herself; in other cases, another woman's fertilized egg will be implanted in the surrogate. In some of these cases, no money changes hands; this is typically when the surrogate mother is related to the couple having fertility problems. In other cases, the surrogate is paid a fee. It is to this latter arrangement—the best known instance of which is that of Mary Beth Whitehead and Baby M[6]—that most have moral objections. And a common objection, and the one that I regard as most worthy of discussion, is that allowing females to rent their wombs will lead to the exploitation of poor women.

Many other cases where the "exploitation" argument is worthy of discussion could be cited. One recent controversy relevant here concerns so-called predatory lenders. These are companies with very high cost mortgages. In some cases, such lenders have approached families with homes from Habitat for Humanity, offering quick cash if these families will trade in their no-interest Habitat loans for mortgages with high rates. Each topic here requires extensive coverage and will not be pursued here. And how plausible the "exploitation" argument is may vary greatly from case to case. What I have done here is to show what is at stake in the debate and how it might go with one particular topic.

The other instantiation of the second argument for inalienable rights points to direct harm or risks to which third parties will be subjected if infringements of certain rights are permitted simply because the possessor of that right gave consent. Allowing one person to kill another simply because of consent is the example I discussed. But that case itself naturally prompts questions about relationships between consenting parties that involve serious risks but not death, or at least not the likelihood of death. Is it justifiable for the state to prohibit such relationships? And if so, are inalienable rights involved? Examples of activities that involve consenting parties and pose risks on the participants include boxing, dueling, street-fighting, and being a subject in some medical experiments. Note that dueling and street-fighting are not legally allowed, while boxing and participation in risky medical experiments are permitted. There are complications, of course. Amateur boxing is less dangerous to the participants than professional boxing, both because of the rules and the additional protective gear worn by amateurs. Here let us focus on professional boxing and compare it with street-fighting. While very few professional boxers are killed in the ring, the activity is nevertheless dangerous to the participants. In addition to the obvious injuries that may occur, long-term neurological damage caused by repeated blows to the head is not uncommon. Why, then, is professional boxing permitted but street-fighting is not? There are at least two relevant differences between the two activities. First, because of the highly organized nature of professional boxing, we can be relatively confident that participation is voluntary and undertaken with reasonable knowledge of the risks involved. Thus, if a professional boxer is killed, society can be reasonably confident that he undertook the risks voluntarily. This is not the case with street-fighting. If a person were killed in this activity, we would only have the word of his assailant that he had participated voluntarily. Second, professional boxing is confined to an arena where spectators pay to watch. This is not the case with street-fighting. This means that the latter is much more likely than the former to trigger a riot in which the well-being and property of many persons are damaged. For both of these reasons, then, relieving a person of responsibility for injuries inflicted to a willing opponent in a street-fight would put innocent third parties at risk. This is not the case, however, if a professional boxer is not held liable for injuries inflicted on his fellow pugilist during a sanctioned match.

It does not follow from what I have just said about boxing and street-fighting that inalienable rights are at issue; I make no claim about that here. The point, rather, is that even though both activities subject willing participants to risks, one can make a case not based on paternalism for proscribing one of the activities while allowing the other. Similar argumentation may show that superficially similar activities are justifiably treated differently by law and social policy; thus, the prohibitions associated with inalienable rights may be narrower than one would expect. That was the point I argued for in chapters 5 and 6 regarding the right to life and its relation to voluntary euthanasia and assisted suicide. It should not be surprising if parallels to this relationship arose in other areas.

The Pursuit of Happiness

Jefferson famously declared that the rights to life, liberty, and the pursuit of happiness are inalienable. In this book I have discussed the right to life and aspects of the right to liberty, particularly liberty of conscience. Why ignore the pursuit of happiness? Two answers spring to mind immediately: one, I am not attempting to develop a complete catalogue of inalienable rights; and two, talk about a right to pursue happiness seems very strange. A brief word, nevertheless, might be said about this right in Jefferson's trio.

Scholars of American history have debated at length the meaning of Jefferson's words. But there seems to be a consensus that Jefferson was stating laconically a political philosophy widely accepted by his fellow countrymen; his intent was principally to harmonize the sentiments of the day.[7] Drawing from many scholars, Pauline Maier shows that other extant documents put, in more words, Jefferson's point.[8] Article I of the Virginia Declaration of Rights, adopted in Williamsburg on June 12, 1776, maintained that people had certain inherent rights, including "the Enjoyment of Life and Liberty, with the Means of acquiring and possessing Property, and pursuing and obtaining Happiness and Safety." And Article I of the Constitution of Massachusetts declared that men have certain natural and inalienable rights, including that of acquiring, possessing, and protecting property and that of seeking and obtaining their safety and happiness. These rights, which Jefferson succinctly called the rights to life, liberty, and the pursuit of happiness, seem to be basic rights. John Locke, in *The Second Treatise of Government*, Chapter V, section 27, called these property in one's own person; and Locke's influence on Jefferson is well documented.[9] So it seems that Jefferson held that people have rights in their own person, and the rights to acquire and possess property and pursue and obtain happiness are among them; and these are rights in one's own person. So understood, the right to pursue happiness seems less strange.

But which, if either, of the arguments I have deployed to defend inalienable rights would apply to this collection of rights in one's own person that Jefferson seems to have had in mind? If one modestly assumes that the desires for survival and happiness are present in all normal human beings, or at least are absent only in the most extreme of circumstances, then it is easy to see why one might hold that the first of the two arguments I have given may apply here. For if the drives for survival are natural and powerful, then it will be very difficult to see how a person can successfully contract not to act on these. And while this is not a historical work nor is it dependent on evidence from history, I am willing to bet that Jefferson, the authors of *The Federalist Papers*—Alexander Hamilton, James Madison, and John Jay—and our other founding fathers held that the desires for continued survival and happiness are natural and powerful.

I end with this speculation. In a well-known chapter of *Taking Rights Seriously*, Ronald Dworkin writes, "Do we have a right to liberty? Thomas Jefferson thought so . . ."[10] Dworkin goes on to say that it is "absurd to suppose that men and women have any general right to liberty at all,"[11] though they have rights to particular liberties. Dworkin's reason for saying this is, in part, due to how he understands rights. Rights in the strong sense cannot be denied to people simply for utilitarian reasons, to promote the convenience and welfare of others. But many liberties can be restricted for just these reasons. To take Dworkin's example, Lexington Avenue can be made a one-way street and people's freedom to drive up it denied simply because this promotes the convenience and welfare of the majority. I agree with Dworkin that if rights were so easily defeated, they would be of much less interest and hardly worth defending.

I suspect, however, that Jefferson did not hold that people have a general right to liberty. As with the right to pursue happiness, Jefferson was being laconic. Basic liberties, plausibly described as rights in one's own person, are what Jefferson had in mind. We know (from chapter 3) that Jefferson held that people have an inalienable right of conscience. That right, the very right to acquire property (but *not* rights to specific pieces of property), and the right to seek happiness by pursuing one's own projects (provided that one does not violate the rights of others) are basic liberties that one cannot alienate. If that is what Jefferson thought, I believe that he was correct.

Notes

Chapter 1

1. My account of the nature of rights here is not original; I borrow from the extensive philosophical literature available. I am most indebted to Sumner (1987), Thomson (1986), Thomson (1990), Wellman (1985), Wellman (1995a), Benditt (1982).

2. See, for example, Sumner (1987), pp. 13, 32, and 36.

3. See Feinberg (1973), pp. 56–58.

4. See Sumner (1987), Wellman (1985), and Wellman (1995a).

5. Throughout this work, I use the terms 'obligation' and 'duty' and their cognates interchangeably.

6. Throughout this work I will speak of *persons* or *individuals* as possessors of rights. I do not preclude the possibility that nonpersons, especially certain nonhuman animals, may have rights. But for purposes of this work, the moral status of nonpersons is not relevant. This will become evident to the reader when the notions of waiving and alienating are explained.

7. These distinctions are explained in Feinberg (1973), pp. 59–60.

8. See Lomasky (1987), pp. 101–103 and Nickel (1987), p. 3. Thomson (1990), pp. 73–76, opposes regarding moral and legal rights as two species of the same genus, but grants that rights can and do have different sources.

9. Sumner (1987), p. 6.

10. Sumner (1987), p. 13.

11. See Gewirth (1982), p. 219 and Thomson (1990).

12. The term 'infringe' is intended to be morally neutral, indicating that the duty correlative with the right has not been fulfilled, but leaving it an open question whether such nonfulfillment was permissible or impermissible. No term seems quite natural here. Other possibilities—instead of 'infringe'—include 'abridge', 'encroach', 'invade'.

13. Thomson (1986), p. 53. See also, Gewirth (1982), p. 219.

14. Feinberg (1980), p. 225.

15. This position is supported by Smith (1995).

16. See Gewirth (1982), Chapter 9.

17. I should say here that it is controversial to say that the possessor must engage in *wrongdoing* in order to forfeit a right. Uniacke (1994), p. 206, argues that there can be forfeiture

without blame. Her examples include forfeiting one's right to be seated at the theater because of arriving late through no fault of one's own, and the forfeiture of parental rights for those who become insane. In order to maintain the connection between forfeiture and wrongdoing, we could say either of two things about the first example: that it involves wrongdoing but no blame, or that this is a case of *losing* but not forfeiting a right. And of the second example, it seems clear that this is a case of losing but not forfeiting a right. Still, I do not want too much to hang on whether my account of forfeiture or Uniacke's is adopted.

18. Feinberg (1980), p. 230.
19. See Uniacke (1994), p. 203.
20. See Bedau (1968), pp. 569–570.
21. Herzog (1989), p. 222.
22. Lomasky (1987), p. 211.
23. See McConnell (1997), pp. 190–194.
24. Fletcher (1996), p. 109.
25. Simmons (1979), p. 76. Later in this same work, Simmons says, "When I speak of consenting, then, I will mean according to another by the consentor of a special right to act within areas within which only the consentor is normally free to act" (p. 76).
26. This case is reported in an Associated Press article, *News and Record* (Greensboro, North Carolina), December 12, 1993.
27. For accounts of this case as reported by the Associated Press, see *News and Record* (Greensboro, North Carolina), October 30, 1996, October 31, 1996, November 4, 1996, and March 11, 1997.
28. *Black's Law Dictionary*, p. 1580.
29. Thomson (1990), p. 38.
30. *Black's Law Dictionary*, p. 72. This is what *Black's* says, but it is in conflict with my account, for it implies that a right which may be waived but not transferred is alienable.
31. Locke (1960/1690), sections 87, 88, and 97.
32. Feinberg (1980), p. 157.
33. Simmons (1993), p. 103.
34. *Black's Law Dictionary*, p. 759.
35. Thomson (1990), p. 59.
36. See Lyons (1994), p. 11 and Nickel (1987), p. 46.
37. Grisez (1970), p. 204. Here and throughout it is assumed that 'inalienable' and 'unalienable' refer to the same concept.
38. To cite but one other example, see Churchill (1994), p. 78.
39. Meyers (1985), p. 2. In an endnote (note 1, p. 197), Meyers contrasts this with an absolute right, which she defines as a right "that can never be abridged justifiably."
40. Meyers (1985), p. 9.
41. For others who hold that, by definition, inalienable rights are not forfeitable, see VanDeVeer (1980a), p. 168; VanDeVeer (1986), p. 236; Becker (1982), p. 212; Nickel (1982), p. 253; Nickel (1987), p. 46; Nelson (1989), p. 519; and Leavitt (1992), p. 115.
42. Meyers (1985), p. 14.
43. See Feinberg (1980), p. 240. It should be pointed out, however, that Feinberg has disavowed what he says here in the "Preface" to this volume, p. xii.
44. Simmons (1993), p. 106.
45. Feinberg (1980), pp. 221–251. This essay was originally published in *Philosophy and Public Affairs*, Vol. 7 (1978), pp. 93–123. All page references here are to the 1980 volume.
46. I take up the issue of the relationship between the inalienable right to life and voluntary euthanasia in chapter 5.
47. Feinberg (1980), pp. 242–246.

48. Feinberg (1980), p. 246. Emphasis in the original.

49. See Stell (1979), p. 8.

50. Feinberg (1980), p. 249.

51. Feinberg (1980), p. 251.

52. Feinberg (1980), p. 250, does say that the state may prohibit the spring rite described earlier, even though the voluntary participants have waived but not relinquished their right to life. One of the considerations he cites to support this claim appeals to the public interest.

53. In the United States, legislation regarding advanced directives (such as "living wills") permit family members and health care providers to withhold or withdraw life-sustaining medical treatment; but it does not permit anyone to kill the patient.

54. See Cantor (1993), especially Chapters 2–3, and King (1996), especially Chapters 2–4.

55. See Cantor (1993), Chapter 2; Meisel (1995), Chapter 10; and King (1996).

56. The upshot of the previous paragraph was that the right not to be killed is not relevant to understanding living wills and other advance directives in medicine. The upshot of this paragraph is that either waiver of any right is not relevant to understanding living wills, or that Feinberg has given an inadequate account of the concept of waiver. I shall argue later (chapter 6) that waiver is not relevant to understanding what is going on when we follow a person's stated wishes as they are indicated in a living will.

57. See Calabresi and Melamed (1972), p. 1092 and Rose-Ackerman (1985), p. 931.

58. Kronman (1983), p. 775.

59. Nickel (1982), p. 254.

60. For one who concurs with this, see Rose-Ackerman (1985): "*Inalienable rights* also need not be exercised, but the right cannot be sold or given away and some uses may be forbidden" (p. 936).

61. Caplan (1995), pp. 13–14.

62. A similar argument against regarding moral duties as absolute is given in more detail in McConnell (1996), pp. 41–42. For a spirited defense of the "specificationist" account, see Christopher Wellman (1995), especially sections 3–5.

63. DeCew (1997), p. 57.

64. For my reasons for opposing dilemmas, see McConnell (1987); Conee (1987); and Zimmerman (1996), Chapter 7.

Chapter 2

1. Sidgwick (1981/1907), p. 298.
2. Thomson (1990), p. 283.
3. Sumner (1981), p. 41.
4. Callahan (1992), p. 52.
5. Kuflik (1986), p. 75.
6. Buchanan (1984), p. 79.
7. Brock (1993), p. 105.
8. Brody (1988), p. 22. Brody uses variables X, Y, and Z instead of P_1, P_2, and R.
9. Brody (1988), p. 22. Emphasis added.
10. Brody (1988), p. 22.
11. Brody (1988), pp. 25, 27, and 28.
12. Brody (1988), p. 33. See also, Brock (1993), p. 125.
13. Brock (1993), p. 106.
14. Nozick (1974), p. 58.
15. Nickel (1982), p. 254.

16. Buchanan (1984), p. 79. See also, Brock (1993), pp. 106–107.

17. This distinction is explained in Feinberg (1980), pp. 110–127.

18. For an excellent discussion of these two accounts of rights, see Sumner (1987), especially pp. 40–51 and 96–97.

19. Among those who seem to endorse the interest conception of rights, see Stoljar (1984) and Lyons (1994).

20. Among those who defend the choice conception of rights, see McCloskey (1975), Buchanan (1984), Lomasky (1987), Sumner (1987), and Brock (1993).

21. Sumner (1987), p. 47.

22. For a discussion of these points, see Sumner (1987), pp. 50–51. For an argument that the interest conception alone can make sense of inalienability, see Kramer et al. (1998), pp. 70–75 and 78.

23. This is not to say that all of the same rights taken to be inalienable on the interest account will also be regarded as inalienable on the choice conception. Rather, it is to say that if the choice account has *conceptual* room for the idea of an inalienable right, then the interest account has room for it too.

24. Sumner (1987), p. 96.

25. See Rose-Ackerman (1985), p. 936.

26. See, for example, VanDeVeer (1986) and Feinberg (1986).

27. See Hill (1991), Chapter 10.

28. Singer (1971), p. 315.

29. For discussions of the "volenti" maxim, see Feinberg (1984), pp. 115–117; Feinberg (1986), pp. 173–177; Stell (1979), p. 8; VanDeVeer (1986), p. 49; and Grisez and Boyle (1979), p. 142.

30. Salmond (1957), p. 531.

31. Simmons (1979), p. 67.

32. For the work that is still definitive on this topic, see Lyons (1965).

33. Perhaps the best known proponent of this position is Dworkin (1977).

34. See Sumner (1987).

35. Rose-Ackerman (1985), p. 943.

36. Calabresi and Melamed (1972), pp. 1111ff.

37. Rose-Ackerman (1985), pp. 950–951.

38. Rose-Ackerman (1985), p. 950.

39. Hardin (1986). For a discussion of Hardin's position, see Kuflik (1986).

40. This particular example is not discussed by Hardin (1986) or Kuflik (1986). It is discussed by Benditt (1982), p. 15, though not explicitly in the context of responding to a collective action problem.

41. See Kuflik (1986), pp. 83–84. See also, Kronman (1983), pp. 767–768.

42. Gert et al. (1996), p. 163.

43. Rawls (1971).

44. See Brock (1993), pp. 33–35. This issue will be addressed in detail in chapter 4.

45. This point is discussed by Rachels (1986), pp. 185–186, in the context of examining the so-called wedge argument against voluntary euthanasia.

46. Hutcheson (1991/1738), pp. 284–285.

47. For a useful survey of important historical figures' defenses of inalienable rights, see Kuflik (1984).

48. Dworkin (1977), p. 198.

49. Dworkin (1977), p. 205.

50. Kuflik (1986), p. 75. Emphasis in the original.

51. Gewirth (1978), p. 77.

52. Hill (1991), p. 13.

53. Hill (1991), p. 15.

54. Hill (1991), p. 15.

55. It should be pointed out, however, that Hill himself does not wish to avoid endorsing the idea of duties to oneself. See, for example, Hill (1991), Chapter 10.

56. Hill (1991), p. 15.

57. Kant (1974/1793), pp. 60–61 and Kant (1965/1797), p. 98 (AK 330). See also, Kuflik (1984), pp. 279 and 282–283.

58. What is explained here and in the following paragraph is taken from Dahl (1988), pp. 75–78. For a related discussion of Kant's ethics, see Dahl (1984), pp. 125–130.

59. Meyers (1985), p. 52. For a full explanation of this account, see Meyers (1985), Chapter 2.

60. For an account of this, see Rachels (1986), pp. 80–82.

61. Quoted in Rachels (1986), p. 88.

62. I ignore here the complications that arise because the AMA statement allows family members to give consent.

63. Here I assume that the right may be overridden or forfeited. If a right were inalienable but could be neither forfeited nor overridden, and if there were no other consideration that could justify infringing a right, then consent would be *necessary* to justify infringement. For purposes of simplicity, I ignore these possibilities.

64. Simmons (1979), pp. 62–63.

65. Simmons (1993), p. 106.

66. Nickel (1987), p. 47.

Chapter 3

1. Thoreau (1981/1849), p. 418.

2. See McGuire (1963), p. 259 and Fuss (1964), p. 111.

3. See Donagan (1977), pp. 132ff.; Ryle (1954), p. 31; Garnett (1969), p. 86; and Childress (1979), pp. 319 and 328–329.

4. D'Arcy (1961), Chapter 1, especially pp. 5–12, distinguishes between judicial conscience and legislative conscience. *Judicial* conscience is concerned with passing judgment on deeds already done. *Legislative* conscience plays a directive role before action takes place; it imposes a rule of conduct on contemplated acts.

5. McGuire (1963), p. 261; Fuss (1964), pp. 117–118; May (1983), pp. 58–59; and Gensler (1985), pp. 161 and 163.

6. Ryle (1940), p. 35.

7. Childress (1979), p. 329.

8. Reprinted in Nickel (1987), pp. 211–229.

9. Nickel (1987), p. 218.

10. Nickel (1987), p. 218. For a discussion, see Nickel (1987), p. 140 and Wellman (1995a), pp. 239–240.

11. Dworkin (1977), pp. 189–190, says that this shows that the right to follow one's own conscience is not a right in the *strong* sense (that is, a right that the government would do wrong to interfere with).

12. Simmons (1979), p. 76.

13. For a contemporary philosopher who seems to endorse the inalienability of the right of conscience, though not explicitly, see Rawls (1971), pp. 206, 212, 217, 370, and 389.

14. See McConnell (1987), pp. 154–173, and Conee (1987), pp. 239–249. It should be noted that even proponents of dilemmas do not typically regard the situation described in this paragraph as an irresolvable moral conflict.

15. D'Arcy (1961), Parts I and II, argues that there is an absolute duty to follow conscience, but nevertheless conscience is fallible. Whether he accepts that this entails that there are moral dilemmas is not obvious.

16. Leland (1991/1791), pp. 1083–1086.

17. Jefferson (1982/1785), p. 159.

18. See *The Papers of James Madison* (Chicago: University of Chicago Press, 1973), Vol. 8, pp. 298–300. All quotations are taken from here. For a discussion of Madison's arguments, see White (1987), pp. 31–34.

19. Kuflik (1984), p. 281, criticizes Spinoza's claims about the inalienability of autonomy for these reasons.

20. It is plausible to suggest that activities such as brainwashing and psychosurgery are relevant to one's right to moral autonomy but not to the right of conscience. What the relationship is between autonomy and conscience is a difficult topic that I do not pursue here.

21. Locke (1983/1689), pp. 26–27. White (1987), p. 33, suggests that Madison was influenced by Locke.

22. Jefferson (1982/1785), p. 159.

23. Leland (1991/1791), p. 1085.

24. Kuflik (1984), pp. 286ff., argues that abdicating moral autonomy is wrong because one might be ordered to perform extremely evil deeds.

25. D'Arcy (1961), Part IV, argues that one has a right to follow conscience based on the assumption (defended by him earlier in the book) that agents have an absolute duty never to act against conscience.

26. Such an argument is given by Barnett (1986a), pp. 186–187.

27. See White (1987), p. 33 and Barnett (1986a).

28. See, for example, Kronman (1983), especially pp. 778–780 and 783–784.

29. See, for example, Buchanan (1984), p. 79.

30. Feinberg (1980), p. 157.

31. See Rose-Ackerman (1985), p. 936.

32. Kuflik (1984), pp. 293–294, mentions this as a reason for abdicating moral autonomy.

33. As Larry May has pointed out to me, this claim is oversimplified. For the process of ridding oneself of beliefs ingrained by socialization may be arduous.

34. See Kuflik (1984), p. 294.

35. Rawls (1971), p. 217.

36. For a related point, see Hill (1991), p. 15.

37. A similar view about agency and responsibility is articulated by eighteenth-century philosopher Bishop Joseph Butler, who says: "[W]e are agents. Our constitution is put in our own power. We are charged with it; and therefore are accountable for any disorder or violation of it" (1983/1726), p. 15. And Rawls (1971), p. 389, says: "Even though men normally seek advice and counsel, and accept injunctions of those in authority when they seem reasonable to them, they are always accountable for their deeds. We cannot divest ourselves of our responsibility. . . ."

38. Price (1991/1778), p. 89.

39. Madison (1973), p. 299.

40. Locke (1960/1690), sections 119, 121, 135, 137, and 149. For a clear discussion of Locke on these issues, see Simmons (1979), pp. 86–88.

41. Rawls (1971), p. 343.

42. Dworkin (1993), p. 15. See also, pp. 161, 165, and 239.

43. See May (1983), p. 58 and Kuflik (1984), p. 288.
44. See, for example, McConnell (1993), Chapter 6.
45. See Simmons (1979), pp. 193–194.
46. Broad (1969), p. 77.
47. See Donagan (1977), pp. 137–138.
48. Rawls (1971), p. 212; and see p. 370. See also, Donagan (1977), p. 138.
49. An important legal case that deals with this issue is *Berman v. United States*, 156 F. 2nd 377 (1946). For a discussion of this case, see Wellman (1995a), pp. 238–241.
50. See McConnell (1993), pp. 136–140.
51. Miles (1992), p. 63.
52. Daar (1993), p. 1245.
53. *Roe v. Wade*, 410 U.S. 113 (1973) and *Doe v. Bolton*, 410 U.S. 179 (1973).
54. Loftus (1990), pp. 721–726.
55. See King (1996), pp. 109–110, 153, and 251.
56. For a discussion of this change in the Virginia statute, see Daar (1993), p. 1279.
57. See Schneiderman and Jecker (1995).
58. See Layson and McConnell (1996) for the argument.
59. *In re Helga Wanglie*: Fourth Judicial District (Dist. Ct., Probate Ct., Div.) PX-91-283. Minn., Hennepin County (1991). For a useful summary of the Wanglie case, see Lo (1995), pp. 79–80 and Schneiderman and Jecker (1995), pp. 51–57.
60. Council on Ethical and Judicial Affairs (1999).
61. *Brophy v. New England Sinai Hospital, Inc.*, 497 N.E. 2nd 626 (Massachusetts, 1986). For a discussion of this case, see Buchanan and Brock (1989), pp. 126–127; Beauchamp and Childress (1994), pp. 522–524; and McConnell (1997), p. 138.
62. *Cruzan v. Harmon*, 760 S.W. 2nd 408 (Missouri, 1988), and *Cruzan v. Director, Missouri Department of Health*, 110 S.Ct. 2841 (1990). For a discussion of this case, see Lo (1995), pp. 197–199; Schneiderman and Jecker (1995), pp. 1–3; and McConnell (1997), pp. 139–141.
63. On these two questions, the definitive work is Buchanan and Brock (1989).
64. Annas (1987).
65. See Daar (1993), pp. 1269–1270, and Layson and McConnell (1996), p. 2618.
66. See Loftus (1990), p. 719, and Wear et al. (1994), p. 153.
67. See Layson and McConnell (1996), p. 2619.
68. Daar (1993), p. 1266.
69. Wear et al. (1994), p. 155.
70. Lo (1995), p. 5.
71. Solomon et al. (1993), p. 19.
72. Caplan (1995), pp. 9–10.

Chapter 4

1. See Faden and Beauchamp (1986), especially Chapter 3, and Beauchamp and Childress (1994), pp.145–170.
2. The two important legal cases in the United States are *Canterbury v. Spence*, 464 F. 2nd Series [D.C. Cir. 1972] and *Truman v. Thomas*, 611 P. 2nd Series [Cal. 1980].
3. See Meisel (1995), Vol. 1, pp. 93–94.
4. *Schloendorf v. Society of New York Hospital*, 211 N.Y. 125, 105 N.E. 91 (1914).
5. *Nathanson v. Kline*, 186 Kan., 393, 350 P. 2nd 1093 (1960).
6. *Canterbury v. Spence* (1972), *Truman v. Thomas* (1980), cited in note 2 above, and *Cobbs v. Grant*, 502 P. 2nd Series (1972).
7. Meisel (1995), pp. 103–109 and Wear (1998), Chapter 8.

8. See Devettere (1995), pp. 93–94 and Wear (1998), pp. 166–169.
9. *Jacobson v. Massachusetts*, 197 U.S. 11, 29 (1905).
10. Gasner et al. (1999).
11. *Cobbs v. Grant* (1972) at 12; see also, at 3.
12. Feinberg (1980), p. 157.
13. See Hagman (1970), pp. 788–789, and Faden and Beauchamp (1986), p. 38.
14. *Tunkl v. Regents of University of California*, 383 P. 2nd Series [Cal. 1963].
15. See Brock (1993), p. 33; N.M. King (1993), p. 401; Lo (1995), p. 33; and Meisel (1995), p. 109.
16. See Meisel (1995), p. 109.
17. See Beauchamp and Childress (1994), pp. 162–163.
18. Hagman (1970), p. 785.
19. See *Danielson v. Roche et al.*, P. 2nd Series [Cal. 1952].
20. See Richards and Rathbun (1993), p. 158.
21. See Devettere (1995), p. 93.
22. When a patient no longer has decision-making capacity, an appropriate surrogate must be designated; and health care professionals have a duty to inform the *surrogate* about benefits, risks, and alternatives independent of whether the patient has validly waived that right.
23. See Sugarman et al. (1998), pp. 209–224, for some of the federal regulations regarding waiver of informed consent for research subjects.
24. See Angell (1984), p. 1116; Brock (1993), p. 33; Kantor (1989), p. 50; King (1993), pp. 400–401; and VanDeVeer (1986), p. 201.
25. See Brody (1988), p. 28; and Brock (1993), p. 105.
26. Meisel (1995), p. 109.
27. VanDeVeer (1986), p. 202.
28. See Sumner (1987), especially Chapter 2.
29. Kantor (1989), p. 51.
30. See Brock (1993), p. 34, and Faden and Beauchamp (1986), p. 38.
31. See Meisel (1995), p. 109.
32. See Kantor (1989), pp. 50–51.
33. See Strull et al. (1984), pp. 2990–2994; and Deber et al. (1996), pp. 1414–1420.
34. Angell (1984), p. 1116.
35. Of course, one hopes that health care practitioners would resist going along with a decision made by the person to whom the right of informed consent had been transferred if that decision were blatantly contrary to the patient's best interests.
36. Kantor (1989), p. 51.
37. See Hill (1991), Chapter 1.
38. Wear (1998), p. 164.
39. There is an irony here. Presumably the Jehovah's Witness's motivation in this case is to avoid religious condemnation. And presumably he believes that religious condemnation occurs only if one consents to a blood transfusion. Yet his apparent waiver is actually consent, though perhaps not informed consent.
40. *Powell v. Columbia Presbyterian Medical Center*, 267 N.Y.S. 2nd 450 (Sup. Ct. 1965). For a discussion of this case, see Veatch (1989), pp. 104–105.
41. See Ost (1984), pp. 301–312; Hull (1985), pp. 183–197; and Meyer (1992), pp. 541–555.
42. See Freedman (1993), p. 574.
43. See Caplan (1995), pp. 65–66.
44. Such "carte blanche" clauses are sometimes part of standard consent forms, buried in the details. That is *not* what I have in mind here. Instead, I am talking about the case

where this is precisely what the patient wants to give to the physician—a blank check to the physician to do whatever he deems appropriate.

45. For an excellent discussion of Hobbes's arguments concerning inalienable rights, see Kavka (1986), pp. 322–333.

46. I thank Kay R. Hagan, J.D., and Rita T. Layson, M.D., for helpful suggestions on an earlier version of this chapter.

Chapter 5

1. See McConnell (1997), Chapter 5, especially pp. 170–173.

2. Thomson (1990), p. 37. Actually Thomson says that the right to life implies a duty not to kill *unjustly*. The qualification is added to allow for cases of legitimate self-defense. I prefer to delete the qualification and include cases of self-defense under the ruberic of forfeiture; that is, the duty not to kill the possessor is suspended because the possessor has forfeited his right to life. See also Meyers (1985), p. 54, though it is not clear that she would limit the right to life to the negative interpretation.

3. Bedau (1968), p. 550.

4. See McCloskey (1975), pp. 417 and 420–421. See also, Wellman (1995b), p. 249, who holds that the right to life gives the possessor a moral-claim right to be rescued from the danger of death.

5. I should add here that advocates of the negative interpretation of the right to life might also agree that a person is morally required to toss a life preserver to another if doing so will save that other person's life. But defenders of this position will deny that such an obligation is based on the drowning person's right to life; there is some other basis for the requirement.

6. *McFall v. Shimp*, No. 78–17711 In Equity (C.P. Allegheny County, Pennsylvania, July 26, 1978). For a discussion, see Huffman (1979), Beauchamp and Childress (1994), pp. 192 and 266–267, and McConnell (1997), pp. 171–172.

7. *Curran v. Bosze*, 41 Illinois 2nd 473, 153 Ill., Dec. 213, 566 N.E. 2nd 1319 (1990). For a discussion of this case, see Hyde (1997), pp. 88–92 and Caplan (1995), pp. 51–52.

8. For the definitive treatment, see Faden and Beauchamp (1986). See also, McConnell (1997), Chapter 3, especially pp. 73–74.

9. There are some exceptions. See McConnell (1997), pp. 81–84.

10. Stell (1979), p. 8.

11. Stell (1979), p. 26.

12. Callahan (1992), p. 52.

13. Callahan (1992), p. 52.

14. R. Dworkin (1993), p. 167.

15. The argument here is based on McConnell (1984), pp. 53–54.

16. On the right of bodily integrity, see Wellington (1990), pp. 101–107 and 118–120, and Chief Justice Rehnquist's majority opinion in *Cruzan v. Director, Missouri Department of Health*, 497 U.S. 261 (1990).

17. *Scholendorff v. Society of New York Hospital*, 211 N.Y. 125, 105 N.E. 92, 93 (1914).

18. I put aside here questions about whether such behavior violates a moral requirement that one has to some third person.

19. See Brody (1988), p. 22.

20. See Faden and Beauchamp (1986), Chapter 4 and McConnell (1997), Chapter 3.

21. Feinberg (1980), pp. 122–124, makes an analogous point but in a different context. Here he tries to show that forbidding a person from selling himself into slavery need not be based on paternalism. The requirement that the consent must be substantially voluntary does

imply a commitment to *weak* paternalism, but such a form of paternalism does not inappropriately restrict personal autonomy.

22. Stell (1979), p. 17.

23. As Lance Stell has pointed out to me, we might operate with a broader sense of 'alienation' and say that a person has alienated something by *abandoning* it. Understood this way, suicide is an instance in which life is alienated by its possessor. For an account of inalienability that is more in accord with my usage, see White (1978), pp. 196ff.

24. Singer (1971), p. 315. For Singer's entire discussion of this topic, see pp. 311–318.

25. Hill (1991), p. 146.

26. Singer does not endorse this as a *premise*; but of course it follows from his premises (2) and (3). Here the suggestion is that one can endorse (4) as a conceptual truth while denying the truth of (2).

27. Hill (1991), Chapter 1, especially p. 15.

28. Hill (1991), p. 15. See also, pp. 88–89.

29. I take it that it is not obvious that *every* alleged duty to the self is also such that others have a duty to the agent regarding the same matter (other than possibly a duty not to prevent the agent from fulfilling his duties).

30. Feinberg (1980), pp. 221–251, attempts to show that voluntary euthanasia need not be precluded by the inalienability of the right to life. I agree with Feinberg's conclusion, though my defense of the position is rather different from his.

31. Angell (1988), p. 1348.

32. R. Dworkin (1993), p. 3.

33. See Buchanan and Brock (1989), especially Chapter 2.

34. See Brock (1993), Chapter 8, especially pp. 205–208; Lo (1995), p. 169; and McConnell (1997), pp. 119–120.

35. An incurable disease is one that medical science lacks the resources to eradicate. A terminal illness is one whose nature is such that it is expected to cause the patient to die. Many illnesses are both terminal and incurable, leading some to think that there is a redundancy in using both expressions. But there is no redundancy here. An example of an illness that may be incurable but not terminal is chronic fatigue syndrome; an example of an affliction that may be terminal but curable is gangrene. There is a difficulty in defining "terminal," however. For legal purposes, it is often defined in terms of life-expectancy—requiring, for example, that the person is expected to die within six months. When it is defined this way, then a condition like amyotrophic lateral sclerosis will be incurable and debilitating but may not be terminal (since it may well have been diagnosed when the afflicted person expected to live more than six months). On these points, see Quill et al. (1992), pp. 1381–1382 and Miller et al. (1994), p. 120.

36. See Quill (1993), pp. 104–106, 117–120, 131–134, and 166, and Shavelson (1995), especially Chapter 5.

37. Quill et al. (1992), p. 1383.

38. When considerations like these are cited in response to the so-called wedge argument or slippery slope argument, they are usually referred to as safeguards. Some of the conditions that I cite here are discussed by Brock (1993), pp. 225–226 and Battin (1994), pp. 173–181.

39. It seems clear that unless the consulting physician is financially and professionally independent of the first, at least some of the concerns about abuse will not be quelled by this requirement. This point is sometimes made in connection with physician-assisted suicide too; see Emanuel (1996), p. 827.

40. The points in this paragraph are made by Battin (1994), p. 174.

41. Shavelson (1995), p. 40.

42. See Rachels (1986), p. 174.

43. Dworkin (1996), p. 145.

44. Dworkin (1996), pp. 144–145.

45. Callahan (1992), p. 54.

46. I allude here to Ronald Dworkin (1993). In this work Dworkin argues that most of us are committed to the sanctity of human life, but we understand quite differently what such a commitment requires of us. These differences show up conspicuously in the debates about abortion and euthanasia. For Dworkin's discussion of the sanctity of life and euthanasia, see Chapters 7 and 8.

47. Teno and Lynn (1996), p. 405.

48. Brock (1993), pp. 227–228.

49. For an extensive discussion of this principle, see Buchanan and Brock (1989), pp. 112–122.

50. See Ouslander et al. (1989) and Seckler et al. (1991).

51. See Quill et al. (1992), p. 1382; Brock (1993), p. 207; and Lo (1995), p. 175. Those who defend only physician-assisted suicide, and not euthanasia, make a similar point. See Baron et al. (1996), p. 11.

52. See Callahan (1992), p. 54.

53. Brock (1993), p. 226.

Chapter 6

1. Brock (1993), p. 204.

2. Quill et al. (1992), p. 1381.

3. Lo (1995), pp. 170–171.

4. See Rachels (1986), pp. 86–87 and 181–182. I should note that to this principle Rachels attaches the qualification, "provided that this does not violate the rights of any third party" (p. 86). As I argue in the text, without such a qualification the permissibility-extension principle is flawed.

5. I do not mean here to have sexual intercourse without consent, for rape can occur in marriage too. Rather, I allude to initiating activities of a sexual nature to determine if one's partner is willing.

6. McConnell (1984), p. 43.

7. Quill et al. (1992), p. 1381. See also, Lo (1995), p. 171.

8. See Blendon et al. (1992) and Quill et al. (1992), p. 1381.

9. Shavelson (1995), p. 102.

10. Quill (1993), pp. 161–165 and 168–173. For a discussion, see McConnell (1997), pp. 134–135.

11. See Quill (1993), pp. 9–16 and 168–175. Emanuel et al. (1998) show that some of these widely supported safeguards for voluntary euthanasia and assisted suicide are not always followed by physicians in the United States. They acknowledge, however, that this may be because euthanasia is illegal in all 50 states, and assisted suicide is illegal in 49 states. That certainly discourages consulting with another physician!

12. See, for example, Emanuel (1996), pp. 827–828.

13. Baron et al. (1996), p. 16.

14. Teno and Lynn (1996), p. 406; Burt (1996), p. 169; and Foley (1997), pp. 55–56.

15. Quill (1993), p. 163.

16. The purpose of the qualification "the consulting physician is appropriately serious" is to acknowledge a problem pointed out by Daniel Callahan (1992), p. 54, namely, that confirming opinions in medicine are often too easily obtained.

17. Battin (1994), pp. 178–180.

18. This provides a response to those such as Teno and Lynn (1996), p. 405, who warn that society's most vulnerable are likely to be the victims of abuse if assisted death is legalized.

19. See, for example, Burt (1996), pp. 165–170, and Martyn and Bourguignon (1997), pp. 393–396.

20. Shavelson (1995), p. 65.

21. Grisez and Boyle (1979), p. 134.

22. Singer (1994), pp. 155–156.

23. Angell (1997), p. 51.

24. Battin (1994), p. 174.

25. Shavelson (1995), pp. 28–29. See also, pp. 66 and 101.

26. Nuland (1994), pp. 152–153.

27. See Gunderson and Mayo (1993), p. 290.

28. Shavelson (1995), Chapter 4, discusses a poignant case of this sort.

29. Pence (1995), pp. 52–53.

30. Shavelson (1995), pp. 122–126.

31. For a sustained argument *against* the permissibility of both assisted suicide and euthanasia based on this line of reasoning, see Cundiff (1992). See also The Hastings Center (1987), p. 129, and Foley (1997), pp. 54–57.

32. This label is suggested in Kasting (1994), where the most thorough and critical discussion of this argument available in the extant literature is provided.

33. See Quill (1993), pp. 38, 90, 156, and 166; Shavelson (1995), pp. 205, 209, and 216ff.; Baron et al. (1996), p. 5; and Angell (1997), pp. 50–51.

34. Lo (1995), p. 169.

35. Teno and Lynn (1996), p. 405.

36. Shavelson (1995), p. 218.

37. See Quill et al. (1992), pp. 1381–1382 and Miller et al. (1994), p. 120 for a discussion of why persons with an incurable, debilitating illness (that may not meet the technical definition of "terminal") should be included. See also, Baron et al. (1996), pp. 10–11.

38. Coleman and Miller (1995), p. 394.

39. See Shavelson (1995), Chapter 4.

40. Shavelson (1995), p. 112.

41. Shavelson (1995), p. 135.

42. For a discussion, see Pence (1995), Chapter 2, especially pp. 41–47, and McConnell (1997), pp. 82–84.

43. Kane (1985), p. 8.

44. Shavelson (1995), p. 155.

45. Shavelson (1995), p. 155.

46. Batavia (1997), p. 1672.

47. See The Hastings Center (1987), p. 128; Lo (1995), pp. 170–171; Meisel (1995), Vol. 1, Chap. 8 and Vol. 2, Chap. 18; and the Council on Ethical and Judicial Affairs of the American Medical Association (1994).

48. Shapiro et al. (1994).

49. Young et al. (1993).

50. Back et al. (1996).

51. Asch (1996).

52. Slome et al. (1997).

53. Emanuel et al. (1998), p. 511, point out that a significant number of physicians *misidentify* what they have done as instances of assisted suicide or euthanasia; thus, the practices of assisted suicide and euthanasia may not be as widespread as studies seem to show. But even if this is true, it points to another problem (discussed below): If acts not accurately labeled

"euthanasia" and "assisted suicide" seem to practitioners morally indistinguishable from them, then it may be that the moral assumptions underlying the conventional view just do not make any sense to those practitioners.

54. Solomon et al. (1993).

55. Truog et al. (1992) and Lo (1995), p. 172.

56. Edwards and Tolle (1992), p. 255.

57. *Brophy v. New England Sinai Hospital Inc.*, 497 N.E. 2d 626 (Mass. 1986). For a discussion of the Brophy case, see Lo (1995), pp. 195–197 and McConnell (1997), p. 138.

58. *Cruzan v. Director, Missouri Department of Health*, 497 U.S. 261 (1990). For a discussion of the Cruzan case, see Lo (1995), pp. 197–199 and McConnell (1997), pp. 139–141.

59. See, for example, Council on Ethical and Judicial Affairs of the American Medical Association (1994), p. 270, where this familiar move is made.

60. *McKay v. Bergstedt*, 801 P. 2d 617 (Nev. 1990).

61. *Barber v. Superior Court*, 195 Cal. Rptr. 484, 147 Cal. App. 3d. 1054 (1983). For a discussion of this case, see Lo (1995), pp. 193–195.

62. For a discussion of this, see Beauchamp and Childress (1994), pp. 206–211; McConnell (1997), pp. 111–114; and Quill et al. (1997).

63. Beauchamp and Childress (1994), pp. 206–211.

64. For a defense of this view, see Aulisio (1995).

65. Thomson (1999), p. 511.

66. Thomson (1999), p. 510.

67. Quill et al. (1997), p. 1770.

68. Edwards and Tolle (1992), pp. 255–256.

69. *Compassion in Dying v. Washington*, No. 94–35534, 1996 U.S. App. LEXIS 3944 (9th Cir. 6 Mar. 1996).

70. Capron (1996), p. 24, makes such a complaint.

71. *Quill v. Vacco*, No. 95–7028, 1996 U.S. App. LEXIS 6215 (2d Cir. 2 April 1996).

72. Miles (1994), p. 1786.

73. Coleman and Miller (1995), pp. 389, 390, and 391.

74. *Washington v. Glucksberg*, No. 117 S. Ct. 2258 (1997) and *Vacco v. Quill*, No. 117 S. Ct. 2293 (1997).

75. *Washington v. Glucksberg*, at 793–796.

76. *Washington v. Glucksberg*, at 797.

77. *Vacco v. Quill*, at 847.

78. *Vacco v. Quill*, at 842.

79. *Vacco v. Quill*, at 843.

80. See Chin et al. (1999), p. 577.

81. Chin et al. (1999).

82. Chin et al. (1999), p. 581.

83. Quill et al. (1992), p. 1383.

84. See Meisel (1995), Vol. 2, pp. 164–185.

85. Meisel (1995), Vol. 2, p. 167 (emphasis added).

86. See Meisel (1991), p. 1498, who notes that there may be difficulties with the reasoning that has been supplied to support this view. And, indeed, the opinions of the Second and Ninth Circuit Courts on the issue of prohibiting assisted suicide (discussed above) suggest that there are insurmountable difficulties with this reasoning; the Supreme Court, however, disagrees, as was explained above.

87. See Beauchamp and Childress (1994), pp. 196–211 and Lo (1995), pp. 141–144.

88. The definitive work in this area is Buchanan and Brock (1989).

89. See Meisel (1995), Vol. 1, pp. 394–408.

90. Here I ignore complications that arise based on two other liberty-limiting principles: legal moralism and the offense principle.

91. Simmons (1993), p. 103, note 7, rightly criticizes my (1984) article for not drawing this distinction. My intent in that article was to focus on the legal case, but some of what I said misled readers about this.

92. Hill (1991), p. 15.

93. Hill (1991), p. 95.

94. Hill (1991), p. 95.

95. Hill (1991), pp. 90–91.

96. R. Dworkin (1993), p. 13.

97. R. Dworkin (1993), p. 24.

98. Dworkin states this point in the affirmative—that it is in the comatose patient's best interests to be allowed to die. I put the point more modestly—that it is not contrary to his best interests. My way of putting the point will remain accurate, even if it is true that irreversibly comatose patients have *no interests*.

99. R. Dworkin (1993), p. 195.

100. R. Dworkin (1993), p. 215.

101. R. Dworkin (1993), p. 97.

Chapter 7

1. See Crespi (1994), pp. 14–15 and 55ff.; Cohen (1989), p. 8; and Radin (1987), pp. 1854–1855.

2. Radin (1987) and Radin (1996), Chapter 2.

3. Sam Seibert and Theresa Waldrop, "Kidneys for Sale: The Issue is Tissue," *Newsweek*: December 5, 1988, p. 38.

4. Michael Kinsley, "Take My Kidney, Please," *Time*: March 13, 1989, p. 88. This case is widely discussed. See, for example, Harris (1992), p. 136.

5. See Devettere (1995), pp. 456–457.

6. This is oversimplified. Locke required the satisfaction of other conditions, including that one not allow that which one has procured to spoil and that one leave enough for others to satisfy their needs. See Locke (1960/1690), Chapter V, section 27.

7. Radin (1987), p. 1851.

8. Rose-Ackerman (1985), p. 950.

9. Munzer (1990), p. 44.

10. Council on Ethical and Judicial Affairs (1995), p. 586.

11. Rose-Ackerman (1985), pp. 935ff.

12. See Spital (1991), p. 234 and Devettere (1995), p. 454.

13. Meyers (1990), p. 198.

14. As is well known, there is a severe shortage of organs for transplantation. In the United States alone (as I write this), the waiting list is over 65,000, more than 60 percent of whom are waiting for a kidney.

15. See Andrews (1986), p. 32, Harris (1992), pp. 131–132, and Radin (1996), pp. 51–52.

16. Devettere (1995), p. 457.

17. Elliott (1995), p. 93.

18. Elliott (1995), p. 91.

19. Andrews (1986), p. 32.

20. If anatomical conditions are right, an adult can donate a portion of his or her liver to a child; the adult's liver will regenerate and the portion donated to the child will grow.

It should be noted that section 274e of the United States Public Health Code counts kidneys, bone marrow, and skin as organs, but not blood.

21. For a discussion, see McConnell (1997), pp. 229–231.

22. See Jonsen, Veatch, and Walters (1998), pp. 412–417.

23. Recently, some have initiated protocols to procure organs from so-called nonheart-beating cadavers. Obstacles for using nonheart-beating donors have been numerous: organs begin to deteriorate immediately when they cease to receive oxygen; time of death is not easily predictable; surgical teams and potential recipients must be in place so that transplantation can begin immediately upon death. For an extensive discussion of the use of nonheart-beating cadavers, see Arnold et al. (1995).

24. See McConnell (1997), p. 230.

25. Peters et al. (1996), pp. 2419–2424.

26. I assume here the so-called dead donor rule: that organs will be procured only from individuals who have died. Another way to expand the pool is to drop this rule and allow the procurement of organs from a subset of individuals who are not technically dead (such as patients in a persistent vegetative state).

27. Veatch (1989), p. 212.

28. Cohen (1989), p. 15.

29. See, for example, Veatch (1989), p. 264 (note 62) and Cohen (1989), p. 15 (note 57).

30. See Crespi (1994), p. 53.

31. This statement should be qualified. The current shortage might indicate not that incentives for potential contributors are necessary, but instead that the current instantiation of the giving policy is flawed and needs to be revised. Another possibility is this: the giving policy gives priority to individual autonomy and it is possible that most Americans simply oppose organ donation. While this latter is a possibility, it appears to be refuted by surveys that have been done. See Cohen (1989), p. 9 and Veatch (1989), pp. 212–213.

32. For a brief discussion of these two versions of the trading policy, see McConnell (1997), pp. 231–233.

33. For a defense of such a policy, see Jarvis (1995).

34. Cohen (1989), pp. 20–21 and Epstein (1997), p. 247.

35. Crespi (1994), p. 27.

36. Cohen (1989), pp. 34–35.

37. Cohen (1989), p. 35.

38. Cohen (1989), p. 28 and Epstein (1997), p. 259.

39. Cohen (1989), p. 28.

40. Epstein (1997), p. 249 and Chapter 12.

41. Crespi (1994), p. 23.

42. Council on Ethical and Judicial Affairs (1998–1999), p. 34.

43. Ellen Goodman, "Pricing 'Donated' Organs is Unseemly," *News & Record* (Greensboro, North Carolina), June 1, 1999.

44. Cohen (1989), p. 2 and Crespi (1994), pp. 36 and 46. To the best of my knowledge, only Richard Epstein (1997) supports allowing living persons to sell their organs. Epstein's contentions are that all plausible general principles allow for alienability by sale, gift, or bequest; that it does not matter whether the transaction takes place from the dead to the living or between two live persons; that it does not matter whether the persons are related; "nor even whether the transplantation is lethal to the donor" (p. 222).

45. Cohen (1989), p. 2.

46. For a discussion, see Rachels (1986), pp. 170–180, Beauchamp and Childress (1994), pp. 229–231, and McConnell (1997), pp. 122–123.

47. Epstein (1997), p. 222 and Chapter 12.

48. See note 44.
49. Cohen (1989), p. 2.
50. Wertheimer (1996), especially pp. 13–28.
51. Wertheimer (1996), Chapters 7 and 8.
52. Wertheimer (1996), Chapter 9.
53. Wertheimer (1996), p. 113.

Chapter 8

1. See Brown (1955), especially pp. 208–209 and Frankena (1955), pp. 228ff.
2. This is demonstrated clearly and convincingly in Richards (1969), especially pp. 393–396.
3. Kronman (1983), p. 778.
4. Kronman (1983), p. 780.
5. Kronman (1983), p. 784.
6. For a thorough discussion, see Pence (1995), Chapter 5.
7. See Becker (1970/1922), pp. 25–26.
8. See Maier (1997), especially pp. 133–136.
9. See Becker (1970/1922), especially Chapter 2, and Maier (1997).
10. Ronald Dworkin (1977), p. 266.
11. Dworkin (1977), p. 267.

Bibliography

Andrews, Lori. 1986. "My Body, My Property," *Hastings Center Report* 16 (October): 28–38.

Angell, Marcia. 1984. "Respecting the Autonomy of Competent Patients," *New England Journal of Medicine* 310: 1116–1117.

Angell, Marcia. 1988. "Euthanasia," *New England Journal of Medicine* 319: 1348– 1350.

Angell, Marcia. 1996. "Euthanasia in the Netherlands—Good News or Bad?" *New England Journal of Medicine* 335: 1676–1678.

Angell, Marcia. 1997. "The Supreme Court and Physician-Assisted Suicide—The Ultimate Right," *New England Journal of Medicine* 336: 50–53.

Annas, George. 1987. "Transferring the Ethical Hot Potato," *Hastings Center Report* 17: 20–21.

Arnold, Robert, Stuart Younger, Renie Schapiro, and Carol Mason Spicer. 1995. *Procuring Organs for Transplantation*. Baltimore: Johns Hopkins University Press.

Asch, David. 1996. "The Role of Critical Care Nurses in Euthanasia and Assisted Suicide," *New England Journal of Medicine* 334: 1374–1379.

Aulisio, Mark P. 1995. "In Defense of the Intention/Foresight Distinction," *American Philosophical Quarterly* 32: 341–354.

Back, Anthony, Jeffrey Wallace, Helene Starks, and Robert Pearlman. 1996. "Physician-Assisted Suicide and Euthanasia in Washington State," *JAMA* 275: 919–925.

Barnett, Randy. 1986a. "Contract Remedies and Inalienable Rights," *Social Philosophy and Policy* 4: 179–202.

Barnett, Randy. 1986b. "A Consent Theory of Contract," *Columbia Law Review* 86: 269–321.

Baron, Charles, Clyde Bergstresser, Dan Brock, Garrick Cole, Nancy Dorfman, Judith Johnson, Lowell Schnipper, James Vorenberg, and Sidney Wanzer. 1996. "A Model State Act to Authorize and Regulate Physician-Assisted Suicide," *Harvard Journal on Legislation* 33: 1–34.

Batavia, Andrew I. 1997. "Disability and Physician-Assisted Suicide," *New England Journal of Medicine* 336: 1671–1673.

Battin, Margaret Pabst. 1994. *The Least Worst Death*. New York: Oxford University Press.

Battin, Margaret Pabst. 1995. *Ethical Issues in Suicide*. Englewood Cliffs, NJ: Prentice-Hall.

Beauchamp, Tom L. and James F. Childress. 1994. *Principles of Biomedical Ethics,* fourth edition. New York: Oxford University Press.

Becker, Carl. 1970/1922. *The Declaration of Independence: A Study in the History of Political Ideas.* New York: Vintage Books.

Becker, Lawrence C. 1982. "Individual Rights," in Tom Regan and Donald VanDeVeer (eds.), *And Justice for All.* Totowa, NJ: Rowman and Littlefield, pp. 197–216.

Bedau, Hugo. 1968. "The Right to Life," *The Monist* 52: 550–572.

Benditt, Theodore M. 1982. *Rights.* Totowa, NJ: Rowman and Littlefield.

Black, Henry Campbell. 1990. *Black's Law Dictionary,* sixth edition. St. Paul, MN: West Publishing Company.

Blendon, Robert, Ulrike Szalsy, and Richard Knox. 1992. "Should Physicians Aid Their Patients in Dying?" *JAMA* 267: 2658–2662.

Broad, C.D. 1969. "Conscience and Conscientious Action," in Joel Feinberg (ed.), *Moral Concepts.* New York: Oxford University Press, pp. 74–79.

Brock, Dan W. 1993. *Life and Death.* New York: Cambridge University Press.

Brody, Baruch. 1988. *Life and Death Decision Making.* New York: Oxford University Press.

Brody, Howard. 1992. "Assisted Death: A Compassionate Response to a Medical Failure," *New England Journal of Medicine* 327: 1384–1388.

Brown, Stuart M., Jr. 1955. "Inalienable Rights," *The Philosophical Review* 64: 192–211.

Buchanan, Allen. 1984. "What's So Special About Rights?" *Social Philosophy and Policy* 2: 61–83.

Buchanan, Allen. 1985. *Ethics, Efficiency, and the Market Place.* Totowa, NJ: Rowman and Allanheld.

Buchanan, Allen and Dan Brock. 1989. *Deciding for Others.* New York: Cambridge University Press.

Burt, Robert A. 1996. "Constitutionalizing Physician-Assisted Suicide: Will Lightning Strike Thrice?" *Duquesne Law Review* 35: 159–181.

Butler, Joseph. 1983/1726. *Five Sermons.* Edited by Stephen L. Darwall. Indianapolis: Hackett.

Calabresi, Guido and Douglas Melamed. 1972. "Property Rules, Liability Rules, and Inalienability," *Harvard Law Review* 85: 1089–1128.

Callahan, Daniel. 1992. "When Self-Determination Runs Amok," *Hastings Center Report* 22 (March): 52–55.

Cantor, Norman. 1993. *Advance Directives and the Pursuit of Death With Dignity.* Bloomington: Indiana University Press.

Caplan, Arthur. 1995. *Moral Matters: Ethical Issues in Medicine and the Life Sciences.* New York: John Wiley & Sons.

Capron, Alexander M. 1996. "Liberty, Equality, Death!" *Hastings Center Report* 26 (May): 23–24.

Childress, James F. 1979. "Appeals to Conscience," *Ethics* 89: 315–335.

Chin, Arthur, Katrina Hedberg, Grant Higginson, and David Fleming. 1999. "Legalized Physician-Assisted Suicide in Oregon—The First Year's Experience," *New England Journal of Medicine* 340: 577–583.

Churchill, Larry R. 1994. *Self-Interest and Universal Health Care.* Cambridge, MA: Harvard University Press.

Cohen, Lloyd R. 1989. "Increasing the Supply of Transplant Organs: The Virtues of a Futures Market," *George Washington Law Review* 58: 1–51.

Coleman, Carl H. and Tracy E. Miller. 1995. "Stemming the Tide: Assisted Suicide and the Constitution," *Journal of Law, Medicine & Ethics* 23: 389–397.

Conee, Earl. 1987. "Against Moral Dilemmas," in Christopher Gowans (ed.), *Moral Dilemmas.* New York: Oxford University Press, pp. 239–249.

Council on Ethical and Judicial Affairs (of the American Medical Association). 1994. "Physician-Assisted Suicide," *Code of Medical Ethics Reports* 5: 269–275.

Council on Ethical and Judicial Affairs (of the American Medical Association). 1995. "Financial Incentives for Organ Procurement," *Archives of Internal Medicine* 155: 581–589.

Council on Ethical and Judicial Affairs (of the American Medical Association). 1998–1999. "Financial Incentives for Organ Donation," *Code of Medical Ethics*. Chicago: American Medical Association.

Council on Ethical and Judicial Affairs (of the American Medical Association). 1999. "Medical Futility in End-of-Life Care," *JAMA* 281: 937–941.

Cundiff, David. 1992. *Euthanasia Is Not the Answer.* Totowa, NJ: Humana Press.

Crespi, Gregory S. 1994. "Overcoming the Legal Obstacles to the Creation of a Futures Market in Bodily Organs," *Ohio State Law Journal* 55: 1–77.

Daar, Judith. 1993. "A Clash at the Bedside: Patient Autonomy v. a Physician's Professional Conscience," *Hastings Law Journal* 44: 1241–1289.

Dahl, Norman O. 1984. *Practical Reason, Aristotle, and Weakness of the Will.* Minneapolis: University of Minnesota Press.

Dahl, Norman O. 1988. "Against Legal Paternalism: Review of Feinberg's *Harm to Self*," *Criminal Justice Ethics* 7: 67–78.

D'Arcy, Eric. 1961. *Conscience and Its Right to Freedom.* New York: Sheed and Ward.

Deber, Raisa, Nancy Kraetschmer, and Jane Irvine. 1996. "What Role Do Patients Wish to Play in Treatment Decision Making?" *Archives of Internal Medicine* 156: 1414–1420.

DeCew, Judith Wagner. 1997. *In Pursuit of Privacy: Law, Ethics, and the Rise of Technology.* Ithaca, NY: Cornell University Press.

Devettere, Raymond J. 1995. *Practical Decision Making in Health Care Ethics.* Washington, D.C.: Georgetown University Press.

Donagan, Alan. 1977. *The Theory of Morality.* Chicago: University of Chicago Press.

Dworkin, Ronald. 1977. *Taking Rights Seriously.* Cambridge, MA: Harvard University Press.

Dworkin, Ronald. 1993. *Life's Dominion.* New York: Alfred A. Knopf.

Dworkin, Ronald. 1996. *Freedom's Law.* Cambridge, MA: Harvard University Press.

Edwards, Miles J. and Susan W. Tolle. 1992. "Disconnecting a Ventilator at the Request of a Patient Who Knows He Will Die: The Doctor's Anguish," *Annals of Internal Medicine* 117: 254–256.

Elliott, Carl. 1995. "Doing Harm: Living Organ Donors, Clinical Research, and *The Tenth Man,*" *Journal of Medical Ethics* 21: 91–96.

Emanuel, Ezekiel. 1996. "Oregon's Physician-Assisted Suicide Law," *Archives of Internal Medicine* 156: 825–829.

Emanuel, Ezekiel, Elisabeth Daniels, Diane Fairclough, and Brian Clarridge. 1998. "The Practice of Euthanasia and Physician-Assisted Suicide in the United States," *JAMA* 280: 507– 513.

Epstein, Richard. 1985. "Why Restrain Alienation?" *Columbia Law Review* 85: 970–990.

Epstein, Richard. 1997. *Mortal Peril: Our Inalienable Right to Health Care?* Reading, MA: Addison-Wesley.

Faden, Ruth and Tom Beauchamp. 1986. *A History and Theory of Informed Consent.* New York: Oxford University Press.

Feinberg, Joel. 1973. *Social Philosophy.* Englewood Cliffs, NJ: Prentice-Hall.

Feinberg, Joel. 1980. *Rights, Justice, and the Bounds of Liberty.* Princeton, NJ: Princeton University Press.

Feinberg, Joel. 1984. *Harm to Others.* New York: Oxford University Press.

Feinberg, Joel. 1986. *Harm to Self.* New York: Oxford University Press.

Fletcher, George P. 1980. "The Right to Life," *The Monist* 63: 135–155.

Fletcher, George P. 1996. *Basic Concepts of Legal Thought*. New York: Oxford University Press.

Foley, Kathleen M. 1997. "Competent Care For the Dying Instead of Physician-Assisted Suicide," *New England Journal of Medicine* 336: 54–58.

Francis, Leslie Pickering. 1993. "Advance Directives for Voluntary Euthanasia: A Volatile Combination?" *Journal of Medicine and Philosophy* 18: 297–322.

Frankena, William K. 1955. "Natural and Inalienable Rights," *Philosophical Review* 64: 212–232.

Freedman, Benjamin. 1993. "Offering Truth," *Archives of Internal Medicine* 153: 572–576.

Fuss, Peter. 1964. "Conscience," *Ethics* 74: 111–120.

Garnett, A. Campbell. 1969. "Conscience and Conscientiousness," in Joel Feinberg (ed.), *Moral Concepts*. New York: Oxford University Press, pp. 80–92.

Gasner, M.R., Khin Lay Maw, Gabriel Feldman, Paula Fujiwara, and Thomas Frieden. 1999. "The Use of Legal Action in NewYork City to Ensure Treatment of Tuberculosis," *New England Journal of Medicine* 340: 359–366.

Gensler, Harry. 1985. "Ethical Consistency Principles," *The Philosophical Quarterly* 35: 156–170.

Gert, Bernard, Edward Berger, George Cahill, K. Danner Clouser, Charles Culver, John Moeschler, and George Singer. 1996. *Morality and the New Genetics*. Boston: Jones and Bartlett.

Gewirth, Alan. 1978. *Reason and Morality*. Chicago: University of Chicago Press.

Gewirth, Alan. 1982. *Human Rights*. Chicago: University of Chicago Press.

Grisez, Germain. 1970. *Abortion: The Myths, the Realities, and the Arguments*. New York: Corpus Books.

Grisez, Germain and Joseph Boyle. 1979. *Life and Death With Liberty and Justice*. Notre Dame, IN: University of Notre Dame Press.

Gunderson, Martin and David Mayo. 1993. "Altruism and Physician-Assisted Suicide," *Journal of Medicine and Philosophy* 18: 281–295.

Hagman, Donald G. 1970. "The Medical Patient's Right to Know," *UCLA Law Review* 17: 758–816.

Hardin, Russell. 1986. "The Utilitarian Logic of Liberalism," *Ethics* 97: 47–74.

Harris, John. 1992. *Wonderwoman and Superman*. New York: Oxford University Press.

Hastings Center, 1987. *Guidelines on the Termination of Life-Sustaining Treatment and the Care of the Dying*. Bloomington: Indiana University Press.

Hauptman, Paul J. and Kevin J. O'Connor. 1997. "Procurement and Allocation of Solid Organs for Transplantation," *New England Journal of Medicine* 336: 422–431.

Herzog, Don. 1989. *Happy Slaves: A Critique of Consent Theory*. Chicago: University of Chicago Press.

Hill, Thomas E., Jr. 1991. *Autonomy and Self-Respect*. New York: Cambridge University Press.

Huffman, Fordham E. 1979. "Coerced Donation of Body Tissues: Can We Live With *McFall v. Shrimp*," *Ohio State Law Journal* 40: 409–440.

Hull, Richard T. 1985. "Informed Consent: Patient's Right or Patient's Duty?" *Journal of Medicine and Philosophy* 10: 183–197.

Hutcheson, Francis. 1991/1738. *An Inquiry Concerning Moral Good and Evil*, in D.D. Raphael (ed.), *British Moralists 1650–1800*. Indianapolis: Hackett, pp. 261–299.

Hyde, Alan. 1997. *Bodies of Law*. Princeton: Princeton University Press.

Jarvis, Rupert. 1995. "Join the Club: A Modest Proposal to Increase the Availability of Donor Organs," *Journal of Medical Ethics* 21: 199–204.

Jefferson, Thomas. 1982/1785. *Notes on the State of Virginia*. Edited by William Peden. Chapel Hill, NC: University of North Carolina Press.

Jonsen, Albert, Robert Veatch, and LeRoy Walters. 1998. *Source Book in Bioethics: A Documentary History.* Washington: Georgetown University Press.

Kane, Francis I. 1985. "Keeping Elizabeth Bouvia Alive for the Public Good," *Hastings Center Report* 15 (December): 5–8.

Kant, Immanuel. 1974/1793. *On the Old Saw.* Translated by E. B. Ashton. Philadelphia: University of Pennsylvania Press.

Kant, Immanuel. 1965/1797. *The Metaphysical Elements of Justice.* Translated by John Ladd. Indianapolis: Bobbs-Merrill.

Kantor, Jay E. 1989. *Medical Ethics for Physicians-in-Training.* New York: Plenum.

Kasting, Gregg A. 1994. "The Nonnecessity of Euthanasia," in James Humber, Robert Almeder, and Gregg Kasting (eds.), *Physician-Assisted Death.* Totowa, NJ: Humana Press, pp. 25–45.

Kavka, Gregory. 1986. *Hobbesian Moral and Political Theory.* Princeton, NJ: Princeton University Press.

King, Nancy M.P. 1993. "Patient Waiver of Informed Consent," *North Carolina Medical Journal* 54: 399–403.

King, Nancy M.P. 1996. *Making Sense of Advance Directives,* revised edition. Washington, D.C.: Georgetown University Press.

Kleinig, John. 1979. "Consent as a Defense in Criminal Law," *Archiv fur Rechts und Sozialphilosophie* 65: 329–344.

Kleinig, John. 1982. "The Ethics of Consent," *New Essays in Ethics and Public Policy: Canadian Journal of Philosophy* Supp. Vol. 8: 91–118.

Kramer, Matthew, N.E. Simmonds, and Hillel Steiner. 1998. *A Debate Over Rights.* New York: Oxford University Press.

Kronman, Anthony. 1983. "Paternalism and the Law of Contracts," *Yale Law Journal* 92: 763–798.

Kuflik, Arthur. 1984. "The Inalienability of Autonomy," *Philosophy & Public Affairs* 13: 271–298.

Kuflik, Arthur. 1986. "The Utilitarian Logic of Inalienable Rights," *Ethics* 97: 75–87.

Layson, Rita T. and Terrance McConnell. 1996. "Must Consent Always Be Obtained for a Do-Not-Resuscitate Order?" *Archives of Internal Medicine* 156: 2617–2620.

Leavitt, Frank J. 1992. "Inalienable Rights," *Philosophy* 67: 115–118.

Leland, John. 1991/1791. "The Right of Conscience Inalienable," in Ellis Sandoz (ed.), *Political Sermons of the American Founding Era.* Indianapolis: Liberty Press, pp. 1079–1099.

Lo, Bernard. 1995. *Resolving Ethical Dilemmas: A Guide for Clinicians.* Baltimore: Williams & Wilkins.

Locke, John. 1960/1690. *The Second Treatise of Government* in *Two Treatises of Government.* Introduction by Peter Laslett. New York: Cambridge University Press.

Locke, John. 1983/1689. *A Letter Concerning Toleration.* Edited by James Tulley. Indianapolis: Hackett.

Loftus, Irene Prior. 1990. "I Have a Conscience, Too: The Right of Medical Personnel Confronting the Right to Die," *Notre Dame Law Review* 65: 699–730.

Lomasky, Loren. 1987. *Persons, Rights, and the Moral Community.* New York: Oxford University Press.

Lyons, David. 1965. *Forms and Limits of Utilitarianism.* New York: Oxford University Press.

Lyons, David. 1994. *Rights, Welfare, and Mill's Moral Theory.* New York: Oxford University Press.

Madison, James. 1973. *The Papers of James Madison.* Chicago: University of Chicago Press.

Maier, Pauline. 1997. *American Scripture: Making the Declaration of Independence.* New York: Alfred A. Knopf.

Martyn, Susan R. and Henry J. Bourguignon. 1997. "Physician-Assisted Suicide: The Lethal Flaws of the Ninth and Second Circuit Decisions," *California Law Review* 85: 371–426.

May, Larry. 1983. "On Conscience," *American Philosophical Quarterly* 20: 57–67.

Mayo, David and Martin Gunderson. 1993. "Physician Assisted Death and Hard Choices," *Journal of Medicine and Philosophy* 18: 329–341.

McCloskey, H.J. 1975. "The Right to Life," *Mind* 84: 403–425.

McConnell, Terrance. 1984. "The Nature and Basis of Inalienable Rights," *Law and Philosophy* 3: 25–59.

McConnell, Terrance. 1987. "Moral Dilemmas and Consistency in Ethics," in Christopher Gowans (ed.), *Moral Dilemmas*. New York: Oxford University Press, pp. 154–173.

McConnell, Terrance. 1993. *Gratitude*. Philadelphia: Temple University Press.

McConnell, Terrance. 1996. "Moral Residue and Dilemmas," in H.E. Mason (ed.), *Moral Dilemmas and Moral Theory*. New York: Oxford University Press.

McConnell, Terrance. 1997. *Moral Issues in Health Care,* second edition. Belmont, CA: Wadsworth.

McGuire, Martin. 1963. "On Conscience," *Journal of Philosophy* 60: 253–263.

Meisel, Alan. 1979. "The Exceptions to the Informed Consent Doctrine," *Wisconsin Law Review*: 413–488.

Meisel, Alan. 1991. "Legal Myths About Terminating Life Support," *Archives of Internal Medicine* 151: 1497–1501.

Meisel, Alan. 1995. *The Right to Die,* Vols. 1 and 2, second edition. New York: John Wiley and Sons.

Meyer, Michael J. 1992. "Patients' Duties," *Journal of Medicine and Philosophy* 17: 541–555.

Meyers, David W. 1990. *The Human Body and the Law*. Stanford, CA: Stanford University Press.

Meyers, Diana T. 1985. *Inalienable Rights*. New York: Columbia University Press.

Miles, Steven H. 1992. "Interpersonal Issues in the Wanglie Case," *Kennedy Institute of Ethics Journal* 2: 61–72.

Miles, Steven H. 1994. "Physicians and Their Patients' Suicides," *JAMA* 271: 1786–1788.

Miller, Franklin, Timothy Quill, Howard Brody, John Fletcher, Lawrence Gostin, and Diane Meier. 1994. "Regulating Physician-Assisted Death," *New England Journal of Medicine* 331: 119–123.

Momeyer, Richard. 1995. "Does Physician Assisted Suicide Violate the Integrity of Medicine?" *Journal of Medicine and Philosophy* 20: 13–24.

Munzer, Stephen R. 1990. *A Theory of Property*. New York: Cambridge University Press.

Nelson, John O. 1989. "Are There Inalienable Rights?" *Philosophy* 64: 519–524.

Nickel, James W. 1982. "Are Human Rights Utopian?" *Philosophy & Public Affairs* 11: 246–264.

Nickel, James W. 1987. *Making Sense of Human Rights*. Berkeley, CA: University of California Press.

Nozick, Robert. 1974. *Anarchy, State, and Utopia*. New York: Basic Books.

Nuland, Sherwin B. 1994. *How We Die*. New York: Alfred A. Knopf.

Ost, David E. 1984. "The 'Right' Not to Know," *Journal of Medicine and Philosophy* 9: 301–312.

Ouslander, J.G., A.J. Tymchuk, B. Rahbar. 1989. "Health Care Decisions Among Elderly Long-Term Care Residents and Their Potential Proxies," *Archives of Internal Medicine* 149: 1367–1372.

Pence, Gregory E. 1995. *Classic Cases in Medical Ethics,* second edition. New York: McGraw-Hill.

Peters, Thomas, Dilip Kittur, L.J. McGaw, Roy First, and Edward Nelson. 1996. "Organ Donors and Nondonors," *Archives of Internal Medicine* 156: 2419–2424.

Price, Richard. 1991/1778. *Richard Price: Political Writings*. Edited by D.D. Thomas. New York: Cambridge University Press.

Quill, Timothy. 1993. *Death and Dignity*. New York: W.W. Norton.

Quill, Timothy, Christine Cassel, and Diane Meier. 1992. "Care of the Hopelessly Ill: Potential Criteria for Physician-Assisted Suicide," *New England Journal of Medicine* 327: 1380–1384.

Quill, Timothy, Rebecca Dresser, and Dan Brock. 1997. "The Rule of Double Effect—A Critique of Its Role in End-of-Life Decision Making," *New England Journal of Medicine* 337: 1768–1771.

Rachels, James. 1986. *The End of Life*. New York: Oxford University Press.

Radin, Margaret J. 1987. "Market Inalienability," *Harvard Law Review* 100: 1849–1937.

Radin, Margaret J. 1994. *Reinterpreting Property*. Chicago: University of Chicago Press.

Radin, Margaret J. 1996. *Contested Commodities*. Cambridge, MA: Harvard University Press.

Rawls, John. 1971. *A Theory of Justice*. Cambridge, MA: Harvard University Press.

Richards, B.A. 1969. "Inalienable Rights: Recent Criticism and Old Doctrine," *Philosophy and Phenomenological Research* 29: 391–404.

Richards, Edward P. and Katharine C. Rathbun. 1993. *Law and the Physician*. Boston: Little, Brown.

Rose-Ackerman, Susan. 1985. "Inalienability and the Theory of Property Rights," *Columbia Law Review* 85: 931–969.

Ryle, Gilbert. 1954. "Conscience and Moral Convictions," in Margaret McDonald (ed.), *Philosophy and Analysis*. New York: Philosophical Library, pp. 156–165.

Salmond, John. 1957. *Salmond on Jurisprudence*, eleventh edition. Edited by Glanville Williams. London: Sweet and Maxwell.

Schiller, Marvin. 1969. "Are There Any Inalienable Rights?" *Ethics* 79: 309–315.

Schneiderman, Lawrence J. and Nancy S. Jecker. 1995. *Wrong Medicine: Doctors, Patients, and Futile Treatment*. Baltimore: Johns Hopkins University Press.

Seckler, Allison, Diane Meier, Michael Mulvihill, and Barbara Paris. 1991. "Substituted Judgment: How Accurate Are Proxy Predictions?" *Annals of Internal Medicine* 115: 92–97.

Shapiro, Robyn, Arthur Derse, Mark Gottlieb, David Schiedermayer, and Mary Olson. 1994. "Willingness to Perform Euthanasia: A Survey of Physician Attitudes," *Archives of Internal Medicine* 154: 575–584.

Shavelson, Lonny. 1995. *A Chosen Death*. New York: Simon & Schuster.

Sidgwick, Henry. 1981/1907. *The Methods of Ethics*. Indianapolis, IN: Hackett.

Simmons, A. John. 1979. *Moral Principles and Political Obligations*. Princeton, NJ: Princeton University Press.

Simmons, A. John. 1993. *On the Edge of Anarchy*. Princeton, NJ: Princeton University Press.

Simpson, Laurence P. 1965. *Handbook of the Law of Contracts*, second edition. St. Paul, MN: West Publishing Co.

Singer, Marcus. 1971. *Generalization in Ethics*. New York: Atheneum.

Singer, Peter. 1994. *Rethinking Life and Death*. New York: St. Martin's Griffin.

Slome, Lee R., Thomas Mitchell, Edwin Charlebois, Jeffrey Benevedes, and Donald Abrams. 1997. "Physician-Assisted Suicide and Patients with Human Immunodeficiency Virus Disease," *New England Journal of Medicine* 336: 417–421.

Smith, Tara. 1995. "Rights Conflicts: The Undoing of Rights," *Journal of Social Philosophy* 26: 139–156.

Solomon, Mildred Z., L.O. O'Donnell, B. Jennings, et al. 1993. "Decisions Near the End of Life: Professional Views on Life-Sustaining Treatments," *American Journal of Public Health* 83: 14–23.

Spital, Aaron. 1991. "Living Organ Donation: Shifting Responsibility," *Archives of Internal Medicine* 151: 234–235.

Stell, Lance. 1979. "Dueling and the Right to Life," *Ethics* 90: 7–26.

Stoljar, Samuel. 1984. *An Analysis of Rights*. New York: St. Martin's Press.

Strull, W.M., B. Lo, and G. Charles. 1984. "Do Patients Want to Participate in Medical Decision Making?" *JAMA* 252: 2990–2994.

Sugarman, Jeremy, Anna Mastroianni, and Jeffrey Kahn (eds.). 1998. *Ethics of Research with Human Subjects: Selected Policies and Resources*. Frederick, MD: University Publishing Group.

Sumner, L.W. 1981. *Abortion and Moral Theory*. Princeton, NJ: Princeton University Press.

Sumner, L.W. 1987. *The Moral Foundation of Rights*. New York: Oxford University Press.

Teno, Joan and Joanne Lynn. 1996. "Voluntary Active Euthanasia: The Individual Case and Public Policy," in Thomas Mappes and David DeGrazia (eds.), *Biomedical Ethics*, fourth edition. New York: McGraw-Hill, pp. 404–407.

Thomson, Judith Jarvis. 1986. *Rights, Restitution, and Risk*. Cambridge, MA: Harvard University Press.

Thomson, Judith Jarvis. 1990. *The Realm of Rights*. Cambridge, MA: Harvard University Press.

Thomson, Judith Jarvis. 1999. "Physician-Assisted Suicide: Two Moral Arguments," *Ethics* 109: 497–518.

Thoreau, Henry David. 1981/1849. *Civil Disobedience*, in Lily Owens (ed.), *Works of Henry David Thoreau*. New York: Averel Books.

Truog, Robert, Charles Berde, Christine Mitchell, and Holcombe Grier. 1992. "Barbiturates in the Care of the Terminally Ill," *New England Journal of Medicine* 327: 1678–1682.

Uniacke, Suzanne. 1994. *Permissible Killing*. New York: Cambridge University Press.

Van Der Maas, Paul J., Gerrit Van Der Wal, Ilinda Haverkate, Carmen DeGraaff, John Kester, Bregje Onwuteaka-Philipsen, Agnes Van Der Heide, Jacqueline Bosma, and Dick Williams. 1996. "Euthanasia, Physician-Assisted Suicide, and Other Medical Practices Involving the End of Life in the Netherlands, 1990–1995," *New England Journal of Medicine* 335: 1699–1705.

Van Der Wal, Gerrit, Paul J. Van Der Maas, Jacqueline Bosma, Bregje Onwuteaka-Philipsen, Dick Willems, Ilinka Haverkate, and Piet Kostense. 1996. "Evaluation of the Notification Procedure for Physician-Assisted Death in the Netherlands," *New England Journal of Medicine* 335: 1706–1711.

VanDeVeer, Donald. 1980a. "Are Human Rights Alienable?" *Philosophical Studies* 37: 165–176.

VanDeVeer, Donald. 1980b. "The Contractual Argument for Withholding Medical Information," *Philosophy & Public Affairs* 9: 198–205.

VanDeVeer, Donald. 1986. *Paternalistic Intervention*. Princeton, NJ: Princeton University Press.

Veatch, Robert M. *Death, Dying, and the Biological Revolution*, revised edition. New Haven, CT: Yale University Press.

Wanzer, Sidney, Daniel Federman, James Adelstein, Christine Cassel, Edwin Cassem, Ronald Cranford, Edward Hook, Bernard Lo, Charles Moertel, Peter Safar, Alan Stone, and Jan van Eys. 1989. "The Physician's Responsibility Toward Hopelessly Ill Patients," *New England Journal of Medicine* 320: 844–849.

Wear, Stephen. 1998. *Informed Consent: Patient Autonomy and Clinician Beneficence Within Health Care*, second edition. Washington, DC: Georgetown University Press.

Wear, Stephen, Susan Lagaipa, and Gerald Logue. 1994. "Toleration of Moral Diversity and the Conscientious Refusal by Physicians to Withdraw Life-Sustaining Treatment," *Journal of Medicine and Philosophy* 19: 147–159.

Wellington, Harry H. 1990. *Interpreting the Constitution: The Supreme Court and the Process of Adjudication*. New Haven, CT: Yale University Press.

Wellman, Carl. 1985. *A Theory of Rights*. Totowa, NJ: Rowman and Allanheld.

Wellman, Carl. 1995a. *Real Rights*. New York: Oxford University Press.

Wellman, Carl. 1995b. "The Inalienable Right to Life and the Durable Power of Attorney," *Law and Philosophy* 14: 245–269.

Wellman, Christopher H. 1995. "On Conflicts Between Rights," *Law and Philosophy* 14: 271–295.

Wertheimer, Alan. 1996. *Exploitation*. Princeton, NJ: Princeton University Press.

White, Morton. 1978. *The Philosophy of the American Revolution*. New York: Oxford University Press.

White, Morton. 1987. *Philosophy, The Federalist, and the Constitution*. New York: Oxford University Press.

Wildes, Kevin. 1993. "Conscience, Referral, and Physician-Assisted Suicide," *Journal of Medicine and Philosophy* 18: 323–328.

Williams, Glanville. 1962. "Consent and Public Policy," *The Criminal Law Review*, 74–83.

Young A., D. Volker, P.T. Rieger, and D.M. Thorpe. 1993. "Oncology Nurses' Attitudes Regarding Voluntary Physician-Assisted Dying for Competent, Terminally Ill Patients," *Oncology Nursing Forum* 20: 445–451.

Zimmerman, Michael J. 1996. *The Concept of Moral Obligation*. New York: Cambridge University Press.

Index

advance directives 59, 112–114
alienable rights 10–11, 23, 34, 46–47, 48, 68, 118–119, 155n
alienation of right of conscience 51–52, 54–55
American Civil Liberties Union 61
American Medical Association 43, 60
Americans with Disabilities Act 62
Andrews, Lori 154n
Angell, Marcia 88–89, 99, 148n, 150n, 152n
Annas, George 147n
Arnold, Robert 155n
Articles of Confederation 48
Asch, David 103, 152n
assisted suicide 95–97, 103–104
  attitudes of health care providers toward 103
  compatible with inalienable right to life 96, 109
  court cases regarding 106–111
Aulisio, Mark 141, 153n
autonomy 28, 29, 40–41, 65, 73–74, 89–90, 91, 92–93, 96, 100–101, 111, 122, 124, 126, 130

Back, Anthony 103, 152n
Barber v. Superior Court (1983) 104, 153n
Barnett, Randy 146n
Baron, Charles 98, 151n, 152n
Batavia, Andrew 102, 152n
Battin, Margaret Pabst 98, 99, 150n, 151n, 152n
Beauchamp, Tom 105, 147n, 148n, 149n, 153n, 155n
Becker, Carl 156n
Becker, Lawrence 142n
Bedau, Hugo 79–80, 142n, 149n
Benditt, Theodore 141n., 144n
beneficence (and prevention of suffering) 90, 92–93, 96, 100–101, 121
Bergstedt, Kenneth 104
Berman v. United States (1946) 147n
best interests principle 114, 115, 154n
"blanket" consent 77, 148n, 149n
Blendon, Robert 151n
Bosze, Jean-Pierre 81
Bourguignon, Henry 152n
Bouvia, Elizabeth 101–102
boxing 138–139
Boyle, Joseph 98, 144n, 152n
Bridgman, Percy 99–100
Broad, C. D. 57, 147n
Brock, Dan 25, 26, 93, 95, 143n, 144n, 147n, 148n, 150n, 151n, 153n
Brody, Baruch 25, 26, 143n, 148n, 149n
Brophy, Patricia 60
Brophy, Paul 60, 104
Brophy v. New England Sinai Hospital, Inc. (1986) 60, 104, 147n, 153n
Brown, Stuart 156n
Buchanan, Allen 25, 26, 143n, 144n, 146n, 147n, 150n, 151n, 153n
Burt, Robert 151n, 152n
Butler, Joseph 45, 146n

Calabresi, Guido 35, 143n, 144n
Callahan, Daniel 24, 82, 92–93, 143n, 149n, 151n
Canterbury v. Spence (1972) 147n
Cantor, Norman 143n
Caplan, Arthur 20, 63, 143n, 147n, 148n, 149n
Capron, Alexander 153n
Cardozo, Benjamin 66, 84
Cassel, Christine 90, 112
Childress, James 105, 145n, 147n, 148n, 149n, 153n, 155n
Chin, Arthur 153n
Churchill, Larry 142n
Cobbs v. Grant (1972) 67, 147n, 148n
Cohen, Lloyd 126–127, 129, 130, 132, 154n, 155n, 156n
Colby, William 61
Coleman, Carl 152n, 153n
Compassion in Dying v. Washington (1996) 107–108, 153n
competence 65, 70, 93
Conee, Earl 143n, 146n
consent
  lacking normative efficacy 8–9, 12, 19, 23, 31, 74, 112
  as permission-generating 9–11, 23, 25, 47, 74, 89
Constitution of Massachusetts 140
contracts
  not morally binding 63–64
  unenforceable 29, 30, 40, 137
consequentialism 33
conventional view (about assisted suicide and euthanasia) 43, 102, 104–106
  criticisms of 103–104, 106–109
Council on Ethical and Judicial Affairs (of the American Medical Association) 60, 119, 127–128, 129, 147n, 153n, 154n, 155n
Crespi, Gregory 126, 130, 132, 154n, 155n
Cruzan, Joseph 61
Cruzan, Joyce 61
Cruzan, Nancy 60–61, 104
Cruzan v. Director, Missouri Department of Health (1990) 60–61, 104, 147n, 149n, 153n
Cruzan v. Harmon (1988) 147n
Culver, Charles 36
Cundiff, David 152n
Curran v. Bosze (1990) 81, 149n

Daar, Judith 62, 147n
Dahl, Norman 41–42, 145n
Danielson v. Roche (1952) 69, 148n
D'Arcy, Eric 145n, 146n
dead donor rule 155n
death (criteria for) 122, 123
death with dignity 90
Deber, Raisa 148n
DeCew, Judith 143n
Department of Health and Human Services 70
Devettere, Raymond 148n, 154n
"Diane," case of 97
doctrine of double effect 105–106
Doe v. Bolton (1973) 147n
Donagan, Alan 145n, 147n
Due Process Clause (of the 14th Amendment) 107, 109
dueling 138–139
duties and sincerity 49–50
duties to disclose information 65, 76–77, 136
duties to obtain consent 65, 74–76, 136
duties to oneself 27, 31, 40, 85–87, 115
  Singer's argument against 86–87
Dworkin, Ronald 39, 57, 83, 88–89, 92, 93, 115–116, 140, 144n, 145n, 146n, 149n, 150n, 151n, 154n, 156n

Edwards, Miles 153n
Elliott, Carl 154n
Emanuel, Ezekiel 150n, 151n, 152n
Epstein, Richard 130, 132, 155n
Equal Protection Clause (of the 14th Amendment) 108–109
euthanasia 15–16, 37, 43–44, 144n
  active and passive 88–89
  concept explained 88–89
  involuntary euthanasia 89
  nonvoluntary euthanasia 89, 116
  voluntary euthanasia 89–92, 95–96, 103–104, 116
exploitation (and the purchase of organs) 130–132

Faden, Ruth 147n, 148n, 149n
Federalist Papers 140

Feinberg, Joel 6, 7, 12, 14–19, 20, 68, 141n, 142n, 143n, 144n, 146n, 148n, 149n, 150n
Flaherty, John 80
Fletcher, George 8, 142n
Foley, Kathleen 151n, 152n
Food and Drug Administration 70
Frankena, William 156n
fraudulent conveyances 119
Freedman, Benjamin 148n
Fuss, Peter 143n

Garnett, A. Campbell 143n
Gasner, M. R. 148n
Gensler, Harry 143n
Gert, Bernard 144n
Gewirth, Alan 39–41, 141n, 145n
Glass, Robert 9
Goodman, Ellen 129, 155n
gratitude 129, 134
Grisez, Germain 13, 98, 142n, 144n, 152n
Gunderson, Martin 152n

Hagan, Kay 149n
Hagman, Donald 148n
Hamilton, Alexander 140
Hardin, Russell 35–36, 144n
harm principle 29–30, 72–73, 87, 88, 90, 114, 120, 136
Harris, John 154n
health care power of attorney 112–114
Henry, Patrick 48
Herbert, Clarence 105, 106
Herzog, Don 142n
Hill, Thomas E. 40, 88, 115–116, 144n, 145n, 146n, 148n, 150n, 154n
Hobbes, Thomas 48, 57, 78, 149n
Hohfeld, Wesley 3
Huffman, Fordham 149n
Hull, Richard 148n
human organs (sale of)
- arguments for allowing 118–120
- arguments for prohibiting 120–122
- futures contracts regarding 125–128
- giving policy for obtaining 122–123
- living contributors 129–132
- policy of presumed consent 124
- taking policy for obtaining 124
- trading policy for obtaining 124–125

Hutcheson, Francis 144n
Hyde, Alan 149n

impartiality 41, 48
inalienable rights
- antipaternalistic argument against 26–27, 30, 71
- concept of 12, 16, 19, 23, 41–42, 47, 135
- conceptual argument against 25–26, 28–30, 71
- distinguished from absolute rights 13
- distinguished from forfeitable rights 13–14
- and duties to oneself 27, 31, 115
- Feinberg's account of 14–19
- and genetic tests 36–37
- impossibility of alienation 50–51, 55, 74–75, 78, 135–136
- inalienable right to life 82–85, 114–116
- Kantian considerations in support of 39–41, 73–74, 88, 114–116
- Meyers's account of 13–14
- modified inalienability 119
- paternalistic position for 72, 82–83
- popular sense of 13, 23, 50, 135
- and the sale of human organs by living contributors 129–132
- utilitarian considerations in favor of 33–39, 72–73

In Re Helga Wanglie (1991) 59–60, 147n
Institutional Review Board 70
integrity 46, 52, 137–138
International Covenant on Civil and Political Rights 46

Jacobson v. Massachusetts (1905) 67, 148n
Jarvis, Rupert 155n
Jay, John 140
Jecker, Nancy 147n
Jefferson, Thomas 16, 40, 44, 48–50, 56, 79, 80, 135, 139–140, 146n
Jehovah's Witness 69, 75, 78, 148n
Jonsen, Albert 155n

Kane, Francis 152n
Kant, Immanuel 39–41, 145n
Kantor, Jay 148n
Kasting, Gregory 152n

Kavka, Gregory 149n
Kevorkian, Jack 95–96
King, Nancy 143n, 147n, 148n
Kinsley, Michael 154n
Kramer, Matthew 144n
Kronman, Anthony 137–138, 143n, 144n, 146n, 156n
Kuflik, Arthur 24, 39–41, 143n, 144n, 146n, 147n

Layson, Rita 147n, 149n
Leavitt, Frank 142n
legal moralism 154n
Leland, John 48, 49, 56, 146n
living wills 17, 18, 89, 112–113
Lo, Bernard 63, 147n, 148n, 150n, 151n, 152n, 153n
Locke, John 11, 48, 50, 57, 118–119, 140, 142n, 146n, 154n
Loftus, Irene 147n
Lomasky, Loren 8, 141n, 142n, 144n
Longmore, Paul 102
Lopatka, Sharon 9, 17, 83
Lynn, Joanne 151n, 152n
Lyons, David 142n, 144n

Madison, James 44, 48–50, 56, 135, 140, 142n, 146n, 154n
Maier, Pauline ~~140,~~ 156n
mandatory rights 12, 19, 30, 40, 52–53, 68
market inalienability 117, 121, 131, 136
Markowitz, Jacob 75
Martyn, Susan 152n
May, Larry 145n, 146n, 147n
Mayo, David 152n
McCloskey, H. J. 144n, 149n
McFall, Robert 80–81
McFall v. Shimp (1978) 80, 149n
McGuire, Martin 145n
McKay v. Bergstedt (1990) 104, 153n
medical futility 59–60
medical research and human subjects 70, 121, 138–139
Meier, Diane 90, 112
Meisel, Alan 143n, 147n, 148n, 152n, 153n
Melamed, Douglas 35, 143n, 144n
Meyer, Michael 148n
Meyers, David 154n
Meyers, Diana T. 13, 42, 142n, 145n, 149n
Miles, Steven 58, 147n, 153n
Miller, Franklin 152n
Miller, Tracy 152n, 153n
Miner, Roger 108
moral dilemmas 22, 38–39, 47
moral risks 53–54, 56, 137–138
Munzer, Stephen 119, 154n

Nathanson v. Kline (1960) 66, 147n
National Organ Transplant Act 117
natural rights 44
Nelson, John 142n
Nickel, James 26, 44, 141n, 142n, 143n, 145n
Niles, Kelly 101–102
Nozick, Robert 26, 143n
Nuland, Sherwin 99, 152n

Oates, Captain 42
offense principle 154n
Oregon Death with Dignity Act 111
Ost, David 148n
Ouslander, J. G. 151n

paternalism 26–27, 137
  hard (strong) paternalism 27, 30, 67, 132
  soft (weak) paternalism 27, 131, 149n, 150n
Pence, Gregory 152n, 156n
permissibility-extension principle 96
persistent vegetative state
  cases involving 59–61, 112, 123
Peters, Thomas 155n
Plato 46
Potempa, Susan 8–9, 17, 83
Powell, Willie Mae 75
Powell v. Columbia Presbyterian Medical Center (1965) 75, 148n
predatory lenders 138
Price, Richard 56, 146n
property rights 34–35, 46–47, 56, 68, 82, 118–120
  modified property 119

Quill, Timothy 90, 95, 96, 97–98, 100, 106, 112, 150n, 151n, 152n, 153n
Quill v. Vacco (1996) 108, 153n
Quinlan, Karen 60, 61

Rachels, James 144n, 145n, 150n, 155n
Radin, Margaret 154n
Rathbun, Katharine 156n
Rawls, John 37, 55, 57, 144n, 145n, 146n, 147n
Rehnquist, William 110–111, 149n
Reinhardt, Stephen 107
religious freedom 48–51
required request law 123
respect 40, 73–74
Richards, B. A. 156n
Richards, Edward 148n
rights 3–7
  absolute 6, 7, 20, 135
  basic 24
  choice conception of 28–30, 44, 116
  contrasted with privileges 3
  and correlative duties 4–5, 20–21, 65–66
  defeasible 7
  forfeitable 6–7, 13–14, 42–43, 135
  in personam 4
  in rem 4
  indefeasible 7, 42
  infringed 5, 21–22, 32
  interest conception of 28, 30, 116
  legal rights 4, 33
  mandatory rights 12, 19, 30, 40, 52–53, 68
  moral rights 4
  negative right 4, 33, 110
  positive right 4, 33, 107, 110
  violation of 5, 32, 96–97
right of bodily integrity 66, 75, 84, 109, 110, 149n
right of conscience 45–48, 93, 110
  arguments for inalienability of 48–53, 136, 137
right of informed consent 37, 65–66
  case against allowing waiver 72–74
  case for allowing waiver 71–72
  exceptions to 66–67
right to life 21, 24, 37, 40, 42, 43–44, 79–85, 109, 112, 136
  Feinberg's account of 15–17
  inalienability of 82–85, 89, 114–116
  negative interpretation of 79–82
  positive interpretation of 79–82
  and suicide 86
right to pursue happiness 139–140
right to self-determination 62, 65, 81, 93, 126
right to self-government 44
right to vote 12, 19, 52, 67
role-related obligations 58
Rose-Ackerman, Susan 34–35, 119, 143n, 144n, 146n, 154n
Rousseau, Jean-Jacques 48, 57
Ryle, Gilbert 145n

safeguards for preventing abuses of euthanasia and assisted suicide 90–92, 97–99, 108
Salmond, John 32, 144n
sanctity of human life 115
Schloendorf v. Society of New York Hospital (1914) 66, 84, 147n, 149n
Schneiderman, Lawrence 147n
Seckler, Allison 151n
self-defense 38, 78, 149n
servility (as a violation of a duty to oneself) 40, 88
Seibert, Sam 154n
Shapiro, Robyn 103, 152n
Shavelson, Lonny 99, 101, 102, 150n, 151n, 152n
Shimp, David 80
Sidgwick, Henry 23, 143n
Simmons, A. John 32, 44, 47, 142n, 144n, 145n, 146n, 147n, 154n
Singer, Marcus 31, 86–87, 144n, 150n
Singer, Peter 99, 152n
slavery, contracts regarding 40–41, 52, 137–138
slippery slope arguments 90–92, 98–99, 110, 111, 130–131, 133
Slome, Lee 103, 152n
Smith, Tara 141n
social contract theory 48–49
Sophocles 126
Spital, Aaron 154n
Solomon, Mildred 63, 147n, 153n
Stell, Lance 82, 86, 143n, 144n, 149n, 150n
Stoljar, Samuel 144n
Strull, W. M. 148n
substituted judgment 93
Sugarman, Jeremy 148n
Sumner, L. W. 4, 141n, 143n, 144n, 148n

supererogation 42
surrogate mothers 132, 138

Teno, Joan 151n, 152n
terminal sedation 100–101
Thatcher, Margaret 118
therapeutic privilege 67
Thomson, Judith 6, 10, 12, 23–24, 79, 106, 141n, 142n, 143n, 149n, 153n
Thoreau, Henry David 45, 56, 145n
tolerance 57–58
Tolle, Susan 153n
transferring patients (in cases of ethical conflicts) 62–63
transfer of rights 11, 23, 24, 47, 68, 78
Truman v. Thomas (1980) 147n
Truog, Robert 153n
Tunkl v. Regents of University of California (1963) 69, 148n

Uniacke, Suzanne 141n, 142n
Uniform Anatomical Gift Act 122
United States Public Health Code 117, 120, 155n
utilitarianism 33–39
  act utilitarianism 33
  rule utilitarianism 33

Vacco v. Quill (1997) 110–111, 153n
VanDeVeer, Donald 141, 142n, 144n, 148n
Veatch, Robert 155n
Virginia Declaration of Rights 140
Virginia Natural Death Act 59
Volenti non fit injuria 31–32

waiver of a right 9–11, 23–24, 46, 69
  Feinberg's account of 14
  necessity of being informed 46, 69, 74, 84–85, 136
  necessity of voluntariness 46, 69, 74, 84–85, 136
  of the right of informed consent 67–68
Waldrop, Theresa 154n
Walters, LeRoy 155n
Wanglie, Helga 58, 59–60
Washington v. Glucksberg (1997) 110, 153n
Wear, Stephen 62, 147n, 148n
Wellington, Harry 149n
Wellman, Carl 141n, 145n, 147n, 149n
Wellman, Christopher 143n
Wertheimer, Alan 132, 156n
White, Morton 146n, 150n
Whitehead, Mary Beth 138
withholding or withdrawing life-sustaining medical treatment 43, 60, 81, 89, 102, 103–104, 107, 110, 113
World Health Organization 118

Young, A. D. 152n

Zimmerman, Michael 143n